Grown &
Gathered.

Grown & Gathered.

BY MATT & LENTIL

plum. Pan Macmillan Australia

DEDICATION

The thought of writing a book has always scared us because what we know today will change tomorrow. This book is full of only the knowledge that we have now. Of what we believe is the best right now. And, if there is a next book, it will be of what we know then. Believe the most recent. We will learn, grow and change – as will our knowledge. So take this knowledge for now, allow it to grow, change and mould into the future like a good sourdough leaven. Because we are always learning, and just when you think you have learnt enough, it's time to start learning again.

This book is dedicated to all of the believers. To all of those who have supported us, and to each person who picks up this book. This book is dedicated to you. We feel so honoured to have the opportunity to share our knowledge with you. It's more than we could have ever dreamed of.

To your future garden, full pantry, warm home, celebrations and happy everyday routines. This book is dedicated to making change, to experiencing life fully, being brave and bold, and to a bright future. We hope that one day 'organic farming' will just be called farming again and 'whole foods' will just be called food.

With our love. We wrote this for you.

We have printed this in the most sustainable way we could, knowing full well that the most sustainable thing to do would be to not print a book at all. But we decided the world needed a book like this and hope that the good it brings outweighs the harm it has caused.

CONTENTS

Our story.

This book is about it all. It's about our experience of learning to live alongside nature, returning to a way of life that people lived thousands of years ago, and discovering how to do that in a modern context. This has been our experience so far. This is a book about our journey.

We live a good life. We are so lucky.

These days, people take traditions – like marriage, sharing dinner times and everyday eating – lightly, but these experiences are the things that make up life. Not in a 'you *must* wear a white dress' or 'you *must* eat dinner before dessert' kind of way, but in an 'it *means* something' kind of way, in a 'making it full of lasting happiness' kind of way. These traditions and experiences, when done thoughtfully, are the key components of life – and the happiest moments of life. When you have a connection with what you are eating each day, in each meal; when you make meals from the produce that you grow; when you share the things you love, and the things that other people love; when you share meals and celebrate them, each experience means something special. It's just a much more fulfilling way to live, a much deeper kind of happiness. And life feels complete.

This book is about our experience of returning to nature and the lessons that we've learnt. It's about connecting to our food and understanding the traditional village life of our ancestors. And it's about what it really means to eat a natural, regional diet. It's about observing, growing, gathering, nurturing, trading, seeking and eating with the seasons. And it's about experiencing the whole process from start to finish – even if only once – and connecting with the people who do it every day.

And it turns out there is a reason why this lifestyle and way of eating, and the resulting happiness, feels different, feels so fulfilling. We have realised that it is in us. That it's innate. It's what our ancestors did.

We will never forget the first time that we made wine. We hand-picked the grapes, stomped on them

and fermented them – and it was the best wine that we had ever tasted. We suddenly understood why, in the past, people had proudly held out their homemade wines. To us, they tasted average at best, but to them, they tasted like the best wine in the world, as if they were the embodiment of all of the wonderful experiences that led to their making. And so it goes with *any* food or drink that you grow or make yourself. There is just something indescribable about experiencing your food in this way. And once we had, there was no going back.

The feeling of experiencing and understanding where everything came from quickly influenced every facet of our lives, enticing us to reduce our waste, learn lost but fundamental life skills, and get to know the people who made everything, from our clothes to our toothbrushes.

We started our separate journeys far away from the farm. We both finished school and uni, and got our first jobs in the city: I worked as a speech therapist, and Matt as a graphic designer. But neither of us felt right. The city was full of lots of *things*, over-sanitation and lunch delivered in plastic tubs. There was something missing.

So Matt travelled solo for a few years, walking and wandering throughout the world, immersing himself in different cultures and the way they experience their food and their lives. It was different to what he had seen before, and there was no forgetting. He returned home to his family's land in Central Victoria, leased a little cottage and a few acres from them, and found his first garden mentor, Brian.

Brian was, and is, a true elder of a man with long white hair and a wispy white beard. Brian knew all there was to know about gardening in a traditional, pre-pH-testing and pre-science kind of way. For six months, Matt and Brian went everywhere together, smelling like freshly collected manure. They tended to rows of garlic and rhubarb, the backyard lemon trees of elderly neighbours, and pruned what felt like every neglected orchard in the district, bringing them back to life. Brian could barter his skills for everything – fruit for expert pruning, garden advice for free meals – and Matt soaked it all in, the consummate apprentice. He stepped out from under Brian's wing armed with the fundamental skills of excellent gardening, a slower and steadier pace than ever, and the mantra: 'Give half the plants twice the love, and get four times the reward.' He will be forever grateful.

But Matt had no money, and Brian couldn't pay him. So Brian reluctantly handed him over to mentor #2, Andy, a man with a plan. Andy turned soil into money, selling rare heirloom (old variety) vegetables to some of the loftiest restaurants in Melbourne. He taught Matt to organically farm *commercially*, with bigger crops, bigger money and bigger business. Andy was a force in the garden and wanted to change the way food was grown on a large scale. But it was all too big. The experience taught Matt new tools, though – how to make it a business.

Both mentors taught him the key skills he needed to begin, but he wanted to create something different: a system that maintained and renewed itself and was a part of his lifestyle, one that made intuitive sense. One that he imagined his Italian grandfather, Quinto, would want. So he started his own little farm on the land beside his cottage. He experimented with the soil – using only waste from battery hen farms and green waste from local councils for fertiliser – applied traditional 4,000-year-old growing techniques he had only read about, and developed a new-found obsession with collecting heirloom seeds.

This is the point that we met, fittingly in Matt's garden. The first thing I noticed was that Matt's passion for food, both growing it and eating it, was palpable. I joined him, and he taught me to grow alongside him. I planted the flowers, and he planted the vegetables. Slowly, as we realised the importance each brought with it, the farm went from a ratio of 10:1 vegetables to

Give half the plants twice the love, and get four times the reward.

flowers, to a ratio of 10:4. They balanced each other like any good relationship. The vegetables were stronger with the flowers, and the flowers grew better with the vegetables. The farm was in balance, like nature.

We started another little farm in an unused block in Melbourne to see what 'urban farming' felt like. I was still a speech therapist in Melbourne, and Matt would go between the urban block and the cottage plot so we could spend more time together. Inevitably, the urban block was sold and we had to vacate. But by this point we'd realised that the city just wasn't for us anyway, and we both moved full-time to the cottage in Central Victoria.

In hindsight, we were doing too many things at once, but we wanted to learn it *all* by experiencing it ourselves. And that's probably why this has all worked, because we are as crazy as each other, and love to experience everything. As soon as we were both living in the country, we slowly began teaching ourselves how to gather more and more from the wild, which felt totally right and intuitive once we were out of the city. We focused more and more on the flowers and veggies in the little market garden we'd planted, and commandeered a host of old fruit trees scattered across the land around our home, including a derelict citrus orchard that Matt's great-grandfather had planted some 40 years earlier.

We started selling the fruits (and vegetables and flowers!) of our labour to Melbourne restaurants from our old ute, without a business name and with a slight ache in our hearts every time a restaurant rejected our offer of homegrown and hand-gathered produce. But we were 'in it' now. This was our life. And it was something we 100% believed in, and worked on 100% of the time.

Our business and life had become one. Matt would spend hours on the phone cold-calling restaurants to convince them that our produce was awesome and that they should try it. We were doing things a bit differently: we were a small grower, and our produce list consisted only of heirloom varieties, wild foods and edible flowers that chefs often hadn't heard of; we were growing 100% seasonally and were gathering foods from the wild; we were proudly not certified organic (see point 12 in *Our 15 Food 'Rules'* on page 133 for our reasons why); we didn't package our produce and only used stackable 100% recycled

crates left over from the tulip industry. At the time, we remember all of this being considered a bit radical. How quickly things have changed.

Then came a critical moment, a life-changing kind of moment. Actually it wasn't so much a moment, but a man. A chef. Douglas McMaster. Dougie took on our produce without question. We told him we were a small farm that wasn't certified organic and didn't believe in being certified, and we only had what was in season – you get what nature gives. He asked us to supply his restaurant without a question. To become his farm. This was a first for us, someone we didn't have to justify our methods, explain our beliefs, or prove ourselves to. So thank you, Dougie, you are one of the reasons we kept going and why we are where we are today.

We soon had a loyal list of some of the best chefs and restaurants in Melbourne. Our produce tasted good. We were teaching chefs about what *natural* food grown in *really* good soil tasted like, and we loved what we were doing. Though we were sometimes frustrated with the lack of understanding of seasonality and produce, we felt invigorated and inspired after each delivery. We felt like we had, in some small way, made a positive impact on the world.

We continued to experiment with watering methods, soils, heirloom varieties and doing everything by hand. We were realising that there was something about farming that science couldn't explain: the way that plants just grow better when each plant is given love and touched on a daily basis (there is now a study that supports this). And our lives were changing based on what we were experiencing.

We started to convert from buying in waste from local battery farms and councils to collecting the food waste from the restaurants and cafes we were supplying, and using only this to feed our farm – completing the cycle, diverting tonnes of waste from landfill, and discovering the sustainable farming of our ancestors. From that point forward, we simply always made sure to collect at least an equal amount of food waste to the amount of produce we'd taken off the farm. We called it 'closed-loop farming'.

The more we gave our produce to people, the more we realised that once people tasted it, met us, their farmers, and experienced their food a little bit more intimately, it made them happier than any food that they had had before. And it made us realise how removed people had become from their food. We were witnessing 'sustainable' cafes blindly supporting chemical farming with their choices of flowers and coffee, and being asked to support 'urban waste systems' that used five times more energy dehydrating food scraps than it would take to simply pick them up fresh and transport them to our fields to compost. People seemed so removed from what actually happens in nature, and from what is *actually* sustainable, that they had things backwards.

It was at this point that it all fitted nicely together for us: people needed to begin to *experience* their food again, just as we had. That was the only way they would begin to understand it. Experiencing our food had changed our lives, and it could change the lives of other people too.

We realised that we had been slowly separated from our food one meal at a time. Once upon a time, our food was either grown by us or by our neighbours. Then it was grown ten kilometres away. Then it was available in nicely packaged parcels in small, local stores. Then came the convenience of the supermarkets. And finally, the ultimate demise: pre-packaged meals and fast food.

It all just kind of snuck up on us. We weren't to know.

But, we decided that the future was bright, and that we had all the knowledge we needed to make the change for us all to eat well, and to live well. The answer was *so* simple: it was time to return to a way of life nearer to one that our ancestors knew, as we had begun to do ourselves. We decided to get legit.

We got a business name, a website and social media accounts and traded the old ute in for a van. Grown & Gathered was born. After initially only delivering produce to our restaurants, we began driving the van to Melbourne and selling vegetables directly to the public. We took on our first intern. And we rented a new house and land where we started our third farm – applying all of the things we had learnt so far. Against all the best advice, we switched our watering system over to small drips during the hottest parts of the day only, and reduced our water use by 80%. We continued to only use food waste to maintain our soil's nutrition, strictly didn't use packaging, and our diet was truly seasonal, living mainly off what we grew or gathered.

The answer was so simple: it was time to return to a way of life nearer to one that our ancestors knew.

At this point, we were, as always, doing too much, but had too much passion to do any less.

Then we had another one of those moments that really changed our lives forever, that made everything we had done up until that point feel like a complete system. It was one of those moments you never forget. We got married. The marriage wasn't why it was life changing (well, of course it was), it was because of our photographer: Shantanu Starick. Shantanu was travelling the world, footloose and fancy free, and he traded his photography skills with us in exchange for food, accommodation and travel costs. In a fashion, he taught us to trade by giving us a taste of what it felt like to remove money from the equation and swap our abundances for his, and, as a result, fully experience what we were doing rather than just handing over money and expecting the job to get done. And we gained a great friend. He gave us so much more than just photography. The equation was easy: trade gives you more than money ever could.

He had given us a taste, and we wanted more.

We first started trading because we wanted to create conversation and to see what would happen if we removed money from the equation. But also, we just wanted to make people happy in the simplest way. We had so much abundance in our lives, why couldn't we use it to fill in the gaps of the things that we didn't grow, gather or nurture?

So we started 'The Flower Exchange' project. Flowers were essential to our ecosystem, essential to our growing, and were the most abundant thing we had, seeing as it was vegetables, not flowers, that were the focus of the business. Additionally, they extended the conversation about where things come from beyond just talking about food. We planned to not sell a single flower for a whole year, only trade them with others for their abundance – whatever that was. We didn't have exact *things* in mind that we wanted to trade, we were more excited by the experiences we would have and where they would take us. All we knew was that we wanted to have conversations with other people, to open genuine communication, instead of simply using money. We were excited to see what it would do to our lives, how they would change, and what we would learn. In hindsight, we had no idea what an incredible journey we were embarking on.

So much happened. Our life together and our business, which at this point were very much one entity, felt complete – like a perfectly joined little circle. We'd love to go ahead and tell you about all of the amazing trades we have had since, from little to big, but you'll have to wait until you get to the *Trade* chapter for that. For now, we will just say that what began as trading only flowers quite naturally led to us trading everything and anything we have in abundance. And that it has absolutely changed our lives.

And so here we are today, growing, gathering and nurturing on the farm, and trading wherever possible for the things that we need but can't grow, gather or nurture ourselves. Someway, somehow, it was all leading here, and we find ourselves with an intricate and complete food system, and, in turn, a way of life that we believe in completely – a traditional system, one that our ancestors would recognise.

The chapters that follow are guides based on the things that we have learnt so far, that can be applied and adapted to anyone's life. They are based on a traditional, pre-industrial food system, but we have taken these old methods and systems and applied them to a modern world. And we see it as the future of food. We believe this is the most mindful, sustainable, balanced and nourishing way to eat and live. This is what our bodies know. This is what they have known for thousands and thousands of years. And it is what has sustained us for all that time before industrialisation changed everything (see *A Very Short History of Food* on page 16).

We hope this book helps you to understand our philosophy of trade, seasonal eating and sustainable living, and communicates the love and passion that we put into everything we do, with the greater good at the core of every decision we make. Our aim is to make it achievable for you. To resonate with you. Because it starts and ends with you. Follow these guides and the world, and you, will both be well.

Whoever and wherever you are, here is to a bright future filled with green beans and homemade passata.

– *Lentil*

The equation was easy: trade gives you more than money ever could.

A very short history of food.

Below is a quick summary of how food has moved in time. We feel that it's essential to understand how things used to be – and how they've changed – to understand where we are now, and why it's important to move back to the beginning, acknowledge the wisdom of our ancestors and adapt it to a modern context.

The very start (~105,000 BC).

Humans were hunting and foraging for fruits, nuts and wild vegetables long before 100,000 years ago, with evidence that they were eating grains (e.g. wild grass seeds, including sorghum grain) as early as 105,000 years ago. It is widely accepted that Aboriginal Australians were practising incipient agriculture and aquaculture on a massive scale at least as early as 40,000 BC (but potentially some 100,000 years earlier), carefully managing the land and its resources with bushfires, dams and specially designed tools and strategies.

The start (~12,000 BC).

Growing, gathering, nurturing and the establishment of the village model: domestication of animals and plants, grain and pulse cultivation – the birth of agriculture as we know it. Food preparations to render grains more edible are well established. Local trade is in full swing; regional specialisation in produce and products is beginning; global trade begins through sailing routes. Drying was one of the earliest food preservation methods, known to have existed as early as 12,000 BC, although probably much earlier – and evidence of fermentation places it as early as 10,000 BC. People begin to consistently ferment fruit to make wine from around 6000 BC.

The middle (~1200 BC).

City states emerge. Advances in food storage enable long-term storage of abundances. Road systems and sailing routes become more developed to allow larger global trade systems. Money and accounting are introduced.

The Industrial Revolution (leading up to the mid-19th century).

Money has taken over, and the idea of 'class' has been introduced. The wealthy are now fussier in their food preferences. A massive shift away from predominantly rural populations to urban populations begins in the 18th century. Canning is introduced in 1810 as a preservation method.

The end — the modern industrial age (mid-19th century to the present).

The aftermath of the Industrial Revolution: dead soils and imbalance. Labour shifts from manual to machine. Mechanisation leads to increased scale of food production, which leads to decreased food costs. Agriculture begins to look at the environment as needing to be controlled, not cooperated with. Post WWI and WWII shift towards chemical pesticides and herbicides to utilise vast munitions stores of ammonia and DDT. Animals are moved out of natural environments and confined inside or in feedlots en masse. The priority of agriculture becomes to constantly increase production while decreasing costs, but quality is compromised. Global trade is now on a massive scale. Over-consumption of meat by large populations is possible for the first time. Genetic modification of animals and plants is introduced. Food 'specialisation' begins, with people now having a preference not just for chicken, but for only chicken legs or chicken breasts, and a new market emerges for the export of 'waste' portions to other nations. A huge division in wealth between nations arises.

The return — back to the start (now).

This is the future of food.

CHAPTER 1

Observe.

Dancing with nature – observing the progression
of changes through the 365 days of the year.

To grow and to live with the seasons means to observe the constant changes in your environment, to respond at the right times, and to thrive off what nature provides. And this begins with observing. It is the first step to everything that follows in this book. We're not going to give you a guide to what is in season at specific times in your specific location. Rather, we are going to guide you on how to live and eat seasonally, no matter where you are, because it is more powerful to know the *how* and *why* part, and you can apply that to any location. We're leaving seasonality up to you.

This book is full of the things that we grow, gather, nurture, trade, seek and eat where *we* are. And that's how it worked traditionally. You grew what you could where you were, and then you ate what you had, sourced a few special things from far away, and that is what made up regional diets and lead to the development of specific cuisines. This book is about our regional diet, and it will be different to yours by a little or perhaps a lot. But you can compare it to your own and apply the principles no matter where you live (see the *Eat* chapter for an explanation of our diet).

We believe in living 100% seasonally, but what does that really mean? It means that you are living alongside nature, that you are, to a point, at its mercy, and you really have little control over the situation. Nature is intelligent, far above and beyond our ability to understand it, and the moment that we think we do, we don't. For this reason, the moment we try to force nature into distinct blocks – like summer, autumn, winter and spring – we fall short. Instead, we must observe and respond each and every day. The moment we think we understand nature and try to lock it into dates, we fail. Humans are different to almost every other animal. We constantly try to control and change nature. But it's not possible. It will continue to change, and we must continue to change with it.

Living a natural life, alongside nature, means stepping outside of the four fixed seasons and constantly observing. It doesn't mean we can't talk of summer, autumn, winter and spring – these are rich terms, full of appropriate meaning – but the key is not being stuck to them on a calendar. Instead, use them as descriptors of a particular time in a particular place, and understand that sometimes none of them will fully apply – there are many times of transition too.

When we realise that we can't categorise and conquer nature, we begin to work with it. We begin to observe and respond to it. It's almost like a dance. It does *this*, and you do *that*. You begin to observe the *progression* of changes through *each* of the 365 days of the year. You understand that these are the true seasons, because things change day to day, month to month, and differently than they did the year before, and the year before that.

This is the first step to growing, gathering, nurturing, trading, seeking and eating, because when you begin to dance with nature, rather than fight against it, everything becomes easier. Your body, health, happiness, the environment and the way you farm all just feel more natural and more balanced – things fit together. It flows, and it makes sense. But this lesson of working with nature and observing can in itself be the biggest challenge. And for anyone who says that it's not, don't believe them.

It is in fact incredibly difficult to put down on paper – and it's something we don't think science will ever be able to explain – although, granted, we do like that it's trying to. It's intuitive, not intellectual. Working with nature is something that your body just knows how to do. It is instinctive, and we need to learn to trust that again.

We want to guide you by showing you what is seasonal to us. But you are in charge of knowing what is seasonal to you, and forming your own seasonal diet. Remember to dance with nature and observe the progression of the 365 days of the year. And if at any moment you feel as though you are fighting nature, you have missed something. Sit, observe and change tack – remember that it is *you* doing something wrong, not nature, as it will always be more powerful and knowing than we are. This is the key to everything that follows in this book.

WHAT TO LOOK FOR: BEYOND SPRING, SUMMER, AUTUMN AND WINTER

When observing a yearly calendar, summer, for example, starts on the 1st of December and ends at the end of February. Although this is a good approximation of a seasonal 'block', the reality is that summer just starts when it starts and ends when it ends. Each year, summer starts at a different time, the rain and wind come and go at different times, as does the heat.

When you live with and observe the seasons, you start to learn to observe what each movement in nature means. There is a certain beautiful, indescribable feeling triggered at each and every stage – smells, patterns and memories of the year before trigger a certain knowing about what is about to happen next. For example, one of our favourite times is when the wild plums are out. It feels like sunshine; the air is hot and dry and the world is alive. The cicadas are loud, and the days are long. The grass is dry and crispy, and the water in the billabong is finally starting to warm up. And equally, we love the anticipation of the first frost. The days are rapidly shortening while we continue to farm our crops, but there is a looming awareness that the summer crops will soon come to their end as they die from the frost, and we prepare to retreat inwards for winter and await the new beginning in spring. Both of these events happen at different times each year, sometimes by as much as two months compared to previous years.

There are certain key moments in nature that we look for where we live. To notice these changes we have to interact with what's around us, observing what is happening each day, as well as how those things affect each other. This really begins with key indicators: weather patterns; stages of flowering for our plants, vegetables, shrubs and trees; fruiting and ripening times in the orchards; and most importantly, what's happening with wild plants, as they are responding directly to nature without any interference.

For example, we know that howling, strong winds occurring at certain times means that the seasons are shifting. After these winds, everything seems to change. The weather might go from fluctuating cool and warm days – a spring pattern – to consistently hot days – summer has arrived. Or, just when it seems the repetition of those summer days will never end, the winds arrive again with the first cool days of autumn right behind them. We know that when our ash trees flower in early spring that the soil has begun to warm again, and it's time to plant eggplant and capsicum seeds into pots to grow the approaching summer's seedlings. And the time that the ash flowers on our side of the river compared to the other side of the river will be different, but on both sides that flowering will indicate the time to plant – no sooner, no later. Nature tells you what you need to do. These are some of the indicators from our own experience of where *we* live. You may not have an ash tree, but there *will* be something. Your indicator might be a blooming wildflower, or the setting of seed in the neighbouring fields of wheat, or the germination of the first spring weeds.

Other key indicators are insects and animals. Which insects are around, when and why? Insects breed and hibernate at certain times of the year, at certain temperatures. They may begin to emerge when certain wildflowers bloom, or when certain plants begin to grow. What are the animals that you nurture and the wild animals doing? What are they eating, and when are they out of hibernation or migrating? Are there large populations of certain animals or insects around and why? Observing these signs tells us a lot. Where *we* are, when the first snakes appear in spring we know the soil temperature is warm enough

to safely plant out summer's crops. In our previous gardens, with less proximity to water and thus a higher risk of a late frost, it would still have been too early. Every location has its own language to learn.

The last key thing to note is that location is important on a micro-level too: different parts of the same property can behave differently, and sometimes drastically so. Take into consideration where your garden beds are located. Are they near water, concrete, trees, hills or open fields? How are the plants and animals responding in each area, at each time of the year? Different areas can be in totally different 'seasons', with soil out in the field still the temperature of spring, while the home garden, up against the warm wall of your house, is already the temperature of summer (we talk more about this in *Grow*). Every location will tell a different story.

A GOOD PLACE TO START

A way to start to observe the effects of all of the key indicators described above is to let some plants – like potatoes, dahlias, herbs, tomatoes and pumpkins – self-seed and grow wild in a few select sections of your growing area. You will easily be able to observe a few key indicators this way. When do the first shoots appear in spring? When do they naturally begin to flower and fruit? Are there differences in different locations? Are different insects attracted to them at different times of the year? And is it the same as your neighbour? One year, in the same backyard, your self-sown pumpkins may begin to sprout naturally in early September, and another year they may not sprout until mid-October. Then you can coordinate everything else, such as planting times, with what is naturally occurring.

The main lesson here is to observe your local environment, no matter how small. It will change from location to location, year to year, day to day. And trust your own observations and your own intuition. Again, this is where it all begins – this is the first step to living with nature and the seasons, and fully experiencing your food.

A year of observations.

We have included some of our observational notes here to demonstrate how things can change from year to year in the same place. These are excerpts from our own personal diaries. There is a lot missing, for sure, and our thoughts are definitely always evolving – to notice more, to think bigger.

Although we have included a calendar year here, our actual diaries begin in late winter (August for us). This is because we see our year starting when we begin to plant seedlings into the greenhouse at the end of winter and prepare for life to begin again in spring. We have included some notes from previous years to give you some sense of our shifting seasons.

We highly recommend starting your own diary and recording your own seasonal observations; it really is the best way to learn about what's going on around you.

Early January (6th)

Summer crackling in the air after New Year's – over 40°C on the 2nd! Some olives have already started ripening, a long way from the harvest though. Zucchinis and cucumbers pumping – started picking. First beans starting, but won't be as good as the late flush in April. Herbs are pumping. The garden finally looks 'full'. Sunflowers beginning to look really good. Zinnias rampant. Dahlias just starting. Late apricots. Early peaches.

Mid-January (12th)

Still hot. Picked first tomatoes and some corn. Fully formed green chillies and capsicums – won't start turning red until March though. Picking out basil tips now to bush out the plants. Delicious! Got the shade cloth over the dahlias this week.* Honey harvest! They're really putting it away – river red gums have been flowering hard.†

* **Late February (28th) 2016**
Still no shade cloth over dahlias, as sun hasn't gotten hot enough and petals aren't burning – don't think we'll bother.

† **Mid-March (15th) 2016**
Went to harvest honey but there was none! Most of the red gums haven't even flowered this year the weather's been so weird. Worst year for honey we've seen.

End of January (30th)

It's been cool lately for summer – below 30°C all last week. Planting for winter begins. Tomatoes have begun to pump. First eggplants! Peaches the cow is in a good milking rhythm. Starting to cut down on Peaches' calf Pip's milk access – she's so fat!

Early February (11th)

Basil and tomatoes are pumping. Cucumbers rampant. Purple peaches and plums. Big row of corn is ready. Beans producing well, but a bit hot for them to really pump. Picking is full on. It's been hot again lately. Now it really feels like summer!*

* **Early February (4th) 2016**
Still only picking every few days, looks like we don't get a summer this year. Have had two weeks of pretty cool weather and so much rain, plants not liking it at all!

Late February (25th)

White grapes ready for harvest. No red wine grapes yet.* First apples could be picked but try to wait for the autumn equinox – they'll be sweeter then. D'Agen plums are on. Gums at peak flowering – they just keep going! Wombok in, to time with chilli, carrot and daikon harvest – no point growing it earlier if you want to make kimchi!

* **Mid-February (21st) 2016**
Shiraz grapes ready to harvest! Baume of 14.4!

Early March (7th)

It's so dry now, but a lovely temperature. A little rain last week but looking dry for weeks now. Fruit is abundant – apples, pears and so many quinces this year! Cider and cider vinegar time from the fallen apples. Figs in full harvest.* Eggplants are really kicking now.

* **Mid-March (15th) 2013**
The first real figs have ripened – only a few though.
Late February (25th) 2016
First figs have ripened! Super early!

Mid-March (18th)

It's so dry, but the tiny sprinkle of rain today was nice. No forage left for the cows. Have brought in some hay for them.* Chillies are ripening now. Spring-planted leeks ready. Hydrangeas still pretty and perfect.†

* **Mid to late February 2016** Lots of forage left for cows and sheep. Those summer rains made such a difference. Have kept a little wild section irrigated for them as a little treat.

† **Mid to late February 2014** Hydrangeas over – too hot.

Early April (7th)

Cape gooseberries still pumping. Second flush of raspberries just finishing. Quinces still abundant, and figs still in season. Still harvesting barely ripe persimmons to beat the possums. Beans peaking again! Eggplants and capsicums rampant – everyone else's have finished fruiting at least a month ago. Love this watering system!

Pumpkins started ripening. First big rains have hit. Wild ducks prolific. Lots of amaranth ready to harvest (for grains). Rice ready to harvest. Starting to get cold. Frost soon? Harvested a little bit of ginger (good time before the cold)! Last chance to harvest honey? – it may be too late.

Mid-April (13th)

Garden is so green again. Time to turn the watering down. Harvested first potatoes! It's like we've NEVER eaten potatoes before this moment – they are magnificent. Garlic shooting. Zinnias, cosmos pumping, dahlias perfect. Ice plant is cranking (loves fringe seasons). Chrysanthemums going well. Seed has set on asparagus. Pumpkins dying off.

Late April (27th)

Olive harvest. Red wine in barrels. 800 litres of dry-grown juice made 400 litres of wine.* Cold has really set in – lost most leaves on the deciduous trees. We are tired. Garden really dying, dahlias almost done but zinnias still happy and pumping! Borage, celosia, cerinthe, Queen Anne's Lace, floss, amaranth, sunflowers, cosmos still happy.

* Early March (8th) 2016

Finally got around to bottling the rest of last year's wine! 400 litres of wine made 35 dozen bottles, give or take (the missing 80 litres was either lees or evaporated from the barrel – the angels share). Super proud of the Shiraz/Grenache barrel – so delicious.

Early May (10th)

It's cold, down to 5°C at night. Grass is just starting to green – have had a super-dry year. Rains only just starting to come often now. Wild mushrooms only just starting this year.* Chrysanthemums abundant. Chamomile and nigella beginning to flower. Harvesting and preserving everything madly, making sure all chillies, eggplants, tomatoes etc. are inside. Preserving last of the olives. Curing sweet potatoes and pumpkins in the sun, before the frost.

* Early April (3rd–5th) 2013

Wild mushrooms have started!

Late May (28th)

The cold weather swept in with a vengeance last Saturday. First frost Sunday morning.* It wasn't a brutal first frost, which was lucky, as we hadn't got all the pumpkins inside yet. That was the first job for Sunday! On Saturday we had just pulled in all the chilli plants whole for picking, picked off all the last eggplants and pulled in a whole tomato plant into the pantry to ripen. Madly foraging mushrooms in the pine forest. Gentle first week of 60 kg, then 210 kg, and 190 kg this week! We've never seen anything like it, and the quality is superb!

* Mid-May (15th) 2013

First frost hit overnight, borage, zinnias etc. all dead.

Early June (5th)

Frosts have settled in. Lemons are fully ripening. Navels are getting close to ripening. Last flower seedlings in, but will just sit there until spring. Planting onions near or after winter solstice to ensure good crop. Have dried off Peaches the cow. Pip was still having a drink given half the chance, but she's a big girl now – time to leave Mum's udder.

Mid-June (20th)

Tidying up the carrots, parsnips and brassicas – the weeds had got ahead of us in the mayhem of autumn. Celery and fennel are pumping – they really love this cold. Wild mushrooms starting to wind up – what a great season.

Late June (29th)

Finally got around to harvesting the last potatoes – a great haul. Realised we missed a lot of sweet potatoes during autumn harvest and they've rotted in the ground. Don't keep in the ground like regular potatoes. Bit sad.

Early July (7th)

It's really cold. Deep winter now. We've got the fire going all day and night. The winter bulbs are brightening our days. And the winter garden is loaded with brussels sprouts, greens and root veg. Winter feasting is happening!

Mid to late July (22nd)

Flowers same as June. Camellias out on a few trees. Silver princess gums flowering and wattle in full swing. Nettles, marshmallow, milk thistle, wild lettuce, dandelion, fat hen and wood sorrel all prolific. Not a lot moving – time for weeding. Mustard greens and chard going well. Rhubarb and navel oranges tasty. Harvesting lemons.

Early August (7th)

These last few days it just began warming up a little – not so many frosty mornings and a few things in the garden are actually starting to move. Still freezing though! Buds of blossom are swelling on fruit trees in a few of the warmer sections.*

* Late August 2013 (24th)

Buds of blossom starting to swell.

Mid-August (16th)

A little rain last week – everything is looking lush. Temperatures are getting up to 15–16°C now and soil temps in the greenhouse closing in on nightshade germination temps (21–29°C). Have started prepping garden beds for spring.

Mid to late August (22nd)

Beginning to warm up a lot, some days feel like spring, others are cold, frosty and foggy. Almond blossom well and truly out.* Apple buds just forming. Wattle almost finished flowering – things are really moving this year! A sea eagle has moved in and started to take chickens. This is crazy! Whistling kites everywhere too. Peaches would normally be calving about now. Giving her a year off. Pip is getting so big!†

* Early September (8th) 2014

First bud burst on almonds, these are always the earliest to pop.

† Early March (4th) 2016

It hit home that Pip is a cow. Literally had to sit down and accept that our baby is all grown up.

Early September (4th)

Apricot and peach blossom beginning. Ash tree flowering – time to plant capsicum and eggplant seeds. All other seeds in the greenhouse now: zucchini, cucumber, corn, pumpkin, tomatillos, gooseberries, huckleberries, some more peas, kale and a few early cabbages. Had a big rain so also planted out a whole bunch of stuff into the ground: spinach, chard, tatsoi, upland cress, lots of roots. Still wintery but lovely sunny days. First asparagus.

Late September (28th)

The first rose has appeared, and everything looks awake all of a sudden! In the past few days the smell of spring is OUT – bees are buzzing and grass is beginning to set seed. First fig leaves and vine leaves are out. Ranuncs are in full swing. Broccoli, kale and fennel taking off. Forgot what it is like when it's warm – feel like we can relax a bit. Sea eagle has disappeared. Yay! Lambs are starting to get big!

Early October (6th)

Have had three days over 35°C with big winds and everything has dried out. Garden is freaking out. It's feeling stressful. Parsnips are sitting well, but all other root veg are thinking about bolting (need to turn the water up). Asparagus is cranking, leeks and garlic going well. Broccoli thundering along, getting spindly though. Beets, parsnips and carrots from the autumn sowing on the move again. Artichokes beginning to do their thing – first harvest now. Meant to be planting next week into the ground, but we haven't finished preparing the beds – makes us feel a bit stressed. But seedlings are all in and going well – the best timing yet! Snakes are appearing.* Bees have started to swarm – have one swarm on the property. Need to pull a bar out of our hive. Larkspurs are out. Violas and borage pumping.

* Early October (10th) 2013

It's super hot now – snakes have started to appear.

Mid-October (16th)

It's so hot, not raining at all – such a dry year. Artichokes are fully out. Kale, beetroot all bolted now. Harvesting the last leeks. Bearded iris and roses out. Poppies popping. Black pearl lillies out. No tulips this year because it was too dry (would normally be finishing flowering now). Violas pumping. Borage has freaked out after the heat. First big harvest of broad beans. Pulling the last carrots and parsnips from winter.

Celery starting to bolt, but still good. Chard looking great. Collard greens are happy and pumping. Feels like we should be planting now, but still a danger of frost? I think we would be fine this year even though it's not November yet. Everything in the greenhouse has REALLY taken off this week. It's time to go! Pumpkins finally sprouting in the greenhouse – slow to germinate this year.

Early November (6th)

Peonies have come and starting to fade now – a few still blooming. FINALLY it has rained, with about three full days of rain, which is just amazing. This is the rain that we remember from years ago. When the snapdragons are big alongside the foxgloves (like now) the rain is always abundant. So happy it arrived!* The onions have started to flower, with heads just starting to pop. Self-seeded potatoes are about 30 cm tall and first flowers are appearing – amazing what the wild tells you. Sweet potatoes are only just popping slips, finally. It's really planting time now – we probably should have done it a few weeks ago this year, but only getting to it now. Pumpkins and potatoes are in the ground, that's a good start. Mulberries are READY!† They are delicious. It's their 'on' year this year. They are full and bursting with flavour! Everything has really bolted now – ready to be pulled out.

* Mid-November 2013

The rain has been prolific, snapdragons are tall and ready to harvest.

† Early December 2014

Mulberries are beginning to ripen and apricots at the same time.

Mid-November (16th)

No more rain. Rains are over?* Potatoes that we planted are growing prolifically, already 30–40 cm tall! Zinnias and dahlias are in the ground. Snapdragons have almost finished. Harvesting first good size root veg. Them + broad beans + edible flowers = happiness. And the peas! And garlic shoots! Love spring.

* Mid-November (16th–18th) 2013

Big rains continue.

Late November (29th)

It's been SO dry again and just not that hot (mainly low to mid 20s). Still eating peas and sprinkling onion flowers on everything now – they're so tasty. Young scarlet runner beans are ON. Super early. What a treat for spring!

Early December (4th)

Zucchinis just started – amazing, didn't realise how much we missed them! Tiny zinnia heads appearing and dahlias still continuing to flower. First garlic is ready to harvest! Love this time of year when everything is in the ground but before everything goes mental.

Mid-December (20th)

We had 40°C heat last week – it's so dry! Summer harvest just around the corner. Everything is pumping – first harvest of cucumbers. Bottled the 50-litre keg of Shiraz in time for Christmas! No early apricots this year – blossoms got burnt by frost in September. But the white peaches are AMAZING! Grey flies are here. Wombok a little smashed. Oh well, they'll be gone soon.* Picking dahlias, zinnias and lots of roots and greens. Garlic out of the ground.

* Mid-December 2014

Grey flies came, sucked life out of greens – two weeks later gone.

Late December (29th)

It's really starting to feel like summer now and New Year's is going to be HOT! Had some great rain this week – a one-day deluge. Perfect timing for summer crops to burst. Late apricots. We missed you! Making a load of jam before we eat them all! The garden is looking fresh and ready to really pop. Super excited for this season.

CHAPTER 2

Grow.

Growing alongside nature.

The world population is on track to hit 11–12 billion some time in the next century. If it does, there will be barely more than a single acre of land left on earth suitable for growing the food for each man, woman and child. So we extrapolated our tomato harvest to the equivalent of an acre, and it equated to over 68 tonnes of tomatoes every year, enough to meet the yearly energy requirements of more than 13 people, with just tomatoes.

To be fair, not all crops yield so intensively. The techniques we are about to share, though, can enable enough diverse *real* food – grains, meat, dairy, fruits, nuts, seeds, herbs and vegetables – to be grown for one person on less than a third of that acre.

And yet science is stressed. Agriculture has become a numbers game. It worries about growth. About getting more for less. It tells us we haven't the space to feed the world. It deeply believes that we are doomed but for the saving grace of chemically managed fields and synthetically produced fertilisers. It's a good story. But it's just not true.

The reality is that we have been farming in partnership with nature for over 10,000 years. Growing things is in our blood. There are even neurological studies to show that getting your hands dirty releases a whole series of positive reinforcement mechanisms in the brain. And also studies that show how working with the soil helps to decrease both allergies and disease. It just seems that there is an ancient evolutionary correlation between working with the earth, and health and happiness.

This chapter focuses on growing your vegetables, fruits and herbs, but the same techniques can be applied to growing anything from grains to pasture to flowers (which we grow alongside our vegetable crops). The theory is entirely scalable, and we have seen it successfully applied to everything from balcony gardens to large-scale farms and everything in between.

We don't believe everyone should be a farmer. But we do believe everyone should grow *something*, no matter how small. Growing things is one of the most satisfying and grounding human activities there is. It reminds us that we can actually feed ourselves. And that's a wonderful realisation to experience.

We would love to see everyone return to a simpler, slower life, more connected to their food again. Such a connection changes the way we see our food, the way we purchase, eat, cook and live. It is a connection to all of the experiences that lead up to – and run so much deeper than – the eating. Food experienced in this way just tastes so much better.

We believe in growing the traditional way, before synthetic fertilisers, pesticides, herbicides and the very idea of waste existed. We want you to forget all the words. Forget 'raw' and 'permaculture' and 'biodynamic' and even 'organic'. Farming should just be farming, growing growing and eating eating – without chemicals and synthetic fertilisers. It was the only way in the past, and will be the only way again in the future.

We see our farming methods as working *with* nature – a natural kind of farming. A farming where things actually become *easier* the more you work with nature and let it do its thing, not harder – unlike the constant battle that is modern agriculture. This isn't hippie rubbish, and it's not so mysterious – our aim is

It just seems that there is an ancient evolutionary correlation between working with the earth, and health and happiness.

to make growing alongside nature approachable and achievable for everyone. We want to make you feel that growing things naturally is possible. Because it is.

Humans have co-evolved with plants and agriculture for thousands of years, and growing food alongside nature is part of our very genetics. It's in you. You've got this.

THE GROWN & GATHERED SYSTEM

Overall, our approach to growing is to see our farm as one cohesive organism that must be in balance to thrive. Likewise, we see our growing system as one cohesive system where there isn't a single piece of superfluous information – every part has a role to play. Our system is driven towards allowing nature to be healthy, and creating a balanced ecosystem that results in high-yielding, stress-free and healthy plants.

For it all to work you must master sun, soil and water, plant a diversity of vegetables and flowers with care and attention, mulch at the right time, allow just the right amount of wildness, and treat your compost and worms with the love they require. If you take this as a whole system, if you follow all of the parts, then you will be rewarded with the most incredibly lush and productive garden that is not only pest free, but also incredibly high-yielding, regardless of its size. One 60 m row of tomatoes on our system provides us with over 100 kg of tomatoes every week, for over 15 weeks each season! One 60 m row of cucumbers provides 140 kg every week, for over 20 weeks! And if something does go wrong – there are pests, our plants look floppy, are diseased, are not thriving – we look at what might be out of balance and treat the cause, rather than the symptoms. We work towards making the whole system and ecosystem work together again. Most importantly, if our garden seems out of balance, we always ask ourselves what *we've* done to cause this problem. Because we are almost always to blame!

Sun, soil, water: The rule of three.

For plants to grow three things need to be right: sun, soil and water. The three interact and support each other, and you simply can't have a thriving garden without perfecting all three. This rule is the key to your success, whether it be growing vegetables, fruits, herbs, flowers, pasture or grains, and no matter where you are located in the world.

We believe that if you give your plants an optimal environment, they will grow faster, produce more and produce for longer. We are constantly giving our plants so much love that they never get stressed. If your plants are never stressed, they never need to spend time recovering, and therefore get to direct all of their energy into giving you higher yields. Everybody wins.

Master sun, soil and water and you're most of the way there.

1. Sun — lots of it.

Have you ever bought seeds or seedlings and read the labels that say 'part shade'? We are here to say forget all of that and start again. Most vegetables and flowers *love* full sun. There are exceptions, but that is the rule. A plant's leaves can be understood as solar panels. The more sun they get, the more energy they have to metabolise the nutrients in the soil and grow. Not only that, but the temperature of the soil has an enormous impact on the speed and vigour with which your plants grow, because a plant thrives best when it can direct all of its energy into growing, rather than just trying to keep warm enough to stay alive. So, don't expect things to grow if they are perpetually stuck in the shade.

Therefore, where you locate your growing area is probably the most important decision of them all. You want to identify the area that gets the most sun: a north-facing site is ideal in the Southern Hemisphere; while south facing is best for the Northern Hemisphere. In a backyard situation, most people prefer to plant next to walls and fence lines to keep a large open space, but that's not always the best decision. If the sunniest spot is right in the middle of your yard, then *that* is where you want to locate your growing area.

The sun moves across the sky differently in each season, so think about where you will get the most sun in each season, and plan your garden around that. The angle of the sun's path is high in the sky in summer — basically directly overhead in the middle of summer — so nearby trees will have less shading effect. Whereas in winter, the angle of the sun's path is very low in the sky, meaning nearby trees can really shade out your winter veggies. So we plant our summer veggies in the spot that gets sun in summer but is shaded in winter, and our winter veggies in the most open area that gets the most sun year round.

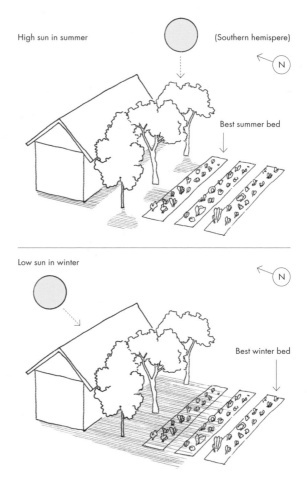

High sun in summer   (Southern hemispere)

N

Best summer bed

Low sun in winter

N

Best winter bed

Brick or stone walls are excellent to grow near because they will actually absorb the sun's heat during the day and gradually release it into your soil throughout the night, stabilising that all-important soil temperature. Painting the wall a very dark colour can enhance the effect even further.

We can also use this theory to stretch the capacity of the local climate. Placing heavy stones, such as bluestone blocks, around plants that need extra heat to grow in your climate – like avocado trees for us – will help to keep the soil temperature around the plant's roots warm.

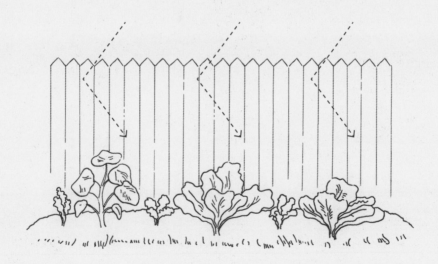

Wooden or corrugated iron fences are also great, as they reflect the sun's rays right onto your growing area, meaning double the sun's energy for your crops. Paint such fences white, rather than dark colours, to get the biggest effect.

CREATING SHADE

The important message here is that all vegetable and flower plants love full sun, but there are some exceptions. Some people say that some greens, such as lettuce or spinach, need shade. However, we have found that as long as you partner them with our natural soil and watering techniques, they are super happy and grow excellently without shade. In our experience, the only things that don't thrive in full sun are some flowers, such as dahlias and hydrangeas, because their delicate petals tend to get sunburnt if not shaded. But that doesn't mean the actual plant itself doesn't love the sun, and they will still grow the fastest and strongest in full sun because that gives them access to the most solar energy possible.

To achieve undamaged flowers, we simply have to interfere with some shade at the appropriate moment. This can be done with the use of cleverly placed shade cloth just before flowering begins, or by planting just the right neighbouring plants, such as corn or sunflowers, to provide shade exactly and only when your flowering plants need it.

The sun is at its most brutal in the hours after midday. So if we plant corn or sunflowers just to the west of the flowers we want to shade, both plants will receive full sun while they are young, when they need it, but by the time the flowers are approaching harvestable size, the corn or sunflowers will have grown tall and will provide shade for the flowers all afternoon long.

The key message is that it is easy to shade sun-sensitive plants, like dahlias, with a sun-loving plant, like corn. Providing shade is easy, but accessing solar energy in a shady spot is impossible. So let your garden bathe in sunshine. You'll be glad you did when autumn sets in and the sun begins to hibernate.

2. Soil — closing the loop.

It is being increasingly said that soil is everything. And it is. Our great-grandparents knew it, and so did countless generations before them. The ancient Chinese farmers revered soil so much that they established a network of canals hundreds of thousands of kilometres long just to capture the soil that their rivers carried down from the Himalayas. They also composted and returned every single scrap of organic waste to the soil because they knew that it needed constant attention and feeding. They — and every other ancient culture beside them, before them and after them — nurtured soil with the utmost reverence because they knew that its very nature required it, and that there was no point trying to argue with nature.

Lately though, since industrialisation and the invention of synthetic fertilisers, farmers have thought they could choose an 'easy route' and bypass nature. It has not turned out well. However, soil is a powerful thing, and it only takes the right ingredients and a little time for its thriving nature to return.

We call our soil management system 'closed-loop farming'. When we deliver fresh produce, we collect an equivalent or greater amount of fresh food waste from our customers, always making sure to collect equal or more than the amount of produce that we harvest — what comes out, must go back in. We incorporate it with the manure from our animals, compost it down and feed it back to our soil the following season, completely closing the loop from fertilising to sowing to harvest and delivery, and back to fertilising again.

When we first established our 1-acre market garden, we naturally ploughed the land using pigs first, and then brought in local composted green waste and two-year-old chicken manure. It was the first and last time we brought in a bulk load of organic matter from outside our closed loop. Ever since, that established fertility has simply cycled perpetually from planting through harvest, delivery, scrap collection, composting, fertilising and back to planting again, and our composting process breaks down any chemicals present in the food scraps, cleaning up the planet one load at a time.

We believe that all compostable waste should become nutrients to grow more food in, not landfill. Then we wouldn't have all this waste, and our agricultural lands would be replete with naturally nutrient-dense soils. Everything would be in balance — a cycle.

A good soil is:

Teeming with life. Nothing can thrive in a dead soil. Plants live off the castings and by-products of all manner of insects, worms, bacteria and fungal life. That living biota digests the minerals in your soil and makes them available to your plants. This is the main reason chemically managed agriculture was always bound to fail: it kills everything, and that includes the soil life. The less you touch, move and dig your soil, the more alive it will be.

Nutrient dense. If it is to produce the sustenance your plants require, that soil life is going to need to feed on something. Your soil should be rich with minerals, dark with decomposed organic matter and perfumed with the distinct funk of life.

Deep. Whoever heard of a 3 cm long carrot? We aim for a workable soil depth of at least 40 cm – now that's a carrot! By workable we mean that you can literally lean forward on a garden fork and slip easily into the soil. Below that 40 cm should be more earth, but it doesn't have to be so easily workable, because your plants have a network of tiny hair-like roots that can penetrate and tap into that firmer, mineral-rich subsoil layer without a problem. If you are going to grow in crates or similar vessels that don't have access to the soil below, throw the 40 cm rule out the window. In that case, we recommend that they are at least 1 m deep with rich soil. Your plants simply need to have access to that kind of deep nutrition to thrive.

Free draining. Plant roots love to be moist, but hate to be wet. A plant's roots can't continue to grow deeper if they are sitting in sub-surface water, and if the roots stop growing, so too does the plant. Most soils are naturally quite free draining. But once you've driven over them a few times, or built a house and then demolished it, and then tried to make a garden there again, they're going to be compressed. A happy, healthy soil is full of tiny capillaries that transport water and air. When we compress the soil we collapse those capillaries, and, in the process, both suffocate the soil life that relies on them and ruin the soil's capacity to drain water away. We'll talk about how to create good drainage later in the *Building Your Garden* section (see page 60), but suffice to say that the spot near the back fence that looks like the Great Lakes after a big rain is not where you want your garden. Well, not without a little work first.

How to create good soil.

Luckily, with the addition of just three ingredients you can turn any soil into a living, breathing home for your plants, rich enough to feed them and structurally strong enough to support them and allow for rapid growth. Those three things are manure, worms and compost. Like sun, soil and water, manure, worms and compost are an interrelated family, and it is only together that their true value is fully realised.

MANURE

Traditionally, not a single gram of nightsoil was wasted. In ancient China, farmers would drive their donkey carts into town first thing every morning to collect everyone's waste. They would place it in enormous clay pots out in the sun and let it sit there fermenting for two years before they spread it out onto their fields. It was a lot of work, but they did it because they knew that what comes out must be returned.

Manure can come from all kinds of different animals, but there are two main categories when we talk about their use in agriculture: grass-eater and grain-eater manures.

Whether from a grass-eater or grain-eater, composted manure will provide your garden with an instant boost, and is essential when regenerating a lifeless soil, building a new one, or simply topping up your soil nutrients for the next season.

Grass-eater manures (sheep, alpaca, horse, cow etc.).

These are ideal for growing in. They are the perfect food for your soil. In fact, they are so gentle that you can plant seeds and seedlings straight into them and they will thrive. Next time you are driving through the country and see five-dollar bags of horse poo, stop and buy some! It's bagged gold, and your plants will love you for it. Always let fresh manure age for a few weeks before use, or the natural composting processes occurring in the manure may damage your plants. But once it's composted down for those few weeks (see *Compost* on page 42 for more information), use any grass-eater manure liberally in the garden. There is no such thing as too much of it.

Grain-eater manures (poultry, pig – or even human!).

These, on the other hand, are a lot stronger and have to be used a little more carefully. They are still *excellent* food for your soil, but due to the diets of these animals being much higher in protein than grass-eating animals, their manure is overly rich in nitrogen (the main building block of a plant's green leaves, but also toxic in high concentrations), which will overwhelm your plants if applied in too great a quantity. Think of it as a thing to sprinkle, not shovel. The concentration of nitrogen in grain-eater manures makes them perfect for when you need to spread a small amount a long way, such as for large-scale farms.

As with grass-eater manures, never use grain-eater manure fresh, always let it age first to undergo an initial aerobic decomposition. This can be achieved by leaving the manure in bags or a large pile for at least two weeks before adding it to your main compost pile to continue decomposition for at least 12 months. This initial aerobic digestion is super important as it will reach the temperatures necessary to kill any pathogens that may be harmful, making your compost safe for use.

WORMS

If it's to experience long-term health, your soil *must* be full of worms. There are thousands of different kinds of earthworms but not all are 'composting worms'. The bait worms you buy from the service station, for instance, won't do the job. But all good nurseries sell shoebox-sized packages of composting worms, and one red and wriggly boxful is all you'll need. Read on to learn a composting technique that breeds them, and, in the *Building Your Garden* section on page 60, we explain how to introduce them to your soil if they are lacking.

COMPOST

Compost is the answer to all of the organic waste matter in the world. In ancient China, Korea and Japan, everything was composted, because everything *could* compost: leather, timber, old cotton and wool clothing – everything!

If manure is for instant gratification, then compost is for the long game. It will increase your soil's ability to retain moisture, improve its depth, drainage and supportive structure and provide a long-term food source for both the soil life and your plants directly. Composting, when done right, breaks *everything* down. By the time the composting process has finished, any chemicals and everything else in that compost will have completely broken down into basic organic compounds, ready to go back into your soil to feed its fertility (see *A Note on Herbicides*, below).

Critical mass.

People are always asking us why their compost piles aren't working. Usually, we blame the makers of those silly black compost bins available at gardening stores. Compost requires a critical mass to get going. You simply can't take the pile out of a compost pile. Without a good pile there just isn't enough insulation to kick off the natural processes required. We believe that about 0.5 m^3 of materials is required to start a new pile, and that would mean that most of those bins would have to be almost full before they even *begin* to compost. So don't feel bad if that banana peel didn't transform into soil in a puff of smoke the moment you threw it in your black plastic bin – there's a little more to it than that, and you weren't to know.

Carbon/nitrogen balance.

When talking about compost, we place scraps and waste into two categories: *brown matter* and *green matter*. Brown matter is generally always brown; it is all the dead, dry stuff. Think small twigs, dry leaves and straw. It is the main source of carbon in your compost. Green matter is not always green, but it is always fresh and moist. Think food scraps, green leaves and fresh manure. It is the main source of nitrogen in your compost. A healthy compost pile requires at least 1:1 brown (carbon) to green (nitrogen) matter, but up to 10:1 brown to

green is equally good, just don't ever use more green than brown. If your compost begins to smell, you have too much green matter to brown matter. Mix in more of the dry stuff and wet it all down, and everything will rebalance itself almost overnight.

What can be composted?

We put everything in our compost pile, and we recommend that you do too: coffee grinds, citrus peels, meat scraps, bones – they're all fine. The only caution is that they are in balance with everything else. If you *only* drink coffee, or you *only* eat oranges, you are going to run into problems, but a healthy, balanced diet will create healthy compost – everything works together! Meat scraps may attract rodents, but so too will any cooked food scraps. We believe that it's better to try and keep such pests out of our compost by securely covering it, than it is to let all that organic matter rot in landfill.

The one thing that we are careful with is seeds – like tomato and pumpkin, and weeds that have gone to seed. Unless you want these plants popping up all over your garden, try to keep their seeds out of your compost pile. We feed them straight to the chickens instead.

A note on herbicides.

There are some chemicals present in modern commercial herbicides that persist no matter how much we compost them. Most have now been made illegal, but there are some, such as clopyralid, that are still universally legal. Food is highly monitored, so food scraps present no risk in your compost pile. Likewise home garden waste, because these persistent chemicals are banned from domestic gardening products too (not that we recommend using chemicals on your garden!). But do ask the question if you are buying commercial green waste compost, as commercially managed gardens do not always follow best practice and commercial products contain the strongest chemicals. All compost producers will test for persistent chemicals so they will know the answer and fingers crossed these last few chemicals will be banned universally in the not too distant future.

Starting a new worm farm.

Composting is a simple thing. However, like most simple things, there are many different ways to do it. We have learnt, after many years, that one way in particular is by far the most effective, and that is composting in the presence of a high worm population, or 'vermicomposting'. In short, a worm farm! It is, to our knowledge, the most efficient and natural system. It releases the least greenhouse gases of any method, most closely reflects a natural process and produces the highest quality food for your plants.

A thriving garden will become, in effect, one giant worm farm, with worms right at the surface, just under your mulch, constantly digesting dead plant matter and creating soil. But that doesn't mean you shouldn't have your own little worm farm as well. Having a worm farm will allow you to compost all of your food scraps and green waste (and, if you want to, much of your neighbours' too). Plus you get wonderful worm tea to strengthen your plants with!

Materials.

1 bathtub or similar vessel with a drainage outlet (we have built these in old IBC tanks with the tops cut off, bathtubs and 44 gallon drums, with equal success; size is key – about 1 m³ capacity is plenty)

4 milk crates (or a simple frame to raise the worm farm high enough to get a bucket under the outlet)

1 bucket of gravel or small stones

1 bucket

4–5 hessian sacks

1 straw bale (any straw will do – you won't need an entire bale, but it's probably worth just getting a whole one anyway and using the remainder throughout the garden)

About 0.3 m³ of compostable organic matter (leaves, coffee grounds (in balance), food scraps, paper, seaweed, lawn clippings, old cotton clothes, basically anything that can naturally decompose – ask your neighbours or local cafes for their compostable scraps)

About 0.2 m³ of soil

1 double handful of worms

1 bag of manure (ideally grass-eater) that has been kept in bags or a big pile for at least 2 weeks

1 lid that fits the vessel and some weights to hold it down

1 drum to store the worm tea

A garden hose to wet everything down

1. Place your vessel up on the crates with the bucket under the outlet. Pile the gravel around the drain, and place a hessian sack over the gravel. Spread a thick layer of straw and twigs on top, followed by a thick layer of soil (at least 10 cm), and then wet everything down thoroughly.

2. Spread your worms on top of the moist soil and cover with another 10 cm of soil – this is where the worms will seek refuge if they need to, a safe place they can retreat to after eating all of your delicious scraps.

3. Now it's just a matter of building the pile up layer by layer. Some soil, some green (wet) scraps, then some brown (dry) scraps, and continue in this way until all your material is in there, ending with a nice thick layer of straw. Always make sure there is plenty of manure amongst the layers, remembering to sprinkle if you're using a grain-eater manure, or shovel if it's a grass-eater manure. Wet everything down a few times throughout the process – although we talk about wet and dry matter, this only refers to its nature as it enters the pile. Once in the pile, *everything* must be moist for the composting process to work.

4. When you've run out of materials, place a few more hessian sacks on top to insulate and retain moisture. The sacks will also protect the worms, allowing them to make their way right to the surface – they will even start eating the hessian! Wet the whole lot down one last time and place a more solid lid on top to keep any pests out.

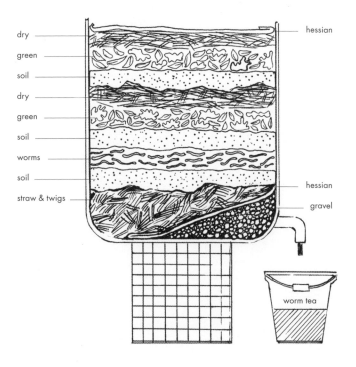

dry
green
soil
dry
green
soil
worms
soil
straw & twigs

hessian

hessian
gravel

worm tea

Notes.

To add new material to the pile. Pull back the hessian sacks and straw and incorporate it into the top layer of compost. Once the worms have broken down the main mass of compost, they will continue to feed on the scraps you add every day.

Remember the 'closed-loop' message. What comes out must go back in. So if you harvest 7 kg of vegetables from your garden one week, be sure that at least 7 kg of compostable material goes into the worm farm that week too. This should happen quite naturally, but it's something to bear in mind. If you find that you aren't accumulating enough scraps yourself, it's time to ask your neighbours and local cafes for theirs (or even start a collection service for your street).

Sea minerals. Initially, we always try to add a bucket of seaweed that we've collected to the pile, and then every few months, if we visit the coast, we collect another bucket. Seaweed is a powerful addition to your compost, and we highly recommend it. Fish bones, scraps and guts are also a wonderful addition and can easily be obtained from fishmongers at the market. Both will add potent sea minerals to your compost and provide a real boost to your garden.

Worm tea. Water your worm farm when you water your garden, so that it is always moist but never wet. You will accumulate a lot of lovely brown liquid in the initial setup process. As it fills up, empty the bucket into the drum for later use. That worm tea is a rich plant food that can be watered down up to 10:1 and sprayed on the leaves of your plants throughout their growth. Constant application of worm tea immeasurably strengthens plants and reinforces soil health.

Scaling up. For larger-scale composting situations, like on our farm, often the only option is to build a compost pile directly on the earth. We collect material throughout the season and then follow the same process all in one go to form a big pile reaching over 2 m high, ensuring any collected food scraps are mixed in with plenty of manure and dry matter, like straw, to keep the pile balanced. The collected material goes through an initial aerobic decomposition before we even mound up the main pile, which is great because it hits the temperatures necessary to pasteurise pathogens, break down common chemicals and, if they've snuck in there, deactivate most weed seeds. We cover it with a thick layer of straw and put an automated sprinkler on top to keep it moist. We leave it for a year to compost down while we begin to collect another year's worth of material. We are missing out on capturing all that lovely worm tea, but we only water the pile just enough to activate the composting process, which ensures the water-soluble nutrients aren't leached away into the soil below.

Times frames. Compost should be left to mature for at least 12 months before use, which ensures adequate time for full decomposition and deactivation of chemical residues and any other nasties. When your first worm farm is full, just start another one next to it by taking some worms from the first one. By the time the second one is full, you'll most likely have completely emptied the first out onto the garden, and can start it fresh again.

To get you started. During the initial period, before the first load of compost is ready, we have found that composted green waste (available from all good nurseries) and aged manure are the perfect combination to establish soil fertility (see the *Building Your Garden* section on page 60 for the rates of application).

3. Water — plants drink when you drink.

When was the last time you drank no water all day and instead spent two hours drinking in your sleep? This is the classic 'treat 'em mean, keep 'em keen' attitude that most farmers and gardeners have taken towards their crops lately, applying an infrequent deep watering overnight and nothing in the heat of the day, in the mistaken belief that this leads to less evaporation, more assimilation and deeper root growth. We believe that it's all backwards and that this leads to dehydration and stress in your plants. Plants aren't so dissimilar to us in their needs and our philosophy is to treat them like we treat ourselves. We eat, they eat. We grow, they grow. We drink, they drink. Because, just like us, if our plants get stressed, they have a far greater chance of getting sick, and that means reduced yields.

Give your plants the most optimal environment possible and we guarantee that they will grow faster, produce more and produce for longer. We are constantly trying to give our plants so much love that they never get stressed. If your plants are never stressed, they never need to spend time recovering, and therefore get to direct all of their energy into giving you higher yields. Everybody wins.

In our garden, the plants drink when we drink: nothing overnight and *little* bits *lots* of times throughout the day, creating a moisture zone right around their roots – right where they need it, when they want it.

We water directly to the base of the plant with drippers, rather than with overhead sprays, because when we're thirsty we like to drink directly from a glass, rather than just spraying water all over our faces. This avoids all kinds of mildew pressures from moisture build-up on leaves, and it also restricts the ability for weeds to grow in the pathways and between your plants.

Even on the hottest days in the deepest heatwaves our plants stand proud and tall in scorching sun, absorbing the glaring solar energy. Why? Because our plants *always* have access to the water they require. Water is the coolant that allows your plants to operate. So long as they can freely access water to circulate through their leaves, they can take even the harshest sun. But even a moment without water when it's needed means their leaves will overheat and burn, and your plant must then spend energy repairing the damage.

> As a guide, in our acre veggie patch in the absolute peak of summer, we water every hour on the hour from 8 am until 5 pm in three-minute bursts. We can dial it up to five-minute bursts in a truly epic heat wave, but that's rare.

Note that there is a key difference between keeping the soil moist and wet here, and there is definitely such a thing as too much water. Some plants require more water, some less. Some soils retain more water, some less. And here we come back to observing. Your plants should never look floppy or wilted; they should look hydrated and robust. Always. Observe them and ensure you deliver just the right amount of water to them. As a guide, in our 1-acre veggie patch in the absolute peak of summer, we water every hour on the hour from 8 am until 5 pm in three-minute bursts. We can dial it up to five-minute bursts in a truly epic heatwave, but that's rare.

Watering in this way has allowed us to reduce our water usage by 80% and the garden has never looked better. We believe it's not just because our plants always have access to water when they need it, but also because all of the water-soluble nutrients in our soil remain right in the root zone where they are needed, rather than being leached deep below the reach of our plants' roots.

Exactly how you achieve the 'little bits of water lots of times' effect is up to you. We use automatic timers and, because everyone is so busy these days, almost always highly recommend a similar system for backyard gardens. Even if you are able to give your garden a regular 15-minute watering every morning and evening before and after work, that's a start. Three ten-minute waterings would be even better. Thirty one-minute waterings, better again.

Planting near large trees.

Try to avoid planting near the root systems of large plants and trees, as they will suck up the water and nutrients destined for your plants. For large trees, the rule of thumb is to look at the height of the tree and stay that distance away from the base of its trunk, as the root system generally mirrors the canopy. Keeping your distance can be tricky in backyards, but keen and constant observation will always allow you to get the delivery of water right. Being extra generous with rich compost and manure on that part of the garden will also help alleviate any nutrient robbing by nearby trees.

Growing with weeds, mulching and companion planting.

Over the years, we have seen how much mechanising and over-controlling things actually makes them harder, not easier. Farming naturally, with the weeds and with the seasons, is *so* much easier once you learn how. A diverse garden that is mainly mulched and weeded to perfection, with just that hint of wildness, is always the healthiest garden.

Growing with weeds. While most of our garden is neatly weeded and mulched, some of it is always allowed to get away. We've learnt to respect and appreciate wildness as much as we respect and appreciate tidiness. A wild patch beside your cultivated garden nurtures small populations of birds, reptiles and beneficial insects and distracts pests away from crops. Experience has also shown us that some flowers and food plants – like sweet potatoes, snapdragons, foxgloves and most flowering bulbs – actually love a bit of competition from weeds and will produce more prolifically when they have it.

For example, we have found that seedlings of tall, fast-growing crops like corn thrive when planted into a freshly weeded bed and simply left to tower above the weeds as they grow – unmulched, untended, undisturbed. When nearing maturity, a small mob of sheep can be let in to graze the weeds without ever touching the tall corn plants – but be wary of leaving them for long, as there's little that's predictable about a curious mob of sheep! We've also found that potatoes thrive amongst wheat. As the potatoes grow taller, the wheat dries out and makes ready-made mulch to pile around your potatoes. Similarly, sweet potatoes seem to do best when planted and ignored, allowing weeds to grow all around them – the competition seems to encourage their growth, rather than hinder it.

We try to prevent weeds and cultivated plants from setting seed in the garden, but we are a bit more lenient in the wild section. We use it as a place to save seeds or let things self-seed (drop their seeds to grow again), whilst being careful not to let things get out of control.

Mulching. We always mulch. Mulch protects your soil from overheating and drying out, and it suppresses weeds and allows your worm life to work right at the surface. Most weeds and grasses make great on-the-spot mulch when pulled *just* before setting seed and then laid down around your plants, as they have drawn up all manner of deep nutrients from the soil during their growth. All of that nutrition will be broken down into your topsoil as the mulch decomposes. Grain straws also make excellent mulch. Any will do: wheat, oat, barley, rice, pea or many others. One word of caution: don't mulch too early in spring, or your soil won't warm up. Always leave your mulch in the paths until the end of spring to allow the sun to directly warm your garden beds, creating the conditions your plants need to thrive.

Companion planting. Taking nature's rich diversity as inspiration, our rule of thumb is that diversity is the best companion planting. But we have learnt some definite 'do's' and 'don'ts'. For example, don't plant pumpkins and potatoes together, or cucumbers and tomatoes together. Gooseberries and tomatoes don't seem to get along either – although cucumbers and gooseberries get along just fine! Do plant dill with cucumbers and brassicas, and tomatoes beside dahlias. We also *always* make sure to plant Queen Anne's lace, cosmos, marigolds and nasturtiums throughout the garden, as they attract beneficial insects and distract pest insects. Sweet alyssum, pennyroyal, lemon balm, catnip, borage and hyssop are also great helpers.

Seeds and seedlings.

Having trouble germinating seeds is like eating chocolate while no-one is looking: everyone does it, but no-one wants to admit it.

Seeds were a complete mystery when we first started gardening: it was a mystery where to get all of the weird, old and interesting seeds from; it was a mystery what to do with them once we did; and germinating them was hit and miss. Now it's flawless.

From the very end of winter through to mid-summer, we plant lots of seeds in trays in the greenhouse, which we later plant out into the garden as strong little seedlings. We also plant many seeds directly into the ground from early spring all the way to the end of autumn. We continue to plant bits and pieces in the greenhouse and the ground as the growing season – spring through autumn – progresses. It's a system, and we discuss details around these planting times in the *Planning Your Garden* section on page 60.

WHERE DO YOU BUY SEEDS?

We only grow from heirloom seeds, and you should too. These are the old varieties of seeds – the ones that grew the food your great-grandparents ate and that have proven to be nourishing and delicious for centuries, sometimes millennia. They have not been altered by scientists and will thus naturally grow stronger plants with tastier harvests. Plus, you can save their seeds over and over again.

There are some wonderful seed companies all over the world, and the more diversity that you can bring to wherever you are the better, we say. Sometimes we need to break our rules on 'local' to diversify that locality. These days, you can jump online and order seeds from whatever faraway land you'd like. They should be, and generally are, approved by customs no matter where you live.

What you *don't* want when purchasing seeds are hybrids (F1 or F2) or genetically modified (GMO) seeds. Plants grown from F1 or F2 hybrid seeds will either not set seed for the following year, or will set seed for a different (but related) plant that you're not going to want (so you can't save these seeds to replant). They are modern plants that your body just isn't as familiar with on a genetic level. GMO plants are an even bigger step away from nature again, and we believe genetic modification is just dicing with danger. These are genetically altered plants, which affect the environment around them and may have negative effects on our bodies too. They don't behave the same way as heirloom varieties – they're either weaker plants, less tasty or both – and so we would suggest they don't offer the same sustenance to our bodies. In our opinion, it's definitely best to steer clear.

WHAT TO PLANT AS SEEDLINGS AND WHAT TO SOW DIRECTLY IN THE GARDEN

The answer to this question is usually dependant on which family or category the plant belongs to. Experience will teach all, but here is what we do:

Direct sow.
- Root veggies, like carrots, beets, turnips, parsnips, radishes and leeks (the long taproots of carrots and parsnips, especially, will usually deform when planted as seedlings, because they get compressed in the process).
- Cut-and-strike-again greens, like rocket, mizuna and silverbeet/chard.
- Soft herbs, like dill, coriander, parsley and basil.
- Beans, broad beans and peas.
- Garlic (plant some of last season's garlic cloves).
- Potatoes (plant some of last season's smallest potatoes).

Grow as seedlings.
- The nightshade family: tomatoes, capsicums, eggplants and chillies.
- The brassica family: broccoli, cauliflower, cabbage, kale, brussels sprouts and kohlrabi.
- Cucurbits: zucchini, cucumber, pumpkin, melons (it's important to note here that cucurbit seedlings that have already sprouted their second set of true leaves – the crinkly edged ones – will produce mainly male flowers and thus a very small harvest, so always plant them young). We also plant these directly into the garden as seed.
- Corn.
- Anything that needs space, like onions, fennel, lettuce, radicchio, witlof, flowers, Jerusalem artichokes, celery and celeriac.
- Perennial vegetables and woody-stemmed herbs like asparagus (for which you plant a crown when it's dormant), globe artichokes, rhubarb, rosemary, thyme, the oregano family and sweet marjoram.

HOW TO GROW SEEDLINGS

We love our greenhouse, but we think it's very important to stress that greenhouses were traditionally created to extend the growing season by establishing good strong early seedlings, not to farm a crop to maturity. We strongly believe that it's best for the environment and our bodies to eat seasonally, which means eating locally grown food that has been grown in a field, in the direct sun.

We highly recommend that you build yourself a little backyard greenhouse. It's amazing what you can do with a few second-hand glass doors and some old windows (see our greenhouse on page 54!).

What vessel do we plant seeds in?

If grown in a pot, seedlings will do best if the pot is compostable, as the whole thing can be planted without disturbing the roots. We prefer coir pots (made from a by-product of the coconut industry) but on a small scale, cardboard toilet rolls are just as good. Alternatively, we have great success planting straight into reusable open seedling trays that nurseries and farms often throw away. This method gives our seedlings' roots lots of room to mature unimpeded and has been the most successful method we have ever used, so long as care is taken when planting to avoid damage to the delicate roots (see *Step-by-Step Guide to Planting Out Seedlings* on page 57).

Do we use potting mix?

We usually plant our seedlings into mushroom waste, which is what it sounds like: a waste product thrown out after being used to grow mushrooms in. It has the perfect open soil texture for little seedlings to push their way through and is very water retentive – great for keeping young seeds moist while they germinate – but it is just an example. You don't need to have old mushroom compost to grow healthy seedlings. We have raised equally successful seedlings in soil we've dug from our garden and in old compost. We've never used potting mixes from the nursery. They're expensive and full of all kinds of stuff that just isn't naturally present in your garden.

The most important thing is that the soil you choose is really friable, so that the young roots can penetrate it easily. The choices are endless, so go seek out what is readily abundant for *you*.

Step-by-step guide to growing seedlings.

1. Prepare your trays or pots by filling them with your chosen growing medium, and then pre-soak the soil with water so that it's already moist for your seeds. Don't miss this step – pre-soaking is key.

2. Place your seeds to a depth equivalent to the length of the seed, and brush some earth back over them. For big seeds, like pumpkin, that's 1 cm. For tiny seeds, like oregano, you basically sprinkle them on top and brush your hand over them to incorporate with the soil. Try and space seeds out in a 3 cm grid. This is completely impossible for tiny seeds, so, in their case, just do your best not to sow too many seeds in each tray – remember that each seed is a potential plant. Do not press down on the seeds, as this will only compress the soil and make it more difficult for the young roots to grow.

3. When all your seeds are in place, give the tray another really deep but gentle soak. Germination is the waking up of the dormant seed, and for that to happen it requires the seed to get *really wet just once*, then to remain *just* moist – like the rest of your garden – throughout the growing process.

4. Place your seedling trays in a warm, protected spot in the sun (on a windowsill or in a greenhouse, for example) and keep them moist. This is where most people go wrong. They just wet their trays once, and then leave them in a hot place and cross their fingers. Inevitably, the trays dry out before the seedlings have a chance to get going. Tend to your seedling trays every day, giving them a sprinkle of water and always keeping them *just* moist – never wet.

5. Once the little green sprouts are up, continue to keep moist, but there is less pressure now because they will have a little taproot down deeper into the moist soil at the bottom of the tray.

6. After four to six weeks, your seedlings will be 15–20 cm tall and ready to plant out.

Step-by-step guide to sowing seeds directly into the garden.

The technique for sowing directly into the garden follows the same theory as sowing into trays, except we plant in what are called drills or furrows to make the task faster and easier.

1. Create a planting space in your garden by clearing any weeds and old plants.

2. Using your hand or a garden fork, loosen a line in the soil at least 20 cm wide and 20 cm deep.

3. Along that loosened line, create a furrow with your hand about 15 cm deep. It will form a natural 'V' shape, wide at the top and narrow at the bottom. For larger applications, a long-handled *ho-mi* – an ancient Asian gardening tool – is a wonderful tool for forming furrows, or even just use the corner of a long-handled, metal-toothed rake.

4. Sprinkle your seeds into the base of the furrow, taking care to space them according to how far apart you'd ideally like each plant to be once mature: for herbs, carrots, rocket and silverbeet/chard, maybe 3 cm; for beets maybe 6 cm; peas and beans do well spaced about 15 cm. Don't worry about sowing depth here, just sprinkle them in the base of the furrow – this technique will work no matter how small the seeds are.

5. Cover the seeds by gently running your hand, *ho-mi* or the back of a metal-toothed rake back along each side of the furrow, causing the soil to gently cascade down the slope and over the seeds. The seeds will be covered by about 2 cm of soil, and a slight depression should remain where the furrow was.

6. Water the seeds in very deeply and then follow the same care as when planting seeds into a tray, keeping the furrow moist but not wet until you see the first sprouts. Continue to keep the little sprouts moist after this point, but again there is a little less pressure now, as they will have a little taproot deeper into the moist soil below.

Step-by-step guide to planting out seedlings.

When it comes to planting out seedlings, care needs to be taken to not damage the delicate roots. Always plant with your hands – no hard tools – into moist soil, and always water your newly planted seedlings straight away to settle them in.

1. Create a planting space in your garden by clearing any weeds and old plants.

2. Using your hand or a garden fork, loosen an area of soil 20 cm by 20 cm by 20 cm. Remember, 'Give half the plants twice the love, and get four times the reward.' – Brian, mentor #1. Always give your seedlings appropriate space. A zucchini will grow 1 m across when fully mature. So you'll need to space zucchini seedlings 1 m apart. On the other hand, kale seedlings can be planted just 30 cm apart. Silverbeet/chard and peas need just 15 cm or less between seedlings, and rocket just a few. Always follow the notes on seed packets, and don't overplant your garden – more plants does not equal more harvest: in fact, you'll likely get much less, with too many plants competing for water and nutrients.

3. If your soil is dry, water it now so that it is moist. Also, water the tray of seedlings you are working with to help protect the roots that are about to get exposed to the air.

4. Put down your tools and carefully remove a seedling from the tray by grasping a small handful of soil around its roots. You want to disturb the roots as little as possible and take as much of the root system as you can with the seedling. Use soft hands. Be gentle. Do not squeeze the handful of soil, as this will compress and damage the roots.

5. Using your free hand, pull back the soil from your loosened spot to about 15 cm deep. Gently hold the seedling in place with your other hand, then brush the soil gently back in place all around its stem. The root ball of the seedling should now be at least 10 cm below the surface of the soil, with soil piled up around the base of its stem.

6. Support the stem of the seedling with the soil around it by laying one thumb on top of the other while touching the tips of your index fingers around the stem and gently but firmly pressing down, as illustrated below. You want to create a *shallow* well around the newly planted seedling. This will help capture water during irrigation or when it rains.

7. Immediately water your newly planted seedling gently but deeply with a watering can or similar shower nozzle. 'Watering in' ensures that all of the disturbed soil settles completely around the seedling's delicate roots. Roots die immediately if they dry out, and good moist soil-to-root contact prevents this from happening.

8. Tend to your newly planted seedling every day, keeping the soil around it moist but not wet. You will know it has established new roots when its leaves deepen in colour. It is now feeding off the soil.

9. Mulch around your seedlings with straw only after they are established and at least 20 cm above the soil to avoid suffocating them.

Potato half barrels.

A potato half barrel is a really fun and easy way to grow over 50 kg of potatoes on less than 1 m². It doesn't have to be in a half wine barrel, any similarly large, structural vessel will do – it's even better if your vessel has only sides and no floor, so your potatoes can tap into the actual ground. A stack of old tyres is a great alternative as they can be stacked on top of each other throughout the process, allowing for a lot of height in a very small space. The depth of the container is important – if it's too deep there won't be enough sunlight for the plants in the initial stages of growth, and if it's not deep enough there's really not much point. This process should begin in early to mid-spring after the danger of frost has nearly passed.

Materials.

1 large vessel, ideally with only sides and no floor

0.2 m³ of compost-rich soil

12 potatoes (save your smallest potatoes from the previous season)

1 straw bale (any straw will do)

1. To begin, fill the base of your vessel with at least 20 cm of compost-rich soil and then evenly space a dozen potatoes on top of the soil. Cover them with another 15 cm of soil. Water it all down, and keep it moist but not wet for the duration of the potatoes' growth.

2. Your potato plants will continually grow lush greenery above the surface of the soil for the next few months. At fortnightly or so intervals, nearly completely cover that greenery with straw, leaving only about 15 cm of growth above the surface each time. Continue until the barrel is completely full, at which point you can just let the greens grow strong and tall out of the barrel.

3. At the end of the season, simply tip the whole thing over and harvest. You can harvest new baby spuds from mid-summer, but the main harvest is in autumn, even after a frost (in fact, you can leave potatoes in well-drained soil all winter and the earth around them will act like a big fridge!). Underneath the straw, and all the way down into the initial layer of soil, potatoes will have formed throughout. It's a super-effective example of maximising space, and perfect for backyard situations where that space is limited.

Evenly space your 12 seed potatoes on top of 20 cm of compost-rich soil and cover with 15 cm more.

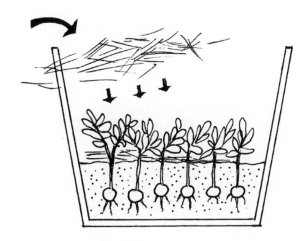

As the potato greens grow up, continue to cover them with a little straw every fortnight.

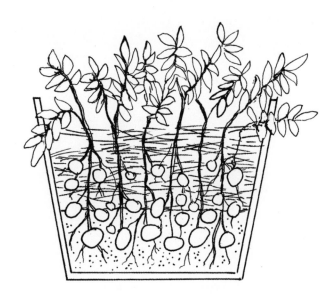

When the barrel is full, leave the plants to grow until autumn and harvest!

Building your garden.

Position your growing area in the sunniest spot. Remember, if you give your plants enough water at the right times, they will all thrive in full sun.

Define your paths and beds. To avoid walking all over your growing area, make the beds no more than twice as wide as you can comfortably reach while kneeling beside them (about 1–1.2 m wide), with 30–40 cm-wide pathways in between. This way, you can kneel comfortably and access the entire bed when planting, weeding or harvesting, without having to put any pressure on the soil.

Establish at least 40 cm of workable topsoil. This is easily achieved by creating raised beds – not necessarily boxed in, just hilled up. You can do it in two ways:

1. For a large area, like our acre garden, we first deep-ripped keylines about 70 cm deep in a checkerboard pattern spaced 1.5 m apart to ensure excellent drainage into the subsoil. We then moved ten pigs across our paddock in 60 m² blocks, moving them every day for ten weeks. They cleared the land back to bare earth and brought the difficult roots of creeping grasses, like couch, to the surface to dry out (it didn't eradicate it, but it made doing so by hand weeding later possible). Then we spread composted green waste across the entire area at a rate of about 1.75 m³ per 100 m², and chicken manure that had been composted for two years over the whole area at a rate of 0.25 m³ per 100 m². Finally, we used a tractor with a hiller attachment to form 80 cm-wide beds (the only time we allowed machinery into the garden). This 'single pass once the soil is broken' mentality ensured that the tractor only compressed the pathways and not the beds, so drainage and soil life were unaffected in the growing area. We have since maintained the hills by hand.

2. On a small scale, it's easy to hill up your growing beds by hand (pictured, top). First, mark out the beds and paths, then fork deeply over the whole area – if your soil is very hard, it will need to be wet down thoroughly in bursts over a few days so that you'll be able to fork deep enough. Forking before digging is very important. It loosens the soil and opens up the natural clefts in its structure. This minimises the damage to the natural capillaries when it comes to digging the path areas and dramatically improves the drainage under the bed areas. When you've finished forking, spread green waste compost and a 2 cm-thick layer of aged grass-eater manure on the bed areas (see page 41 for more information on manures). Finally, take a spade and work your way along the marked pathways digging about a 30 cm depth of soil out of the paths and onto the adjacent bed area.

Building raised beds guarantees proper soil depth and drainage, and in the process builds your soil's nutrition and structure. It also creates a space you won't have to disturb ever again, meaning your soil's tiny organisms, bacteria and worm life will thrive.

Introduce worms. Grab some composting worms from your worm farm (see page 44) or a nursery. Dig a few 30 cm-deep holes around your growing area and bury a handful of worms in each. A shoebox full of worms should be enough for 50 m² as they will rapidly multiply!

Establish an irrigation routine. Our preferred method of irrigation is to use automated drip lines. They allow for an enormous reduction in water use by applying water exactly where and when your plants need it. We use 30 cm-spaced drip emitters on lines spaced 40 cm apart. For our 80 cm-wide beds, we run two parallel lines (pictured, bottom right). For a 1–1.2 m-wide bed, we would run three (pictured, bottom left). We link parallel lines together at both ends to ensure an even flow of water. An automatic timer is absolutely worth the investment. By using an automatic timer combined with our use of drip emitters, we have been able to reduce our water use by over 80%.

Mulch. Finally, mulch your paths and beds with a thick layer of straw. Remember, don't mulch too early in spring; allow the soil to warm up first, and be careful when mulching around newly planted seedlings so as not to suffocate them.

FREE FORM BEDS

Building new beds

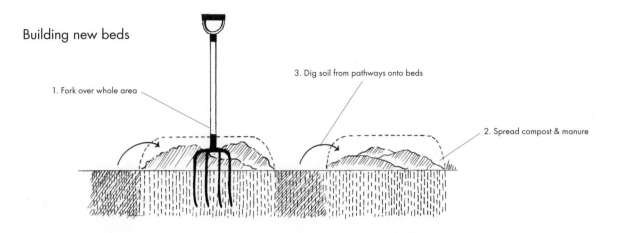

1. Fork over whole area
3. Dig soil from pathways onto beds
2. Spread compost & manure

Drip irrigation pattern

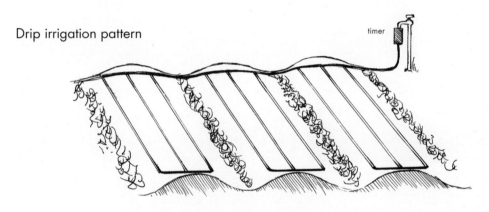

timer

EDGED BEDS

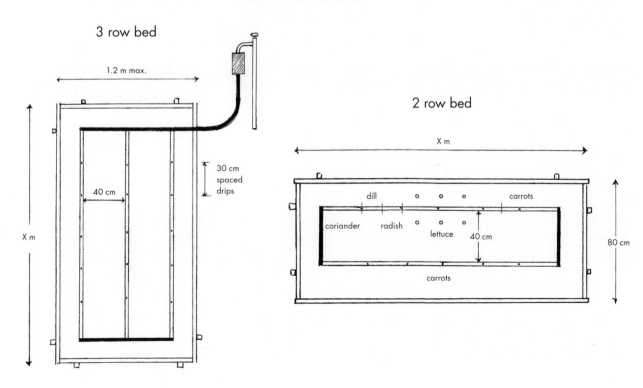

3 row bed

1.2 m max.

40 cm

X m

30 cm spaced drips

2 row bed

X m

dill   carrots

coriander   radish   carrots

lettuce   40 cm

80 cm

carrots

Planning your garden for a year-round harvest.

One of the most common questions we get asked is: 'What do I have to do so that I can harvest all year round?' And our response is always the same: 'You can't expect to harvest something every week if you don't plant something every week.' – Brian, mentor #1.

Admittedly, there is a little more to it than that, but the heart of the lesson is to *plan*. Our yearly plantings must be timed and managed so that we not only *always* have something ready to harvest now, but also *always* have something growing up to harvest *next*.

It's a fine balance that takes time to get right, and we will never stop learning. But as long as you make sure to plan your garden and plant a diverse range of plants you love, there will always be something to feast on.

Here we outline a plan for a home garden in a temperate climate, suitable to feed a family of four from about 140 m² of land. This is just an example – scale it up or down to meet your needs, and alter it to suit your climate. Don't feel fixed to it. If there is something you love, plant twice as much of it. If there is something you hate, don't plant it at all. And if you are really pushed for space, just pick some of your favourite things and plant only those. There are also less common plants we haven't even mentioned. If you miss them, add them to your plan. It's *your* garden, and it should reflect you and your tastes and nurture you as you nurture *it*.

Before planning, an important thing to note is that winter behaves differently to other seasons. Nothing really grows in winter. This doesn't mean everything dies – in fact there are numerous vegetable plants that can be frozen solid and continue to live happily – it just means that they don't physically grow very much, they simply sit there. Think of your winter garden as one big fridge, with all of your winter vegetables sitting in suspended maturity, ready to harvest whenever you so desire.

To achieve this, your garden must be fully loaded *before* the cold sets in, and all of your winter vegetables and herbs must be fully mature – harvestable – by late autumn. It's infuriating to read planting guides that suggest you plant things in the depths of winter. It's just not the case. Winter is a time for rest, not planting.

Yearly planting plan for a family of four in a temperate climate.

This plan requires 110 m² of garden space, which equates to about 140 m² including paths. In the planting tables we will refer to centimetres (cm) of *this* or metres (m) of *that*. This indicates how much of a given thing to plant along your rows. As discussed in *Building Your Garden* (see page 60), space your rows 40 cm apart, and plant seeds and seedlings along those rows, as per the *Step-by-Step Guides* on pages 56–57.

Towards the end of winter – the season begins.

Before we begin to plant directly into the garden in spring, we start sowing our first seeds into trays in the greenhouse in the last weeks of winter. These are the vegetables and flowers that take a long time to grow, so benefit from this early start. This is also the time to plant sweet potatoes and potatoes in soil in the greenhouse to sprout (see pages 58 and 264).

All of the above will be mature enough to plant out in six to eight weeks' time – see the mid-spring planting guide on page 66.

This is also the time to dig up, divide and re-plant horseradish, rhubarb, globe artichokes and cardoons, and to plant asparagus crowns.

Sow into trays in the greenhouse in 3 cm grids.

Basil, chillies, eggplants, capsicums, tomatoes	10 seeds of each
Cabbage, wombok, cauliflower, kohlrabi	12 seeds of each
Kale	20 seeds
Lettuce	1 tray
Potatoes	12 little potatoes for your potato barrel (see page 58)
Sweet potatoes	7 sweet potatoes to sprout (see page 264)
Cosmos, marigolds/calendula, nasturtiums, Queen Anne's lace and any other favourite flowers	10 seeds of each

Early spring – the first garden planting of the season.

Our first major planting happens in early spring. This is the time that we are harvesting the winter root vegetables, brassicas, greens, onion shoots and garlic shoots that we planted last summer and autumn. Our stores of pumpkins, potatoes, sweet potatoes, apples and quinces are still abundant, too. Those stores won't last forever though, and, as the soil begins to warm up, our winter vegetables will rapidly set seed and become woody. If we're lucky, the first broad beans and peas are ready to harvest too, but only just.

So, to avoid a serious vegetable drought, we must plant more crops now, which we will begin to harvest in late spring and continue to harvest through to mid-summer. Spring is still far too cold for many plants to tolerate, but some plants can, such as the herbs, greens and roots outlined in the table opposite.

Now is also the time to begin raising seedlings of the fast-growing summer crops – zucchini, pumpkin, cucumber and corn – and also to begin weekly sowings of lettuce, radishes, greens and soft herbs directly into the garden, vegetables that grow fast and can be harvested only once.

WEEKLY SOW

Sow every week from now until early autumn. As you begin to harvest these plantings, re-sow with more weekly plantings but in a different order, so as not to grow exactly the same plant in the same spot twice. Continue in this fashion, harvesting and over-sowing, until mid-autumn.

Asian greens, like pak choi and tatsoi	30 cm of each
Coriander, dill, radishes	15 cm of each
Lettuce	15 seeds into trays in the greenhouse 8 seedlings from the greenhouse into the garden, in a double row spaced 15 cm apart (start with the tray you planted towards the end of winter – see table opposite)
Spinach	45 cm – sow for the next 6 weeks only, then start again towards the end of summer through autumn (summer is too hot for spinach to thrive)

Sow the following seeds directly into the garden.

Beets, parsnips, turnips	5 m of each – when you begin to harvest these plantings, start from one end and re-sow weekly with carrot seed over where you have harvested
Carrots	13 m – when you begin to harvest this planting, start from one end and re-sow weekly with beet seed one week, then turnip, then parsnip, then beet again and so on, over where you have harvested
Chives, parsley, mixed salad greens (e.g. mibuna, mizuna, mustard, rocket, sorrel and tatsoi)	2 m of each
Leeks	8 m
Lemongrass, marjoram, mint/peppermint, oregano, rosemary, sage, thyme	Sow seeds/plant seedlings in big pots or half barrels to avoid them taking over the garden!
Silverbeet/chard	3 m

Sow into trays in the greenhouse in 3 cm grids.

Corn	15 seeds every fortnight for the next 6 weeks
Cucumber	15 seeds
Pumpkin, zucchini	10 seeds of each

Mid-spring – planting for the main summer harvest.

This is our second major planting. The crops we plant now will be ready for harvest in mid-summer, just as our early spring planting is coming to its end.

We perform this planting only when the risk of really cold nights – and frost – has passed. There is nothing worse for summer crops than being exposed to really cold weather early in their growth. We call it 'cold-checking'. Plants that have been cold-checked will never grow quite as rapidly or as large as plants that haven't, resulting in a smaller harvest.

So don't rush this planting. We use our tomato seedlings as indicators, and wait until they are about 20 cm tall. Then we plant out all of the seedlings from the greenhouse as outlined below. Use your discretion. If a seedling isn't mature enough for life in the open, leave it to grow for another week or two. Often our eggplants or capsicums fall into this category.

We also plant companion plants such as marigolds throughout the garden. Continue to sow more lettuce, radishes, greens and soft herbs every week (see the *Weekly Sow* table on page 65).

It's garlic harvest time. Set aside the *biggest* garlic cloves for planting out for next year's crop. It seems counterintuitive, because they're the ones you want to eat, but this technique will constantly improve the quality of your harvest, because the biggest cloves grow the biggest bulbs.

Plant the following seedlings into the garden.

Basil	5 plants; 30 cm spacing
Cabbage/wombok, cauliflower	6 plants of each; 60 cm spacing
Chillies	3 plants; 60 cm spacing; will benefit from staking
Corn	9 plants in a 3 x 3 grid; 30 cm spacing; plant every fortnight for the next 6 weeks
Cucumber	8 plants; 30 cm spacing; will benefit from a 45° trellis
Eggplant, capsicum	5 plants of each; 60 cm spacing; will benefit from staking
Kale	10 plants; 30 cm spacing
Kohlrabi	6 plants; 30 cm spacing
Potatoes	Plant 12 potatoes into your barrel (see page 58)
Pumpkin	5 plants; 90 cm spacing in all directions (plant away from other plants to avoid a pumpkin invasion)
Sweet potato	Plant out 60 slips; 30 cm spacing (it can sometimes take a little time to get the slips up and ready to plant out, but get them in the ground as soon as they are (see page 264 for more details)
Tomatoes	4 plants; 90 cm spacing; will benefit from a vertical trellis
Zucchini	6 plants; 90 cm spacing in every direction
Cosmos, marigolds/calendula, nasturtiums, Queen Anne's lace and any other favourite flowers	As many seedlings as you like throughout the garden

Sow the following seeds directly into the garden.

Bush and pole beans	4 m; seeds spaced 15 cm apart; will benefit from a vertical trellis

A few weeks into summer – brussels sprouts, celery and celeriac.

Some things require more time to grow than others. For that reason, a few weeks into summer, sow trays of brussels sprouts, celery and celeriac into the greenhouse. These are all very slow growing and need some extra time compared to the rest of our winter plantings, which we will get to in a few weeks, in mid-summer.

Now is usually the time to harvest onions and French shallots (which you plant in autumn the year before, see page 69). Store them for eating from now and all through winter, but only do so when their tops have fallen over. And save the seed heads of both for breaking apart and planting in autumn.

Sow into trays in the greenhouse in 3 cm grids.

Brussels sprouts	12 seeds
Celery, celeriac	20 seeds of each (these are very small seeds, so just sprinkle very lightly across half a tray and gently work into the soil)

Mid-summer – planting for the winter harvest begins.

Amongst the abundance of mid-summer, it's very important to remember the cold of winter, and to begin readying winter's crops. Weekly sowing of lettuce, radishes, greens and soft herbs continues (as shown in the *Weekly Sow* table on page 65).

Sow into trays in the greenhouse in 3 cm grids.

Broccoli	40 seeds
Cabbage/wombok, cauliflower, fennel	20 seeds of each
Kale	30 seeds
Kohlrabi	10 seeds

Sow the following seeds directly into the garden.

Beets, parsnips, turnips	7 m of each
Carrots	21 m
Chervil	1.5 m
Parsley	3 m
Silverbeet/chard	4 m

Late summer – the final planting for winter harvest.

This is the last major planting into the garden and is completed a few weeks before the start of autumn. Except for broad beans, peas, onions and garlic, this is the last chance to get everything in the ground with enough time to grow before the cold sets in.

It is also time to sow trays of onion seed into the greenhouse to plant out as pencil-thick seedlings in autumn.

When the truly cold weather arrives in early winter, the summer harvest will promptly end. This planting provides the crop that will see you through to mid-spring, but *only* if it's completed a few weeks before the first day of autumn.

Plant the following seedlings into the garden.

Broccoli	20 plants; 60 cm spacing
Brussels sprouts	6 plants; 30 cm spacing
Cabbage/wombok	10 plants; 60 cm spacing
Cauliflower	9 plants; 60 cm spacing
Celeriac, fennel	14 plants; 15 cm spacing; double row
Celery	8 plants; 30 cm spacing
Kale	14 plants; 30 cm spacing
Kohlrabi	7 plants; 30 cm spacing

Sow the following seeds directly into the garden.

Salad greens (rocket, mizuna, mibuna, sorrel)	3 m
Mustard greens	1 m
Upland cress	2 m
Pak choi, tatsoi	1.5 m of each

Sow into trays in the greenhouse in 3 cm grids.

Onions	200 seeds

Autumn.

We use autumn and winter to settle in some plants with a long growing period, so that when spring hits they are really ready to take off. Crops planted now also assist to bridge the harvest gap in late spring before the first new harvest is ready.

It's time to plant out the garlic cloves and French shallot seed heads that you set aside back in early summer, along with the onion seedlings from the greenhouse, but only if they have reached pencil thickness. Plant seeds of shelling peas, snow peas, sugar snaps and broad beans, and continue weekly sowing of lettuce, radishes, greens and soft herbs (as shown on the *Weekly Sow* table on page 65) until mid-autumn.

The time for planting is over by the end of autumn. All of your potatoes, sweet potatoes and pumpkins should be stored away and the autumn harvest – like tomatoes, eggplants, capsicums, cucumbers and zucchinis – preserved on the shelves. Your winter crops should be fully grown. It's time to rest.

Sow the following bulbs/seeds/seedlings directly into the garden.

Broad beans	4 m; seeds spaced 15 cm apart
Garlic	140 cloves; 10 cm spacing; triple row Plus 2 m sown thickly in a furrow, to be harvested as immature shoots throughout winter and spring
French shallots	50 seeds from saved seed heads; 15 cm spacing; double row Plus 5 whole French shallot bulbs, which will sprout next year's seed heads Plus 2 m seed French shallots sown thickly in a furrow, to be harvested as immature shoots throughout winter and spring
Onions	100 seedlings; 10 cm spacing; triple row
Various peas (sugar snaps, snow peas, shelling peas)	4 m; seeds spaced 15 cm apart

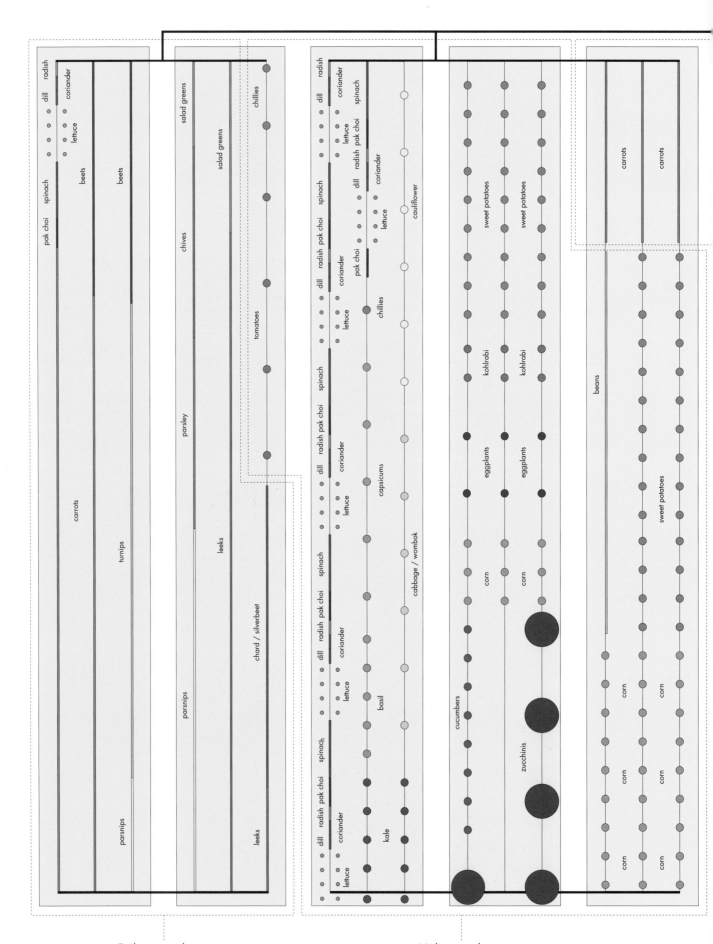

Early spring planting

Mid-spring planting

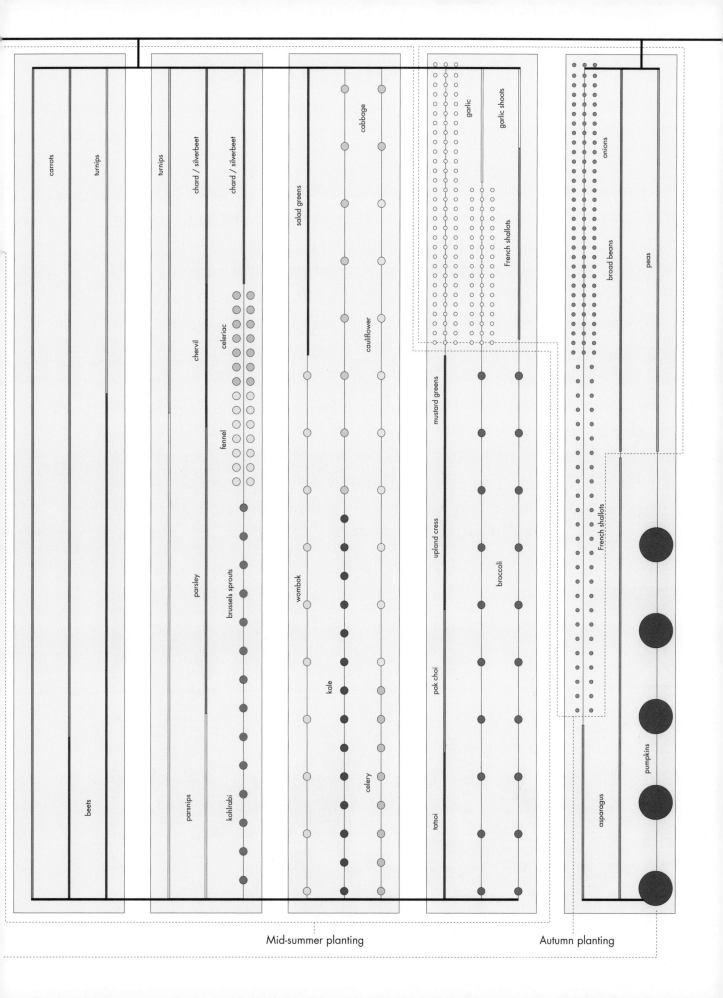

Mid-summer planting

Autumn planting

Fruit tree maintenance.

Fruit trees are awesome. You only need a few trees to supply all of the fruit that you need, and there really is nothing like homegrown fruit. For a backyard situation, we highly recommend choosing a few of your favourite fruits and planting a tree of each up against a sunny fence or wall, espaliering them as they grow. If you have more space, put in one or two trees of some of the other things that you love. But be prepared – a tree allowed to get as big as it likes can easily yield hundreds of kilograms of fruit.

We shape free-standing trees into an open vase shape because we find this maximises air movement and light throughout the canopy, but we've also seen incredible yields per acre on closely planted trees that have been heavily trellised. There are a million ways to treat a fruit tree. Whichever way you choose, follow the below advice to keep them happy and healthy.

FEEDING

Annually, spread a few centimetres of compost below the tree from near the trunk all the way to the drip line (the outer edge of the tree canopy) and mulch heavily with straw. Always leave a small gap between the trunk and the compost and straw to avoid collar rot. Feeding and mulching in this way not only maintains the tree's nutrition, it also suppresses weed competition, protects the all-important roots near the surface and maintains worm activity right where you need it at the surface.

PRUNING

Whole books exist on the subject of fruit tree pruning, but we try to forget the doctrines and just focus on a few key principles:

Intervene as little as possible. In fact, we believe that if you plant a very young tree seedling (under one year old) and leave it alone from day one, you can probably get away with never pruning it at all. A tree planted in this way will generally grow happily and healthily, naturally fitting in with the prevailing conditions. So, as long as you never move it to another location

or prune its branches, it should grow in a natural and orderly shape and remain in great health. But rest assured, if a tree has been pruned once, then it must be pruned regularly, or its branches are sure to become overcrowded, and ultimately the tree will begin to suffer.

Timing. We prune stone fruit trees during summer after their fruit has been harvested; apple, pear and quince trees during their winter dormancy; and citrus trees in late spring, or whenever the flower buds can be easily identified.

Always prune flush to the next branch. There is nothing worse than leaving little stubs all over a tree, as it seriously depletes the tree's ability to efficiently circulate nutrients and energy. If you have an old tree with this burden, clean it up by pruning them off right up against the next main branch. Use a small

chainsaw or pruning saw for large branches and very sharp secateurs for smaller ones.

Remove dead wood. Dead wood can be a huge burden for a fruit tree and, like little stubs, has an enormous impact on how efficiently the tree can circulate its energies. Remove it all back to the next living branch junction.

Remove any inward-growing branches. You're farming light – your trees need that solar energy – so you want to create an open shape in the centre of the tree to allow for maximum sunlight to reach all of the leaves and for air to easily circulate around them. It's an easy shape to achieve, simply remove any branches that point into the centre of the tree back to the next branch that doesn't.

Remove any branches that are crossing over. We could stop at inward-growing branches, but often there are also some outward growing branches that are getting in the way of each other as well. These will impede air circulation and potentially damage hanging fruit from adjacent branches. Prune branches that cross other branches back to the next branch that doesn't.

Maintain fruiting branches. Finally, to keep mature trees within a manageable size and ensure good fruit production we need to maintain the canopy each year. For citrus trees, remove a fifth of all the branches – selecting the longest and leggiest – right back to the trunk each year. For apple, pear, quince and stone fruit trees, only cut back those branches that are getting too long and have already fruited. Prune them right back to one bud near their base, from which will grow a new fruiting branch.

There is no fixed art to pruning fruit trees, and a lot of it comes with experience. But following the above principles means you can't go too wrong, so be brave and you'll learn a little more about your trees every year.

CHAPTER 3

Gather.

From the wild.

To gather food from the wild is to connect with a different, more intensely deep part of our genetics. It focuses our minds. It exposes us to the earth's incredible natural abundance. And it fixates every molecule of our bodies on the absolute time-and-place seasonality of things. There is a very special feeling that comes with identifying and using wild foods: they have amazing flavours and textures that are just so different to cultivated foods, they are perfectly imperfect, and they grow so superbly without any effort on our part. Gathering from the wild satisfies a feeling that is so innate and there is just a wonderfully simple and satisfying joy in learning what is safe, and what is not, and how to use all of these beautiful new foods!

That said, it is key to note that while humans have been hunting and gathering from the wild for far longer than they have been growing, nurturing or trading, modern humans are now largely agricultural beings. The domestication of plants and the birth of agriculture occurred so many thousands of years ago (see *A Very Short History of Food* on pages 16–17) that it has literally changed our brains and our physiology. Today, we thrive best by cultivating food, and the experiences this brings, *alongside* hunting and gathering from nature. So while we feel that gathering from the wild is super important, it is only one component of our diet, and we recognise that nature's abundance is not limitless.

The art of gathering got quite lost on the journey to modern society, and then more recently the opposite has happened, and parts of the wild have been pillaged almost beyond recovery by a new enthusiasm for it. We feel that our approach to gathering needs to sit somewhere in between, where we recognise how incredible gathering from the wild can be, but acknowledge that we can only take a little bit, in balance with what nature can give.

Most of what we gather or hunt are invasive pests, whether plant or animal – introduced species that are causing unnatural imbalances in the native ecosystem – and it's nice to know that we are helping to control these invasive species, and so helping to restore the balance. We can't tell you everything here, but start slow, learn how to identify, learn how to harvest responsibly and go from there. This is just a little guide to some of the most easily identifiable things that we take from the wild. Learn what is abundant around you and find yourself a local mentor who can help – nothing is better than real life experience under the guidance of a knowledgeable mentor.

SUMMER

Wild plums, blackberries and other wild fruits. European settlers introduced a host of incredibly invasive edible fruiting plants all over the globe. For those with smaller seeds, like wild plums (a relative of regular plums that are very small and quite sour) and blackberries, birds swallow the seeds whole when they eat the fruit, thus spreading the plants far and wide very rapidly. Less naturally, when freeways are built, they often cut through properties that become abandoned as a result. So the wild remnants of many hundreds of orchards can still be found on the sides of roads throughout the world. So long as you can be sure the plants haven't been sprayed with poison for control purposes (usually quite apparent from dieback, but recent sprays may not be so obvious – do some local research to be sure), these are easily identifiable and very safe foods to forage.

Carp. Introduced to Australia in the late 1850s, carp are now completely out of control in our rivers, and have caused the demise of many native fish species. Consequently, carp have a bad reputation in this country, which we think is a little unfair on the poor carp, who are just doing what they do. Carp are thought to be inedible in Australia and described as tough with a muddy taste. Indeed, if you pull a carp straight out of the river, let it flap around on the ground for half an hour, then kill it and cook it, that is exactly what you'll get – and what you deserve. But give carp a little love and they are *incredibly* delicious, nutritious and tender. In fact, they are our favourite freshwater fish!

To properly prepare carp, you must first purge them of their muddiness. The easiest way to do this is in an old bathtub, but a large tub or cooler will work too, so long as the fish can move freely and float horizontally as it normally would. We've found that it takes three days to completely remove the 'river' taste, and you will need to aerate the water by running a tap or hose at a constant trickle (you can also use a basic fish tank aerator), or change the water periodically (it's not an exact science, but if your carp is looking lethargic or gasping at the surface you've left it too long – please be careful). Also, sprinkle some oats, barley or other whole grain in the water to keep them fed.

Once purged, gently remove the fish from the tub with a bucket or net and immediately use the *ike jime* method to dispatch it and then sever its 'throat' to bleed it out (see diagram below).

This is a very simple, instant, and – importantly – painless method for killing the fish, after which the flesh is totally relaxed and never tough. Your carp is now ready to scale, gut and cook (see page 304 for our favourite cooking technique).

Carp are most active over the warmer months and whole dried corn kernels soaked overnight (especially in milk), hard cheese or worms are the best baits. You can never catch too many carp – the more that are removed from our waterways the better – so we (and our dogs and chickens) enjoy them throughout the summer.

Salt. Gathering your own salt is not so difficult, or mysterious! It would be reasonable to think that all salt is harvested near the ocean, but a great deal of the salt we eat actually comes from inland salt deposits. So much modern, dry land was once ancient seabed (even the Himalayas were once under the ocean), and so much subsurface water moves through saline aquifers before feeding inland lakes. Those inland salt lakes are the easiest places to gather your own, and it's a fantastic experience. It has to have rained in the previous few months for the salt lakes to 'work', but, provided the weather has been favourable, we usually gather salt in mid-summer, once the spring rains have been and gone and the water level has retreated. We visit our salt lake every year or so and stock up – a little salt lasts a *long* time!

AUTUMN

Game.

Autumn is our main hunting season. We prefer to hunt during daylight, usually at dusk and dawn, and catch animals while they are calmly feeding and unaware of our presence. We find this to be a much more natural and humane process than 'spotlighting' (hunting at night with a spotlight to startle the animal), which can cause a great deal of unnecessary stress. The meat will also be more tender, because the animal is totally relaxed at the moment before death.

Ducks. Wild ducks land and feed on our farm year round. They have finished breeding and raising their young by autumn, and are well fed in preparation for the colder weather. We take about half a dozen each season, enjoying them fresh through the autumn, and freezing some for winter. Wild ducks are smaller than farmed ducks, and the meat is much darker, much more intensely flavoured and usually leaner. Always bleed your ducks out from the throat immediately, and, for the most tender flesh, rest them in the fridge for a day or three before cooking (see recipe on page 321).

Rabbits and hares. Since their introduction in the 1860s, rabbits and hares have become a big problem in the area where we live, contributing to soil erosion and competing for resources with native species. We hunt them all year round to contain the population, but the best time for eating them is in autumn when they have fattened up for winter. Hare and rabbit are very different in flavour. Rabbit meat is finer and lighter (similar to chicken), while hare is much darker (similar to beef but more gamey). But both are delicious. Like ducks, always bleed rabbits and hares out from the throat immediately, and, for the most tender flesh, rest them in the fridge for a day or three before cooking (see recipe on page 318).

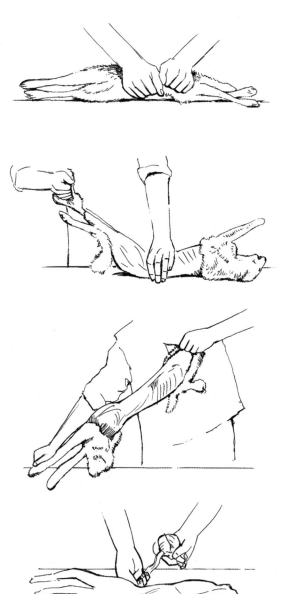

1 Slippery jacks, saffron milk caps and a couple of young crab brittle gills

2 Saffron milk cap

3 Young crab brittle gills, slippery jacks and saffron milk caps

4 Young crab brittle gill

Albacore tuna. We don't live near enough to the ocean for seafood to be a major component of what we eat. But we do feel that diversity is incredibly important for thriving health, so we still include one tuna a year in our diet. There really are plenty of fish in the sea, but albacore tuna is one of the most sustainable around Australian shores. Plus, they are bycatch for most Australian fishermen and are considered almost worthless in comparison to more highly prized tuna species like bluefin, so it is nice to offer them a little appreciation! Tuna run past the south coast of Australia from the end of summer through to the beginning of winter, so at some point during this time we get our hands on a mature albacore from an experienced fisherman. One that we know has used a pole and line to catch it, and the *ike jime* technique to kill it. We preserve the whole fish (minus a little sashimi) as per the recipe on page 233, and that one fish provides our entire seafood intake for the year (except for a few trips to the coast!).

Wild mushrooms.

Autumn is wild mushroom time! Foraging for wild mushrooms is so much fun. In season, mushrooms are always present in radiata pine plantations because the pine trees rely on a symbiotic relationship with the mushrooms to grow, so the mushroom spores are introduced when the trees are planted. We forage for three varieties of mushrooms in our forest (a massive timber plantation), with saffron milk caps being by far the most common. The others are slippery jacks and crab brittle gills, which we find in varying quantities each year – you just never know how the season will go.

Wild mushrooms fruit after the autumn rains, at which point the moisture and temperature reach their critical tipping points in the forest. Usually, the season lasts from mid-autumn to the beginning of winter, about 12 weeks. We've experienced seasons that lasted only half as long, but interestingly, we harvested just as much as normal – it was like the forest had to get it all out of the way at once!

There is an ongoing debate on whether to pull from the stem or to cut at the base when harvesting wild mushrooms. Neither is likely to matter. Whatever you do, though, always leave some mushrooms in the forest so that they can drop their spores and complete the lifecycle – growing many more mushrooms again the following season. We highly encourage deeper research into wild mushrooms. We find them to be an endlessly enthralling phenomenon.

There is only so much we can communicate through words and pictures alone. Misidentifying mushrooms can be quite literally deadly, so please only use this as a guide and find yourself a mentor to actually take you into the forest. Always cook mushrooms well, and always follow the number one mushroom foragers rule: if you don't know, throw. Note that some pine plantations/forests have chemicals 'air-dropped' over the whole area at intervals. Ask before picking.

Saffron milk caps. (*Lactarius deliciosus*). Normally just referred to as pine mushrooms or red pines, saffron milk caps are easily identified by their bright orange cap, stem and gills, and even brighter orange sap – nothing looks quite like them. They taste like bacon and eggs when cooked in butter with some salt and pepper. In season, these are the most prolific mushrooms we find. And they are *so* good.

Slippery jacks. (*Suillus luteus*, *Suillus brevipes* and *Suillus granulatus*). Although slippery jacks are usually quite common in pine plantations, for whatever reason they're not so much in ours. They are a love-them-or-hate-them kind of mushroom. Not for their flavour, which is subtler than the rest but still delightfully earthy and sweet, but for their texture, which is, as the name suggests, incredibly slippery when cooked. They have a light to dark brown cap that is *very* slimy, a light yellow stem and a particularly sponge-like yellow underside rather than gills. Being sponge-like, they soak up flavours particularly well, and they are an absolute delicacy floating in chicken stock. Peel before cooking.

Crab brittle gills. (*Russula xerampelina*). These are adored by everything in the forest. Finding some that haven't been either nibbled on or downright demolished is like finding a needle in a haystack. But it is a beautiful moment when you do. They have deep maroon to purple caps, bright white stems and pale yellow gills that are very brittle – hence the name. As the name also suggests, they are super crustacean-like to eat, and they maintain their firm and crunchy texture when cooked. We call them the 'fish and chips of the forest', and they are our absolute favourite.

Autumn fruits.

Prickly pears. In a nod to Lentil's Maltese ancestry, we do our best to collect some prickly pears each year. Once you get past the graininess, they are mildly but pleasantly sweet and quite melon-like (in Malta, they are actually mostly used to make liqueur!). Prickly pears are an invasive species, but aren't out of control in Australia any more. Pick them when they are fully coloured and peel to eat.

Olives. Yes, olives grow wild where we live! Like blackberries and wild plums, olives have a small enough seed that birds swallow them whole and spread them far and wide. There are many old olive groves near us, and consequently there are many wild trees too. Wild olives are wonderful. They are smaller than farmed olives, but the varieties vary in size and flavour. They tend to fruit a little less prolifically, too, but their flavour is particularly intense. We generally mix the varieties and make enough brined olives (see page 210) to get us through the year. They are magnificent.

WINTER AND SPRING

Wild greens/edible weeds.

Wild greens are most prolific from the end of autumn when the rains begin, through winter and into spring until the rains dry up again. But winter is when they are most abundant, as they thrive in the cooler weather. They're also nice and young then, which means they are at their sweetest and most tender. Even though we have a whole garden full of delicious vegetables, we gather these wild greens because they have such unique and delicious flavours.

Some general rules for picking wild greens:

- If you want them at their sweetest and most tender, pick wild greens young.
- Avoid thick stems, as they are generally tough, even after cooking. The leaves and the little connective stems attached to them are the tastiest parts.
- Never pick anything you can't identify.
- Never pick anything that might have been sprayed with poison – especially important in urban areas.

Edible weeds were eaten regularly by our ancestors, but over time we have forgotten how to identify them. Below is a guide to a few of our favourites.

Dandelion. (*Taraxacum officinale*). Also known as 'wild chicory', dandelion leaves make a great addition to salads. But, for us, dandelion's real strength lies is in its root, as a substitute for coffee. Dandelion can be identified by its rosette of heavily serrated 'lion's tooth' leaves, and very recognisable bright yellow flowers. The root is at its plumpest and most tender from the end of autumn until early spring, before it begins to run to flower. We dig them up, clean them thoroughly, chop them into smaller pieces and dry them in a 50°C oven until crisp. Once dry, they can be used as is for dandelion tea or, our favourite, roasted for a few hours at 150°C then blitzed in a high-powered blender to make dandelion 'coffee'. You can also buy regular chicory seeds, grow chicory, and do exactly the same thing with *their* roots. Delicious.

Fat hen. (*Chenopodium album*). This is one of our favourites. When you find a patch of fat hen, you really find a patch of fat hen! It is especially prolific in autumn and spring, and its furry, slightly grey-tinged, green leaves – that look like blunt prehistoric spearheads – are readily identifiable. When cooked, it is nutty and silky, and the most perfect substitute for spinach of all the wild greens. The perfect green for our beans and eggs recipe on page 262.

Mallow. (*Malva parviflora*). Mallow, which is shaped like folded lily pads, is everywhere. It has slightly fuzzy, dark green leaves with crinkle-cut edges, a lighter coloured underside and seven veins radiating from its stems. It is smooth but quite dry in texture when cooked, with a nutty, spinach-like flavour. Best eaten sautéed, in a risotto, in a stew, or even juiced – generally just use it as you would spinach (although it takes a little longer to wilt during cooking). Ideal for our Szechuan rice bowls with wild greens (see page 324).

Stinging nettle. (*Urtica urens*). To us, nettles are the absolute pinnacle of edible weeds. They are the most annoying to pick, but the most rewarding to eat. They're also a great source of protein and one of the richest sources of chlorophyll on the planet. Nettles can be identified by their serrated, furry, teardrop-shaped leaves that grow on an upright plant with a central stalk. Leaves should be a vibrant dark green and give a sharp sting if you brush past them.

1 Pickly pears

2 Young
dandelion plant

3 Fat hen

4 Mallow

1 Stinging
nettles

2 Wild radish in
flower

3 Wood sorrel

4 Pine needles

5 Seaweed

sheer abundance – for us – wild radish is probably the most common weed that we eat and it pairs beautifully with wild mallow in our Szechuan rice bowls with wild greens (see page 324).

Wood sorrel. (*Oxalis*). This has to be the most common – or at least one of the most well known – wild weeds. It is easy to identify due to its distinctive flavour and shape, with small clover-like leaves – shaped like three hearts joined together – on long stems. Its flowers are usually yellow, but can also be purple, pink or white. The flower, stalk and leaves are all edible. Wood sorrel tastes pleasantly sour and vibrantly lemony and is excellent raw in salads, cooked in tarts or with fish, or dried and used as a tangy herb. The flowers especially, but also the leaves, make for a brightly flavoured garnish as well.

YEAR-ROUND

Pine needles. (usually *Pinus radiata*). These are another bounty of the forest that we love to collect when we are gathering mushrooms, but they can be collected and used year-round. We highly recommend soaking green pine needles in olive oil for three days to make a fantastically fragrant dressing. Use it in place of olive oil to add flavour to salads, vegetables, grains and beans.

Seaweed. There are so many varieties of seaweed growing along the world's coastlines, and none are poisonous, so gathering them is very safe. Always collect fresh specimens, not seaweed that has been washed ashore for days! Ideally, cut it from above its holdfast (where it connects to the rocks or seabed) yourself, and only collect from the open ocean, not small bays where the water may not be as pure. It is worth doing a little further research to try to identify the most delicious species, but species aren't always easy to identify, and there are just so many of them that it can get a little confusing. However, a basic understanding is still pretty useful. It's also worth experimenting and tasting what's around you, and discovering what's delicious and what's not. We collect seaweed whenever we visit the coast and not only eat it ourselves but add it to our compost (see page 45).

So wear gloves to harvest, or grab them firmly enough to crush the little 'hairs' so they can't sting you. Nettles taste earthy, like an intense silverbeet, and are best cooked in soups and stews. They maintain the most incredibly bright tone of green after cooking, too, making them ideal for our wild mushroom and weed ravioli (see page 306). Blanch them in hot water to remove their sting before handling. They're also great dried and used as tea (very cleansing!).

Wild radish. (*Raphanus raphanistrum*). Wild radish is a beautiful wild brassica that grows prolifically on our farm. We love it. It can be identified by its hairy – almost to the point of being spiky – rosette of broad-lobed leaves, which become massive, though remain edible, in the favourable conditions of autumn through spring. Even young leaves are too coarse and spiky to eat raw, but they are neither of these things after cooking. Instead, they are vibrantly green and completely tender once cooked, and taste like a less pungent version of broccoli. They make a unique and sweet substitute for any recipe that calls for kale or silverbeet/chard. The flowers are edible and are incredibly sweet and pretty too. Due to its

CHAPTER 4

Nurture.

A symbiotic relationship between humans, animals and nature.
Eggs, meat, dairy, honey.

Raising animals has changed us. Not just the way we farm, and the way we eat, but *us*. The relationships we have formed with our animals are some of the most fulfilling that we've ever had. Keeping animals comes with challenges, for sure, but it is incredibly rewarding, and the joy of participating in our animals' lives has enriched our own lives immeasurably.

When we set out on this journey, we acknowledged that a small amount of animal food has always been present in traditional diets, and that this small amount played a vital role in wellness (see the *Eat* chapter for more information), but we were particularly uncomfortable with what we saw of modern, conventional animal raising. We wanted to learn what it meant to raise animals *well*, in a way that nurtured the animal and was in balance with nature.

So, like with our growing techniques, we went back to the start – to a simpler time and a gentler approach. And we found what we were looking for. We have long since learnt that animal husbandry can be a truly beautiful thing. That it doesn't have to mean suffering, and, in fact, can be a truly balanced relationship between humans, animals and the grander scheme of nature.

THE ROLES OF ANIMALS IN TRADITIONAL AGRICULTURE

Humans long ago realised that you can grow more plant food in a given area than you can animal foods. But they also realised that if you wanted nature to really do its thing you added animals, because their manures and their specific behaviours – grazing, rooting, scratching and pollinating – all enlivened plants and soils and stimulated growth. Animals were also good workers in the fields, able to pull and push much greater loads than us. Besides all of that, eggs, dairy, honey and meat were prized for their concentrated nutrition, and wool, leather, down and bone were invaluable materials. Traditional animal husbandry always revered its flocks, and when you meet a good farmer today, the devotion they have for their animals is still apparent. It's a relationship. And there's a balance. For the animal, there is safety, an abundant food source and guaranteed continuation of its species. For the human, there are any of the above tasks, foods and materials. Traditionally, the animal's health and enjoyment of life was always paramount, because a healthy, happy animal is not only easier to work with, but provides the most superior work, food and materials. It was an approach that is worlds away from industrialised modern farming and a place we believe animal husbandry must return to.

A SYMBIOTIC RELATIONSHIP: NATURE, ANIMALS AND US

A new (old) approach to animal husbandry.

In many ways, we treat our animals like we treat ourselves. We need food, water, company and shelter; they need food, water, company and shelter. But we also must observe our flocks, and get to know them, so that we can empathise with them and know what it means for *that* animal to lead a fulfilled life. We can then answer questions like, 'How do we replicate its *natural* environment and natural lifespan?' and, 'How do we nurture its natural behaviours?' Then we can provide the conditions that allow them to thrive, and also know what is normal behaviour and what is abnormal behaviour so that we can keep everyone happy and healthy.

With time and experience, you will begin to see the slightest shifts in behaviour that might indicate early signs of illness, or that it's time to implement a change. You'll notice a sick sheep with a mild cough months before it has serious problems, and you can catch that cough early and naturally medicate so that further problems don't develop. We watch our animals every day. We touch base with them every morning, keep an eye on them from a distance throughout the day, and touch base with them again every evening. It's a joy to do, to watch them grow and play and just freely be themselves – animals are much more honest in their behaviour than most humans!

To us, every animal is as important as the next. We once had a lamb with a badly broken leg. In modern high production farming it would have been euthanised. Can you imagine being put down for a broken leg? We gave him anti-inflammatory herbs and raw cow's milk bolstered with egg yolks, and we splinted that leg as best we could and got young 'Paddle', as he became known, back out with his mum as soon as possible. And he is now as fat, fit and well as all of the other grown lambs. In short, you can't just leave a mob of sheep in the back paddock and hope they'll be okay. It's a relationship, and we love it.

Nurturing animals is awesome. We can't imagine a life not directly involved with the production of our animal foods anymore. When done in a traditional manner, where animals are allowed to exist in their natural state, nature is balanced, farming is balanced, and our diets are balanced. Animal foods make up only a small fraction of our diet, as they always have in traditional diets, but we have found that a small amount makes a big difference (see the *Eat* chapter for more details).

Of course, not everyone can raise their own animals – although if you can experience it even just once, please do – but please source your animal products responsibly and honestly, and don't eat too much of them. We believe it is a far more powerful act to choose to eat well-produced animal foods, and thus support those good farmers, and increase the demand for better farming practices, than it is to not eat them at all.

HOW TO BEGIN?

When taking on a new animal, we *always* seek the advice of a mentor. Naturally, a big reason for writing this chapter is so that not everyone has to make the same mistakes that we have, but, when embarking on nurturing a new animal, please find yourself a physical guide(s) too, because if you're like us, there's nothing worse than the feeling that you've caused even the slightest hardship to your flocks!

With that in mind, here are our key tips that you may not discover elsewhere – things we've learnt that keep our animals, nature and us in perfect balance:

General rules for all animals.

Choose old breeds. We have found that heritage breeds of *all* animals are by far the most robust and are better foragers across *all* conditions. They are so much closer to their wild equivalents and, as such, still have the ability to look after themselves when you give them wild-like conditions. Like modern, hybridised vegetables (as discussed in *Grow*), modern animal breeds are invariably sculpted towards one product-oriented quality or another, be it more milk, better tolerance of confinement, more wool or more meat. But an old-breed cow produces plenty of milk, an old-breed chicken produces plenty of eggs, an old-breed sheep grows plenty of wool, and an old-breed turkey has plenty of meat. Old breeds produce food that – like an heirloom plant – tastes better and is more in balance with nature. And they are better for you because of it. They most closely resemble the animals our ancestors worked with, and on the deepest of levels they just feel right.

Do not overstock your land. As a general guide, every acre of very well-managed pasture can support one mature cow or five mature sheep or goats without supplementary feed. They would need little else but water and minerals (see page 97). Or, the same area of land will support five mature pigs or 50 chickens, but both would require free access to a grain and seed mix (see *Poultry*, opposite) for extra protein, as well as water and minerals. These numbers should give you an idea of the possibilities, but it all depends on so many factors: soil quality, pasture quality, pasture diversity, balance of trees to pasture, rainfall, slope, the breed – the list is endless. These are best-case scenario numbers and would require an active rotational grazing system (see the next point) to be in place. Start small, get your systems down and observe what your land can support, bearing in mind it might take two to three years before you start to notice problems stemming from overstocking. Watch what your animals graze and forage, keep an eye on their condition and supplement with additional feed – such

as lucerne and grain – as needed while you find the right balance. Land capacity can be greatly improved by sowing ideal grasses or forage for your climate and terrain to increase the nutrient density of your pasture – this is very location specific, so you'll have to do some local research on the appropriate varieties for *your* area.

Crash graze (rotational grazing). We are big advocates for crash grazing – regularly moving your animals to new pasture in small blocks. It's too complex a subject to properly tackle here, but we highly recommend you do further research into the subject. Using this method, cows can be confined to an area using just one or maybe two electric wires. Sheep, however, require mesh fencing or electric netting – they are sneaky things. And poultry definitely require mesh fencing or electric netting. Move your animals daily if you can, weekly if not, and no less than monthly in the worst-case scenario. Crash grazing is by far the most natural way to manage your pasture and the health and happiness of the flock or herd, and we can't recommend the process highly enough. In our system the cows graze a given area first, followed by the sheep, followed by the birds.

POULTRY

We keep chickens and ducks for eggs and meat, and are about to embark on keeping turkeys. They are all fantastic helpers in the garden, working over the garden beds in their dormant season, and also provide down for pillows and doonas. We absolutely love our birds and can spend hours watching them do their thing. Each species has its own little quirks, but to keep them healthy, happy and producing abundantly, all poultry require free access to the following:

Grain, pulse and seed mix. Three-parts whole grains to one-part pulses for balanced protein – use whatever is most abundant in your locality. We use wheat, barley and oats for the grains, and lupins, peas and lentils for the pulses, plus some seeds, like sunflower, flax, sesame and pumpkin. We allow them to eat as much as they want, which, as an example, averages out to around 130 g per chicken per day, depending on how much forage they have (see *Space to Roam* on page 97). Soaking the mix in soured raw milk, water (ideally, acidulated with a little apple

cider vinegar) or whey increases the nutrient value, plus we often soak the mix in boiling water briefly during winter to give the birds a hot breakfast – this keeps them laying despite the cold weather.

Seaweed meal and unrefined salt. These provide important minerals, such as potassium, phosphorus, magnesium, calcium, sodium, chlorine and sulphur. Provide both the salt and seaweed meal in separate low feeders, as with the grain mix and shell grit (see below), so the birds can pick at them as needed.

Shell grit. Coarsely ground seashells provide all-important calcium for eggshell production.

Clean, fresh water. All animals need clean, fresh water to be healthy. We use the rainwater from our tanks (our birds don't need chlorine or fluoride in their diets any more than we do) and change it regularly.

Space to roam. Old-breed poultry are great foragers. Our birds eat less of the grain we offer them when they have more space to self feed, choosing instead to forage and scratch across the land for green plants, wild seeds and insects. In a backyard situation, just let them roam as much as possible – the larger and more naturally diverse the area, the better. If you don't have the space to let them roam, they will be missing out on a lot of nutrition normally provided by insects, so be sure to supplement their feed with some high-protein additions like milk, meat and fish scraps, or bone meal. The latter are often available from butchers and fish markets – including the bone meal that accumulates in butchers' saws.

Water for water birds (ducks, geese). These birds don't just love to paddle, they love to root around for grubs in the shallows too. So the bigger the 'puddle', the better – ideally, a pond. Try to keep it clean, as it is literally their bath.

Dust for land birds (chickens, turkeys). If these birds don't have access to dry earth to bathe in, it is impossible for them to groom themselves and you will surely end up with lice and mite problems. Again, it doesn't need to be a huge space, just ensure that they have access to dry earth throughout the day – this is often forgotten for backyard chickens! Without a sheltered dust area, a few days of rain can be enough to cause major problems. To help with lice and mite control even further, we also sprinkle our chicken's favourite dust bath areas with diatomaceous earth – a very fine powder made from ancient fossilised algae that is a natural anti-parasitic (available from any good feed store). We dust the sheep, cows and dogs with this periodically for the same reason.

A safe place to roost. We have multiple chicken houses and each chicken has its chosen perch in its chosen home. The birds go into their houses on their own at dusk – we just lock the door behind them and open it in the morning. Our bird houses have floors so that foxes can't dig under them, and they can also be moved around to work in with our rotational grazing system. Chickens love a high place to roost, whereas ducks will sleep on the floor.

In the wild, fowl don't normally form groups larger than 20 birds, so we provide enough pens for them to replicate this behaviour. It is thought that they can't easily remember more 'faces' than this, so when more than 20 birds are forced to roost in one space the pecking order breaks down, causing a lot of stress and fighting. Sometimes more will roost in one, but we always give them the choice. This is one reason why the label 'free-range' definitely does not equal good. Free-range regulations allow for thousands of birds to roost in the one space, guaranteeing stress and aggression. Actually, the term 'free-range' doesn't even mandate that birds have access to a large *outdoor* space – only that their shed is a certain size. Please choose poultry and eggs that have been raised on small farms that raise animals well – look for the terms 'pastured', 'pasture-raised' or 'biodynamic'. Or raise your own. Large-scale poultry farming is a nightmare.

A place to lay. This has to be large enough for them to quietly hang out in, have nice thick, clean straw on the bottom, and be a little private – something with a top and sides and a small entrance is perfect – so that they feel comfortable and safe – this really makes a huge difference. Twenty birds will happily share one laying nest; in fact, they usually do in the wild. If they don't seem to be getting the point, leave a golf ball in the laying box to encourage them to lay in that spot.

Scraps. Poultry love food scraps, which provide a free and significant boost to their dietary protein and overall health. We throw all of our food waste from our kitchen and some of the waste we collect from restaurants to our birds. They get everything from bones and meat to vegetable and fruit scraps, but we try to keep out coffee and tea and definitely chocolate.

Some additional notes on poultry.

Boys. It's just natural! Of course, it's not always possible to have a rooster in your backyard due to the noise, but, if you can, provide a male for your girls. One rooster or drake needs at least six chickens or ducks in his harem to accommodate their sex drive. This is very important to avoid frustrated birds. If you are trying to hatch chicks to grow your flock, six to ten is a good number for maximum fertility. We aim for one rooster or drake with about ten mature hens or ducks per house, and up to another ten immature birds. Provided the mature males are all getting along, we let the flocks mix during the day and they all return to their respective houses each night. Fertilised and unfertilised eggs are exactly the same to eat, it just means that if you did incubate the eggs, or a hen did sit on them, they would grow into baby chicks. If you don't want chicks, of course, broody hens can easily be discouraged simply by constant removal of the eggs she's trying to sit on.

Incubation. We have stopped incubating eggs ourselves in an incubator. Birds just do the job so much better, and things work out so much more perfectly. Every season – from mid-spring to late summer – a few of our girls will get clucky and start sitting on eggs, so we provide them with a clean separate area with water, seaweed meal, grain etc. and their own space to roam. We give them 12–14 fresh fertilised eggs (store them narrow-end down while you accumulate them) to sit on. They sit for three weeks and always hatch and raise their chicks well. We give the chicks access to a mix of ground seeds, grains and pulses, salt, seaweed meal and water and leave them to grow with their mother. As early as four weeks, she may push them away. If this happens, we simply return her to the flock and leave the chicks in the separated area to raise themselves. We slowly increase how coarsely we grind the chicks' food and introduce shell grit. Eight weeks later, when the chicks are 12 weeks old, we integrate them with the rest of the flock. Chickens can hatch duck eggs and ducks can hatch chicken eggs, but only one or the other at a time, because chicks take 21 days to incubate and ducklings take 28 days.

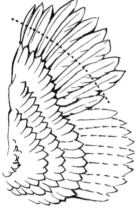

Poultry in the garden. We use our birds to tidy up the veggie and flower beds, but only after the crops have all been pulled. During production, they wreak too much havoc with mulch and young seedlings and are more of a hindrance than a help! They will also flatten hilled beds, so be prepared to re-hill your garden beds post poultry.

Guinea fowl. These guys are great for keeping snakes away!

Turkeys. Turkeys are said to be excellent bug eaters (great for pest control), minimal scratchers (so they won't destroy your garden beds), and excellent foragers (so you don't have to feed them as much).

Wing clipping. Cut the flight feathers of one wing of each bird to prevent them from flying away or over fences. It's super easy and totally painless (see diagram on the left).

GRAZING ANIMALS

We keep milking cows for dairy and mowing grass, and Wiltshire sheep for mowing, meat and wool (which they naturally shed). The cows are like pets; they are part of the family. The sheep are wilder, requiring a less complex relationship. Despite this, we love them all equally. This is how we do it:

Form a bond. Grazing animals kept primarily for meat are very easy to raise. If kept for milk, though, you must create a much stronger bond with the animal. It's not harder, but it's definitely more involved. This happens with time. Be patient as you get to know your new milking animal, and work up to hand-feeding her and being able to calmly walk her around *before* she kids/lambs/calves for the first time. Like all animals, food equals friendly. Spoil them and they will love you. Our cows love fruit, like apples, peaches and pears, and will do anything for it. That's why one of our cows is called Peaches.

Allow a bond. We believe in calves and lambs growing up with their mums, and so allow the babies to feed for as long as they want while they transition to pasture.

For milking animals though, you obviously don't have to let them take all of the milk. In a commercial dairy, calves will only get about 5–6 litres of milk a day and are fully weaned by the time they are two months old. To create a really strong bond, we allow our calves to feed freely for the first three months, by which stage they will be eating a large amount of pasture. When they start taking more than half of the day's milk (about 10 litres), we transition to a single evening milking and begin to separate mum from calf during the day (for the 12 hours leading up to milking) by a metre-high, ring-lock, non-electrified fence that they can kiss each other and hang out over. This way we only milk once a day and mum and calf get to spend plenty of time together. You could wean your calf at any point after two months, but we think the later the better – the bond between mum and calf is strong for almost 12 months.

Milk by hand. We are big advocates of hand milking. It builds such a strong bond with your animal and a fantastic connection with your food. It just feels innate. We lubricate our fingers with ghee or butter when we milk.

Provide the basics. We give our grazers free access to clean water, good pasture, seaweed meal, unrefined sea salt and diatomaceous earth. It is said that it's a good idea to also give access to lime, dolomite, dusting sulphur and copper sulphate, especially with Australia's ancient soils, which tend to be copper deficient compared to Europe, where many of these animals' genetics herald from. But when we did this, our stock never touched them. We treat our pasture like we treat our garden, so if you have a healthy pasture this may not be necessary.

Dust against external parasites. As with poultry, diatomaceous earth is an incredible natural weapon against lice and mites. Dust your animals' coats regularly.

Use herbal medication whenever possible. Our number one medication is a 'herbal ball' – a mixture of diatomaceous earth, crushed garlic, oregano oil, unpasteurised honey, lemon juice and apple cider vinegar. Roll it together and force it down. It cures all of our runny nosed or slightly 'off' animals overnight.

Be wary of lucerne and grain. Cattle, especially, are not clever eaters and will sometimes overeat this very rich feed, giving themselves potentially deadly bloat. If your animals do appear bloated – lethargic and literally swollen around their bellies – consult a livestock veterinarian immediately. Olive oil poured down the throat will ease non-life-threatening cases. If you do feed lucerne and/or grains, never allow your animals to feed freely. Ration a small amount to each animal each day. We have often fed a small bucket of lucerne to our dairy animals during milking, not because they need it, but because they love it so much. Sheep are much smarter eaters; they tend not to overeat anything – although we have never kept hybrid sheep, so it may differ with them. Our sheep are Wiltshire horns, and they actually prefer grass over *everything* else, so we used to just let them graze around the garden without fencing it off. So long as there was grass, they'd just eat that. But we've since learnt the hard way that they will, at a push, devour potato leaves, gooseberry leaves, melon leaves and most greens – although they will *never* touch pumpkin leaves, making them an invaluable maintenance crew around the pumpkin crop. The lesson: experiment with sheep around your crops, but keep a close eye on them.

Abattoirs. Probably the biggest smudge on the meat industry is the abattoir system and the live transport it requires. It's hard to see a solution except for well-managed on-farm slaughter, but it's a very difficult situation, as this is currently illegal in Australia – animals must go to abattoirs if they are to be sold for meat. We have many friends who raise the most loved and cared for commercial animals, only to shed a tear every time they watch them walk into the abattoir to meet their end – a place so far removed from the peaceful pastures they were reared on. It just shouldn't end that way. We have come to appreciate that the good death of an animal is almost more important than a good life. So if you can access homegrown and home-killed meat, done without causing stress to the animal, please utilise it.

BEES

We keep bees more for the pleasure of the experience than the bonus of honey and bee pollen. The honey and bee pollen are great, we just don't make that the focus. Bees pollinate nearly every vegetable and fruit that we grow, so ensuring that they are around is just common sense. Bee populations globally are under threat from modern chemical-based agriculture, so keeping bees to maintain the health of the species is more important than ever.

Try an old-style hive. We have a top bar hive and highly recommend it because it's so easy to work with. We have seen the best results when the bees are initially given an inch or so of foundation comb on each bar to build off to ensure they build straight. Provided the bees build straight comb, a top-bar hive is a joy to work with. If they build comb all over the place, though, it can be really frustrating – very much speaking from experience here! We'd also like to experiment with a Warré-style hive, but it's unclear how appropriate they are for Australian conditions. Both the top-bar hive and the Warré are intuitively designed hives that do everything they can to support the natural behaviours of the honey bee, as opposed to being designed to maximise honey production. We'd prefer the happiest bees, rather than the biggest honey harvest. All that said, there is no reason a modern Langstroth hive can't be a joy to work with for both the bees and the keeper – the key is to learn from a wise and gentle mentor, and they each have their own preferences.

Location is everything. Always set your bees up in the shade with a clear take-off and landing path. The fewer obstacles in their way at take-off and landing means the most efficient flight path, and therefore the most energy for honey and pollen collection. Avoid facing the entrance towards a commonly trodden path, or you're likely to end up with unnecessary contact. Also avoid facing your hive due south in the Southern Hemisphere or due north in the Northern Hemisphere. East facing is great as the morning light gets your bees buzzing early.

Lose the fear. Bees are super docile, unless you are robbing them of their honey, so don't fear them. Also, like us, they have good days and bad days, so observe the hive and wait for a good day to harvest.

Collect bee pollen, but not too much. We collect bee pollen every now and again with a pollen catcher. It's very simple. We just leave it at the hive entrance for a day and collect enough pollen to last us for a couple of weeks.

Don't harvest too frequently or too late. We occasionally rob the honey stores – but never take more than a third – always between summer and early autumn, and then always leave the bees alone with plenty of time to stock up for winter when there are fewer flowers and they have much less energy to collect nectar.

Take your time and do it right. When we rob the hive, we are always very careful not to break the honeycomb or expose any honey, because bees will stick to it and that's that. Done right, harvesting honey causes zero deaths. As soon as we have finished harvesting, the bees just get straight back to work as if nothing has happened. Happy hive, happy keepers.

CHAPTER 5

Trade.

Because the longest lasting happiness happens when we share.

Although we have learnt to grow, gather and nurture enough food to feed ourselves, we still continue to source some food and goods from others to diversify our diet and life. To do this we have embraced an idea that has been almost forgotten, a skill that has been all but lost. Trade.

By trade, we mean the exchange of goods and services without money – to barter or swap. It's based on the traditional village model, where trade was always a part of life. People traded within their villages – and sometimes from far away – to enrich their regional diet, and their lives, gaining things and skills that *others* grew, gathered, nurtured or were particularly proficient at, in exchange for things that *they* grew, gathered or nurtured or were particularly proficient at. In this way, abundances were shared, excesses were distributed and things got done in the most efficient and effective way.

In the modern world, though, the exchange of goods and services for money has come to completely dominate the economy, and the skill of trading without money has been lost. So we set out to re-learn it. Along the way, we have discovered that trade always seems to give you so much more than you expect. The journey has been full of humour, happiness, cringing, smiling and, overall, very happy hearts, because trade is like that little extra ingredient added to a great meal that makes it so much better. It isn't essential to survival, but it's something that we guarantee will change your life in the happiest way.

Studies have shown that when you see or buy something new there is a part of the brain that lights up and makes you feel happy. But they've also shown that this happiness is incredibly short lived. The first time you see the thing you've bought, you get a *big* chemical spike of happiness. But then, with each successive time you see it, the spike of happiness gets smaller, until you are driven to purchase something new. Experiences, on the other hand, have been found to lead to much more profound, long-lasting spikes of happiness. And we have to agree. For example, we've gained such long-lasting personal satisfaction from growing, gathering and nurturing our own food, and this in turn has made *eating* food a more profound experience. It all adds up. And the same goes with the experience of trade.

We are social animals, and traditionally, in our villages, we acknowledged this by eating *together*, celebrating *together*, growing, gathering and nurturing *together* and trading for skills or things we didn't have. Quite aside from the tasks themselves, the *togetherness* was the key – the *human* experience. Unfortunately, though, in our modern world, we have lost this communal connection. Instead, we rely almost entirely on money, and have lost these experiences along the way. Today, it is so easy for our lives to be driven by money and career, and we can become so bound up in a perpetual, insatiable desire to go newer and bigger and grander that we sometimes forget the whole point. We sometimes forget that it's actually real human experiences, not money or things, that make us happy.

In our modern world, it's so easy to forget that there are people behind the food we are eating.

Conversation is no longer needed, because money can directly result in a product. The human connection in these exchanges can get lost.

There's also a flip side to this: the modern phenomenon of 'self-sufficiency', where you set out to produce *everything* that you need. We don't see this as achievable, or balanced either. In the village model, this was never done. Every great culture – large or small – has recognised that the greatest success and the surest survival relies on the strength of the collective. We produced what we could, and then shared both our physical and human resources within our village. We relied on each other because it simply wasn't efficient to do everything yourself. We all have different strengths and weaknesses, and so we're simply stronger when we share. By trading our abundances with each other, everyone's necessities were taken care of, and community was built, and if you ask us, that's what it's all about.

So that's what we believe in: growing, gathering and nurturing our necessities, and trading for as many of the other things that we need as possible. We are all people, who all have something in common and all have something we can teach or share with each other. We believe life is easier, more fulfilling and happier when we have each other, and when we swap and share our abundances.

When you trade, genuine human interaction is unavoidable, because a trade is only possible with conversation. You *must* discuss what a fair trade is. You *must* discuss the exchange of goods. Whereas with money, you can just hand over the money and get a product in return, no conversation required. Sure you end up with the same product, but with a *remarkably* different experience. And this is what we want to highlight here: the *experience*, that human connection, is the most important thing. When we have more human interactions – talk to strangers, have great conversations – we believe that society is at its strongest. When we realise that we are all more similar than we are different, when we begin to understand each other more, see each other's points of view, share skills and have empathy, we all become happier, and we all become stronger human beings.

> We believe life is easier, more fulfilling and happier when we have each other, and when we swap and share our abundances.

WHAT IS OUR
EXPERIENCE OF TRADE?

We started by only trading flowers, and we had no idea where trade would lead us, or what it was really about. We chose flowers as the initial focus of our 'trade project', as they were the most abundant to us. They were, and still are, a hugely important part of our garden ecosystem, but were more undervalued than anything else. So we began a project called 'The Flower Exchange', with the idea that we wouldn't sell a single flower for a year and see where it would take us. We continued to drive our van down to deliver our produce to Melbourne's chefs, but now we extended our offering: we additionally filled it with veggie boxes, for people to buy from the van, and flower bunches to trade.

This really was one of the best times of our lives. That initial experience of trade was so much fun, and we had so many conversations with strangers. We were sharing not only the things people wanted to trade – from banana bread to homemade soap – but also having great conversations, learning about other peoples' lives, hearing their stories and sharing knowledge and skills. It really opened us up to the world around us, to see people's perspectives, to empathise with others' experiences and to recognise how similar we all really are. We are all just people. And there was something in this that made us so truly, contentedly happy. Sometimes as a society we feel we want to keep it *all* for ourselves – that isn't happiness. This was happiness.

Trade is now a key part of our lives. We trade anything and everything that is abundant to us, and couldn't imagine our lives otherwise. We trade our homemade wine for sacks of grains and beans and chocolate; flowers for coffee and olive oil; our help harvesting for nuts; and our skills and knowledge for other skills and experiences. We always set out just to cover our necessities, but we always end up with much more. We've discovered that's just the way trade works. When everyone is sharing their abundances, it's just natural that you give generously. With money, we have found it to be the opposite – you're always trying to hold on to as much as you can.

But trade extends far beyond produce. Trade means sharing meals and recipes, ideas and inspirations,

> When everyone is sharing their abundances, it's just natural that you give generously. With money, we have found it to be the opposite – you're always trying to hold on to as much as you can.

pickles and preserves, and skills and craftsmanship. This sharing is an experience of both teaching and learning that has truly enriched our lives. Most of the experiences we have had through trade have been completely unexpected. Certainly none of them would have happened had we just used money. Again, we would still have all of the same *things* but none of the accompanying *experiences*.

Our stories of trade vary so greatly, from small moments to big moments. But we can truly say that each one, each person, has changed our lives. Even if a trade was challenging, it taught us something, pushed us to have that human interaction, and to understand someone else.

One of our first exchanges was for a cake – orange and rosemary – and we can still see the smiling face of the woman who handed it to us. The cake was still warm and wrapped in brown paper tied with twine. We don't remember the flowers we traded for it (maybe a bunch of zinnias?), but the truth is that when we ate the cake later, it tasted terrible. Truly. Ha! But, that absolutely didn't matter. It didn't diminish our happiness, or make us feel dissatisfied with the trade. That woman had given us so much. She had put love into baking that cake and thought about using recycled packaging. We'd had a great conversation, and she had so much appreciation for our flowers. It was worth it. We shared empathy, a human connection. We shared an experience.

One of the most life-changing trades we have had was for our weekly coffee supply. The first time that we traded flowers for coffee was with a man named Andy, who owns a coffee roastery called Small Batch. We still remember it clearly. He came to the van with his three-year-old daughter on his shoulders, and we sat cross-legged on the grass and talked about what we did. From the outset, there was a mutual love and respect for each other's passions. Andy was one of our kind – someone full of energy and with a big heart. We set up a meeting in the roastery, and Andy gave us all of his time, sharing with us his coffee-making secrets and, most importantly, talking to us about the reality of the coffee world – where and how it is grown, and how it is imported. And we took him lots of vegetables and flowers, and shared with him stories from the farm, and the knowledge of how we farm.

We were so excited to share with each other the things we were most passionate about. We left feeling inspired and we think somehow our businesses were shaped by each other, even if just a little. Andy began to import more organic coffees, and we began to understand the importance of supporting farms from far away, rather than totally excluding these foods from our lives (see the *Seek* chapter for more information). We started an ongoing relationship where we would trade our flowers for coffee, and we felt good about where the coffee came from. We felt good about supporting the farmers behind it, and we felt good about the trade and the conversations. We learnt so much.

And then there's the wine, all that *wonderful* wine. You generally know where money will take you, but you never know where human interactions will lead you. That is the joy in trade. One day we met an amazing couple, Andrew and Kerrie, who lived across the river from us. They had left Melbourne long ago to purchase some acres and plant vines. They ran the vines commercially for a time but then decided to let them go wild – unpruned, unwatered, untouched. It was our dream to find vines like this to make our own wine, vines that were growing happily and healthily with zero intervention. The fruit was so intense in flavour, and completely natural and organic. So we began to trade. To pick the grapes and make some wine, we exchanged vegetables and flowers from our farm and some of the wine we made. This was an amazing trade! It allowed us to make our own wine and learn so much by doing it. And for them, as they didn't grow vegetables, it provided them with fresh produce. Additionally, they were just so pleased that their vines were being put to use, that the space was being activated, that there was life there again. They taught us so much about grapes and about making wine. We shared great conversations and became friends. I don't think that they really have any idea how much they changed our lives. But they really truly did, in so many great ways.

Trade has filled us with a mixture of awe, surprise, adventure… so many things. We have laughed and cried, cringed and grinned, been repeatedly blown away and had our minds opened wider and wider. The enchanting people who we have met along the way, and the awe-inspiring things that they do, stand out more than anything else. We truly feel extraordinarily lucky. And we feel as though the world must be a bright place if it has all of these amazing people in it. We promise if you only trade once, it will change the way you experience the world. It just will.

HOW TO START: SOME TRUTHS AND SOME GUIDELINES

One question we always get asked is: 'How does it work?' We remember, a few years ago, feeling just as perplexed as you probably feel right now, and that's totally normal. We felt achingly awkward when we started. Once, early on, we gave our whole hearts filling someone's home with flowers, only to walk away with one little fridge magnet made from scrabble tiles. We felt distinctly empty, meek and confused. Since then, we've come to realise that this is just the reality in our modern world – a lot of people just don't get trade. It's not their fault, and they aren't trying to take advantage of you, trade is just a skill that has been all but totally lost. And it's a skill we need to allow time to re-learn.

The two biggest things to remember are:

Forget about money. If you go into a trade thinking about the monetary value of the exchange, or if you are doing it because it is the cheaper option, stop now.

Think beyond yourself. It's not just about you; it's about both people. Just like when you plant a tree, you don't plant it only for you. You are planting it for all of the people who will experience that tree, so if you rent a house, plant that slow-growing fruit tree anyway, people will love you for it in the future. Trade is about the giving, not just the getting, so think about the bigger picture. Think beyond you. Think about what you can give and what you might learn in return. Remember, we work best together.

A good trade requires two things:

A conversation. You must discuss what is considered to be a fair trade between both of you, and what you are both happy with.

Sharing abundances. Generally, we undervalue the things that we have, and yet they can be so valuable to someone else. Those things that you enjoy doing, that come easily, whether a skill, something you make, something you produce, or the knowledge that you possess, are great things to trade with others who have different skills, different talents, different things. Both parties get more than they would expect.

General guidelines.

How do I know if a trade is fair? Quite simply, a fair trade is when both people are happy. And it largely relies on honesty and openness. If at the end of the exchange someone isn't happy, then that's okay, you can always work it out, but only if both people are being honest and open. Generally, it's just like making friends, you can tell almost immediately if you want to trade with someone else – if you will be on the same page.

Don't expect added bonuses. You can't go into a trade expecting more than what's been talked about. As we've said, you are *probably* going to get more than you expected. You are also *probably* going to give more than the other person expects. But none of this is guaranteed. Your experiences are not predictable, and, most of all, we can't tell you what they might be, because your experience of trade will be totally different to ours. The extra experiences you get from trading are total bonuses. They are always unexpected and unintentional. They just happen naturally. Let them. But don't be disappointed if not every trade blows your mind. Sometimes it really is just a straight up this-for-that exchange. And that's fine too, because even just that genuine human interaction is an experience that a simple monetary exchange could never have created.

Nothing is off the table. We have had all kinds of bizarre trades suggested to us, and we love it. One of the strangest trade suggestions was from a lady who wanted a bunch of flowers in exchange for two kittens. Not one, it had to be two. It still makes us laugh now. But hey, that was probably just what was abundant in her life at the time. We didn't take the kittens, but we're pretty sure we still gave her flowers, because the great story and the laughter were enough for us.

Step outside your comfort zone. We guarantee that you'll probably feel silly, stupid, nervous or all of the above the first time you trade. You will probably feel uncomfortable. These are all totally normal feelings, because we have lost touch with the art of trade. See it for the 'new' skill that it is and realise that you are not alone – we are all in this together. Step outside of your comfort zone. It's warm out there.

SOMETHING TO LEAVE YOU WITH

Trade is not predictable. It asks us to be real and honest and vulnerable, and is an amazing human experience because of it. Trade *will* make you happy – a long-lasting kind of happy – but we just can't tell you exactly how, because our experiences are all different. We believe the world would be a better place if trade was more prevalent in it, because it reminds us that we are all just people who are more similar than we are different, with emotions, skills, needs and abundances to share.

For us, trade has made our lives feel full. It has made our lives feel full in the best kind of happily contented, life-is-good way imaginable. Amongst everything we do, it is trade that has implanted the most thorough contentedness in our hearts. It has allowed us to connect with the most amazing people, to empathise more, to continue learning every day, and to fill our lives with all of the things we need and more. There is just a total honesty, vulnerability and joy in trading.

We're not saying that you shouldn't use money, but we *are* saying trade your abundances, because trade is awesome and we believe it would make a great component to everyone's life. It might just bring you more joy than you ever expected and change the way you see and experience the world in the best possible way.

CHAPTER 6

Seek.

'5% foods' – sometimes foods from far away.

The ability to access any form of produce from anywhere and at any time is a modern phenomenon. Traditionally – in the village model – people had a nearly 100% regional diet: growing, gathering or nurturing foods locally, with the seasons, and trading their abundances. The experience of eating foods grown in faraway lands was rare. Such foods spent many months travelling by sea or overland, and supply was sporadic and unreliable. These were the flavours that were savoured, yearned for, used sparingly, and joyously celebrated with. They were the spices of life – quite often literally!

Our current system of global trade, however, has totally reversed this situation. We can now consume foods from far away easily and often, and this means that things are *way* out of balance. With that in mind, we'd like to introduce the concept of '5% foods'.

These are the foods that aren't produced in season in your local region, usually for climatic reasons. Traditionally, these foods were also a part of the trade/bartering system discussed in the previous chapter, but these foods didn't come from inside the village, they came from distant lands. In our modern world – where we can get anything, at any time and from anywhere – we need to consider how to both consciously seek out these few special celebration foods, as well as to consider the role they play in our diet.

Our level of easy access to these foods normalises our flippant consumption of them and makes it almost impossible to really appreciate where they are from, how they have been farmed and how far they have actually travelled. But as much as we try, we can't separate ourselves from nature: someone *is* on that land producing those foods, and they *did* travel across oceans to reach us, whether we as consumers are conscious of it or not. So we believe in a 95% regional diet, with 5% 'sometimes foods from far away' (see the *Eat* chapter for more details). These 'sometimes foods' play a supplementary role, as opposed to being a main food source.

Why? Because if that 5% is more like 50%, it is not only unsustainable due to massive energy expenditures in global logistics, but, more importantly, it makes it almost impossible to be connected to our food. If we have no connection to that entire part of our diet, if that much of our relationship with our food turns 'long distance', it also becomes all too easy to become detached from the real implications of food production. It becomes all too easy to forget that the produce we eat is actually connected to a place, connected to the health of its local environment, to the health of the soil. It becomes all too easy to stop caring about the farmers producing it, the distance that it has travelled and its environmental impact. It also becomes all too easy to simply think only of our personal enjoyment, rather than acknowledge any of these grander consequences, because, for better

or worse, our minds are amazing things and we can, and do, invent justifications for the things that we enjoy. It's just what humans seem to do. We can be super weird.

Environmental factors aside, should we really be eating so much of these foods from far away just because we can? Is it actually good for us? Well, we would have to say no. If something's not in season regionally to you, you just shouldn't be eating that much of it. It's not a way of eating that the human body has ever been exposed to in its hundreds of thousands of years of evolution, and so it's just not something that we've adapted to. On the flip side, all kinds of beautiful things happen when you live and eat in line with your natural environment. When you eat what's around you, it's like a deeper part of you wakes up. You become part of your environment all the more. And you feel well. Eating locally, with the seasons, is what our bodies know and so limiting 'faraway foods' allows us to feel a deep connection and nourishment that exotic treats could never provide (we discuss this more in *Eat*).

There are many things that we have decided to go without because they aren't grown near us – you will notice this in our recipes – but we do still choose to have a few special foods from far away, to savour and for celebrations – especially for desserts, which we see as celebration food. In our experience, this way of eating adds to special occasions, making them all the more special. Additionally, global trade can be a truly beautiful thing when done well. It can uplift poorer communities, strengthen and support good farming practices, celebrate cultural diversity, strengthen our humanity, and support wonderful endeavours. It *can* be beautiful. But it can also be insane.

To be honest, sometimes we do wonder – and have long discussions about – whether we should cut these foods from our diet altogether. Do we really need them? We still fight with ourselves as to whether it's more sustainable to cut these foods out entirely, or to support and advocate for good farming practices of these global foods – such as coffee – that are currently being consumed in such large quantities. This is a question we will continue to sit on and contemplate. For now, we have decided to continue to source these foods, but to do so in the most conscious way possible

> All kinds of beautiful things happen when you live and eat in line with your natural environment. When you eat what's around you, it's like a deeper part of you wakes up.

by only supporting well-farmed and responsibly sourced produce. By supporting products that are farmed well, we are increasing their demand and therefore encouraging better farming practices among other producers. Plus, just like the traditional village, we trade for these foods whenever possible (see the *Trade* chapter for more details). Trading for these foods directly with people who know the farmers also allows us to bring the 'human' back into a part of our diet where it is easily lost, bringing with it all of the beautiful experiences that only trade can. It also enables us to get to the truth of these foods. That is, where they are *actually* from, and how they were *actually* farmed.

So while we now have the technology and logistics networks to export and import on a whim, we believe that it's time for a dietary rethink. There are currently countries that export produce for one price, just so they can import the same type of produce for a cheaper price. Economical dogma has become the only measure. Not quality, or ecology, and definitely not humanity. For too long in our modern world it has been seen as progressive to be able to get anything from anywhere and at any time. It's not. Our bodies and nature just can't sustain it. To eat seasonally and regionally, as it was always done, is in fact much smarter.

TWO POWERFUL QUESTIONS

When sourcing produce or eating out, ask two questions:

1. Is it grown locally?

2. Is it farmed *well*, in the sunshine, in a natural way?

Try to shop at places that you know source seasonal produce (e.g. farmers' markets, local veggie boxes, or make a farmer friend). If your neighbour has a great garden, ask if you can swap something. And get a seasonal chart for your area. If coconuts aren't grown near you, replace coconut oil with butter. If bananas aren't either, eat apricots. And the same goes if something isn't in season, replace it with something else that is. Then decide on those few foods that you really can't do without and source them well – again asking those two essential questions.

WHAT WE SEEK

As mentioned, we grow, gather, nurture and trade so much of our own food that we could easily go without these 'sometimes foods', and often do. After the commercial harvest failed one year, we went 18 months waiting for organically grown Australian ginger – it spurred us to begin growing some of our own in a pot in the greenhouse! And we went three years without buckwheat – we may have been the most excited people ever when we finally found a local organic grower! But, every now and then, we do choose to experience some 'faraway foods' to add to life's joys and celebrations. Here is our list:

Some spices. We try to grow most of our own spices and are always trying to grow more – the flavour is unmatched. In our temperate climate, we've been able to grow many of our own spices such as: chillies; cumin, fennel, mustard, caraway, nigella and coriander seeds; kaffir lime leaves; lemongrass; plus a whole world of herbs. What we can't grow, we seek – they are very compact and a little goes a long way!

Coconut oil and coconut paste. Coconut is a tropical plant, and so, for us, always comes from far away. However, it is delicious, so we indulge sometimes.

Psyllium husk. We just haven't found a way around this one yet. All psyllium husk comes from the subcontinent, and we're yet to find anything that performs quite as well in our wholegrain flour mixes. Fortunately a little goes a long way.

Coffee and tea. In Australia, and many other countries, we largely don't have the combination of altitude and climate required to grow coffee and tea well. In saying that, there are a few select Australian growers, however they are still far away for us.

Chocolate. Much like coffee and tea, Australia lacks the conditions suitable for commercial cacao production. There are a few Australian growers making headway, but again, they are still far away from us.

Unrefined sugar. Always Australian grown. We are lucky to source some of the most amazing, nutrient-rich (unstripped) sugar that exists, however it's from the very far north of Australia. So we try to mainly use honey from our bees wherever possible and are experimenting with beet sugar!

Miso and tamari. We buy these for now, but we're learning to make them from locally grown soybeans! It's a fantastic – but long – process.

Fish sauce. Just like the soy products, we're working on it!

If we could only buy a sailboat, fill it with all of these things – enough to last us many years – and sail home, then we would. And one day we might. Or we might just cut them out altogether. But we would miss those little bits of special foods, which we savour and use to celebrate, and we'd definitely miss our morning coffee! So for now, we will just do our best to support all those legends out there growing and making incredible things in faraway lands.

HOW TO SEEK 'FARAWAY FOODS' WELL

Many of these points apply to sourcing things well in general, whether grown close to home or far away.

Get as close to the producer as possible. Buy produce with the least amount of middlemen involved. The coffee that we use, for example, is sourced directly from the coffee roaster, who visits the coffee farms himself and has a relationship with the farmers. We then get to discuss with him the origins of the coffee. Was it farmed organically? Is the farmer behind the coffee being supported? Are the workers paid a fair wage?

Trade where you can. There are so many benefits to trading (see the *Trade* chapter). In this scenario especially though, it can allow you to learn more about the farmers, farming practices and origins of the food that you are sourcing. Additionally, it just opens up a great conversation and allows you to give feedback to your farmers and for both parties to share ideas.

Ask where it's from. Generally, if someone can tell you where it's from and something about the farm or farmer that means they have taken the time to source the product thoughtfully.

Ask if it's produced well. Find out if the produce is chemical/spray free. Sometimes the best products aren't labelled organic. These might come from well-managed but uncertified farms, or be picked or gathered from the wild. You may need to ask.

Never source staple foods or fresh foods from far away. Remember we are talking about *sometimes* foods here. Your staple grains and beans, fruits and vegetables, meat and dairy should *all* be sourced locally. No matter where you are, no matter what the season, regionally grown produce is as diverse as it is delicious. Choose it.

Buy foods that are as concentrated as possible. Coconut paste is one example of this – it contains the equivalent of about four cans of coconut cream in the space of less than one! That means it requires one quarter of the energy in transportation. Thankfully, almost all 'sometimes foods' simply *are* as concentrated as they can be because they've been traded this way for many thousands of years.

Make sure you aren't sourcing produce from far away that can be sourced locally. Often on the shelf there will be two products sitting side by side, but one is local and one is from far away. Choose local.

Be honest about distance. Australia is so big that eating 'Australian grown' does not always mean that we are eating locally. For us, foods grown in some parts of Australia definitely fall into the 'sometimes foods from far away' category.

A FINAL THOUGHT

Our modern world of money, career, fast-paced lifestyle and our recent 'needing everything I want when I want it' attitude just isn't serving our innate needs to eat and live seasonally, our happiness, the health of our bodies, or the health of the environment. If we can just take these lessons from the traditional village model and put them to use – eating a predominately regional diet, bringing trade back into our lives, seeking our 'sometimes foods from far away' with awareness and humanity – we will not only enjoy the eating part of life that little bit more, but we, and the planet, will also be much healthier.

CHAPTER 7

Eat.

Eat a natural, regional diet,
90% plants, properly prepared.

Our regional diet consists of food made for sharing and celebrating every day: year-round staples combined with fresh ingredients from around us; preserves from seasons past; something a little bit special we have sought or traded with a great person; a jar of something fermenting on the bench; or a homemade stock ready to go. This is what food is about. It's the diet of our ancestors, and it is what all of the previous chapters lead to: eating.

SO WHAT EXACTLY IS A NATURAL DIET?

It is all of the things you have read about so far in this book. It is about produce that has been grown, gathered and nurtured with the seasons. It is about nutrient-rich foods and great experiences. And it is great for your body and for nature, bringing the two into balance.

A natural diet is one that works with what nature gives you. It means that you must grow and eat a diverse mix of plants, because for the soil to be balanced you must grow a range of crops, including vegetables, trees, flowers, pulses and grains. It will be mainly plants, because plants produce more food per acre than animals, and, in harmony with the fierce efficiency of nature, we have no reason to cultivate more land than we need. But for the soil to be balanced also requires a mix of animals, because their manures, the farm tasks they help with and their specific behaviours – grazing, rooting, scratching – all enliven soil activity and stimulate growth. A natural eater, utilising what is around them, will assimilate these animal foods into their diet too. Finally, when we place ourselves in nature, we observe seasonal abundances, which, like the rest of nature, we respond to. So we hunt game and gather wild greens, fruits and fungi until balance is restored. And so this becomes our diet.

It is a diet that is seasonal and full of wholefood ingredients, mainly plants. It is incidentally balanced, full of variety, sustainable and local. All foods are produced well, are 'organic'. You don't even think about it, just as nature doesn't think about it. And with each season that passes, your body is well.

WHY DO WE BELIEVE IN THIS?

We believe that the past holds the key to our health and wellness. What we have eaten for thousands of years is what our bodies know, and it is what is good for us. So we eat and live as our ancestors did. It is what our bodies and minds are used to – it is innate. And, for us, this is what we have experienced. Eating this way – having a natural, regional diet, full of real wholefood ingredients and seeking and trading for what we don't have – has made us healthier, happier and more balanced than we ever believed possible. In the past, this diet and way of life was pivotal to some of the healthiest and longest living populations in the world. And it still is to this day.

When we look at traditional diets as a whole, something special happens. Nutrients come together better than science can currently explain. When we eat as our ancestors did, when food is both produced well *and* prepared well, it naturally provides you with complete nutrition, and brings you into balance with nature while it's at it. When your diet works with nature, each component comes together to give your body everything it needs to be nourished and healthy. Well-produced wholefood ingredients are full of nutrients that are in balance with each other, which helps us to efficiently absorb them. Fermentation and naturally occurring good bacteria allow your gut to stay healthy, and good fats and oils keep your nervous system well. As the seasons move around you, and your diet balances itself naturally, you almost become a bystander to it. Food can just be food, and you never need to worry about nutrition again.

Some examples:

- There is a vitamin called K2 (essential for holistic bone, cartilage, vascular, skin and prostate health – and probably much more), which is present in high concentrations in wild or pastured animal foods and fermented soy and vegetable foods. Very little is present in modern feedlot, grain-fed animal foods and none in unfermented plant foods! Naturally raised, wholefood ingredients and traditional preparation are key.

- Fermented foods have been found to improve gut health and aid in reducing allergies and disease.

- Soil, real soil, is full of natural living bacteria such as *Mycobacterium vaccae*, which has been found to enhance serotonin, the neurotransmitter essential for regulating our moods. Additionally, the bacteria have been found to improve gut health and immune function. Seems we are naturally predisposed to getting our hands dirty.

- Studies show that fermenting grains makes their nutrients and minerals more bio-available, as well as helping to reduce allergic reactions. For example, the wild yeast fermentation of wheat, such as using a sourdough culture (see page 142), has been found to almost fully break down the gluten protein that causes allergic reactions.

- Modern hybridised grains and vegetables have completely different nutrient profiles to their ancestors, and not for the better. For example, einkorn – wheat's ancient cousin – outperforms modern wheat in its levels of nearly every vitamin and mineral (it contains over 30 times the concentration of vitamin A!). Likewise, multiple studies show a decrease of between 20% and 100% in vitamin and mineral content across the board for fruits, vegetables, grains, pulses, nuts and seeds in the last 40-plus years – a downward trend that seems to have been occurring since the middle of last century. The causes: modern farming methods geared towards unnaturally fast production of the heaviest possible yields (the over-stimulated plants having no time to absorb the nutrients they used to), and modern plant breeding that has favoured shelf-stability and appearance without any concern for nutrition.

We believe that a natural diet full of well-produced wholefood ingredients allows your health, your mind and your happiness to truly thrive. Modern agriculture and food production methods have changed so profoundly that many foods are not only deficient in nutrients and minerals, but are also, at times, actually toxic. We need to return to living and eating more traditionally. Remember, food should always be fun, and life should always be full of experiences. This is not just a 'diet'; it is a way of life. And it will make you both healthy and happy in the most natural, fulfilling way.

OUR REGIONAL DIET

Vegetables, fruits and fungi, both wild and cultivated, are the foundation of our regional diet. They provide flavour and diversity and have long been respected as key to thriving health. Then come whole grains – their storage durability and nutritional density have long seen them rise to the top as the traditional human staple. But every fourth season, traditional farmers knew they needed to grow a crop of pulses, which helped to absorb atmospheric nitrogen into the soil and restore balance to their fields. So they ate about three-parts grains to one-part pulses.

Poor or rocky soils, or mountainous terrain, meant that not all sections of land were easily cultivated, so traditional farmers ranged animals, such as cows, goats and sheep. They knew animals were far less efficient at producing food for a given area of land than grains and pulses, but it at least allowed something to be garnered from the land. Plus, the larger animals, such as cattle, horses and pigs, could be used to work their fields, and they would gather the manure of these animals (and their own) to spread out onto their fields each year, concentrating the nutrition of the surrounding country where they needed it most. Animals were most useful alive, so only occasionally did meat reach the dinner table, and when it did it was considered incredibly sacred. It was always only a small percentage of their diets, but it was essential to health and wellbeing.

Nuts, seeds and spices also provided vitamins, minerals, proteins, fats and oils, antioxidants and antimicrobial elements. They were also valued for their medicinal and anti-inflammatory properties, and are thought to have become so ingrained in traditional diets as much for their health-giving qualities as for their flavour. They were harder to cultivate than grains and pulses but provided delicious diversity, and they have long been prized as supplemental foods.

The diagram on page 130 illustrates our regional diet, based on what we grow, gather, nurture, seek and trade, with an explanation below. Your regional diet will be different based on exactly what *you* are able to grow, gather and nurture where you live. You may have access to wild berries at a time that we don't, or you may be able to hunt wild deer. You may raise pigs and goats instead of sheep and cattle. But in all cases, the balance of food categories – 90% plants and 10% animal products, with 95% locally produced and 5% from far away – will remain the same.

Winter – which really starts whenever the first frost hits – is a special season that is almost totally different from all the rest. We turn inwards, resting more, having fires and sharing more celebration meals with the people we love. It's full of heavier and more comforting foods. We eat more grains, because it's what our bodies crave. And we eat more preserved fruits, vegetables and fungi, because there is less variety of fresh vegetables, very minimal fruit and wild fungi is no longer available in the forests. Interestingly, there are more wild edible weeds available, which balances out the lack of variety in the garden. Meat consumption is at its peak, as we eat richer, more warming dishes from our autumn stores. These meats are predominately darker and are higher in certain vitamins, like B vitamins, that your body needs to bolster itself against the cold. There are some dairy products available, which are mostly preserved, like ghee, cultured (sour) cream and cheeses. These are naturally more concentrated fat sources, again helping our bodies to produce more heat, to 'burn warmer'. Interestingly, it is also a time that we eat fewer eggs, as chickens lay less in winter. So one form of animal product increases as another decreases – a balance.

Spring is a constant fluctuation between winter and summer, with brutally cold days following the brutally hot. It really feels like an in between time. Our bodies start to wake up and get more energy from the sun and adjust again to more fresh foods. We are perpetually observing, looking for whether wild reptiles are out of hibernation and for which trees are flowering, to gauge soil temperatures and find the next planting time. There is a burst of new greens and growth on many plants and vegetables, but there is also a big gap, where we have eaten the last crops from winter, but the new spring crops haven't reached maturity. This is a natural time of cleansing for your body, the one gap in the year where there are mainly only young greens available, and little else. We rely more heavily on preserved foods at this time – mainly for variety, as greens can get a bit boring. There is less meat, but this is the time that mothers are giving birth and raising their young – as the grass is at its greenest and growing at its fastest – so fresh dairy is plentiful. Again, there is a balance: less of one animal food, more of another.

Summer is colourful and bright, a time when the days are long and the sun gives us energy, so we need less food to stay warm. We eat lots of fresh vegetables and fruit, as they are abundant. We eat less grains, as we don't crave them, and less meat, as the animals are still raising their young. We occasionally eat wild carp from the river – they are prolific at this time – or our preserved tuna, or one of our young male birds to keep the flocks in balance. We eat lots of eggs, as the chickens love the warmth and lay more often. It's busy and things are perpetually harvested, planted and preserved. We hardly eat preserved or stored vegetables and fruit at this time, as everything is abundant and fresh – though occasionally we do, because they offer such delicious variety.

There is a clear link between nature and our bodies: when nature is balanced, so is our diet, and so too are our bodies.

Autumn, our favourite season, has a crossover of almost everything and total abundance. Game animals have fattened and reached a peak in their populations, and our bodies need them to prepare for the cold. Many summer crops are still in season through early to mid-autumn, with some new autumn crops bringing even more variety. It begins to get cold, but we continue to harvest and preserve as if it was summer. We continue to eat a lot of fresh fruit and vegetables, but this is also the *best* time for foraged foods. Plenty of rain and the perfect temperature mean that we see lots of wild greens, nuts, fruit and wild mushrooms. If we are going to kill a larger animal that we have nurtured, we do it now, because then we can preserve the meat through winter.

Then suddenly it's really cold, frost has hit and many of the crops from summer die or go dormant. With lactation cycles of mothers naturally drying up, fresh milk begins to run low, and we start to eat more preserved dairy products. You need more of these heavier fats as it gets colder, so, again, the timing is perfect.

Our diet has become natural and intuitive. In spring we crave asparagus and eggs, naturally, and in summer all we want are fresh foods like tomatoes and cucumbers. There is just something special about how nature works, it is more intelligent than we are – and we will continue to learn about its ways until the day we die. There is a clear link between nature and our bodies: when nature is balanced, so is our diet, and so too are our bodies.

Your natural diet will vary from ours, because your seasons will be different, your local crops will be different, and your local wilderness will be different. But that is the whole point, as *that* is what you are meant to be eating. Even if you don't grow, gather or nurture your own food, try to think about what you *would* be, or what other people around you *are* growing, gathering or nurturing at different times of the year, and use this as a guide. Subtract and add, and make it work for you.

Our regional diet.

	Winter. (Eat more)	Spring.	Summer. (Eat less)	Autumn.
35% (Stored year-round)	Whole grains	Whole grains	Whole grains	Whole grains
	Pulses (mainly cooked), nuts & seeds	Pulses, nuts & seeds	Pulses (mainly sprouted), nuts & seeds	Pulses, nuts & seeds
90% Plant foods / **50%**	Fresh vegetables (very little fresh fruit)	Fresh vegetables (very little fresh fruit)	Fresh fruits & vegetables	Fresh fruits & vegetables
	Preserved fruits & stored vegetables & mushrooms	Preserved & stored fruits, vegetables & mushrooms	Preserved & stored fruits, vegetables & mushrooms	Preserved & stored fruits & vegetables
	Wild greens & mushrooms	Wild greens	Wild fruits	Wild fruits, greens & mushrooms
5%	Sometimes foods from far away	Sometimes foods from far away	Sometimes foods from far away	Sometimes foods from far away
10% Animal foods	Dairy	Dairy	Dairy	Dairy
	Nurtured red meat & pork, preserved pork	Nurtured red meat, pork & poultry, preserved pork	Nurtured poultry, preserved pork	Nurtured red meat, pork & poultry, preserved pork
	Wild duck, rabbit & hare, preserved tuna	Wild fish, preserved tuna	Wild fish, preserved tuna	Wild fish, duck, rabbit & hare, preserved tuna
	Eggs	Eggs	Eggs	Eggs

WHOLEFOOD INGREDIENTS

Below is a list of some of the key wholefood ingredients that we use in our recipes. Cooking with these will help you to create the same flavours and experiences that we achieve in the recipes to follow.

Water. Rainwater or spring water – it is essential to have access to unchlorinated water for your health and the health of your ferments.

Vegetables, fruits, fungi and edible flowers. And lots of them! Grown in nutrient-rich soil or gathered from the wild.

Whole grains. Soaked or sprouted first, or when flour is required, always milled fresh in a stone mill.

Pulses. Always soaked or sprouted first.

Dairy products. Full-fat dairy! Always use full-fat, pastured dairy products from well-raised animals.

Eggs. Pastured eggs from home-raised or similarly spoiled chickens.

Meat and fish. Gathered from the wild or raised and killed respectfully, naturally and stress free.

Fats and oils. We use extra-virgin olive oil, ghee, butter and lard or other rendered fats, and occasionally cold-pressed seed oils like sesame and sunflower. These are all whole forms of natural fats, which help our digestion, skin and nervous systems, and some contain vitamins that are otherwise hard to get.

Nut and seed meals/flours. We always grind flaxseed meal and LSA fresh in our high-powered blender, as they oxidise rapidly once ground and lose their nutritional benefits. If you need to buy pre-ground versions, try to find fresh, refrigerated stock.

Spices. We use the seeds as whole products or mill them fresh.

Salt. We only use unrefined salt, as refining strips away all of the trace minerals.

Coffee, tea and chocolate. Responsibly sourced from farmers who grow well.

Honey. Unprocessed honey – not heat-treated. Raw honey contains live enzymes, pollen, vitamins, minerals, antioxidants and antifungal properties, which are largely denatured when heat-treated.

Sugar. We always use unrefined sugar unless stated. The person who produces our sugar juices their sugarcane and dries that juice – and that is our sugar. It's full of all of its natural vitamins and minerals and tastes like nothing else. Or we use rapadura, but even rapadura is still processed, with some minerals stripped. So even 'unrefined' sugars are still processed to some degree.

PREPARING FOOD WELL – NUTRIENT-RICH FOOD

To ensure that our food is as nutrient rich as it can be, we prepare our wholefood ingredients in a traditional way, the way our ancestors did. They knew how to take raw, unrefined and sometimes quite indigestible foods and transform them into the most nutrient-rich foods possible. Eating in this way takes things a step further in terms of working with nature. Eating the most nourishing food means that you need to eat less and produce less, putting the least toll on nature and instead working *with* it. You are truly getting the most out of your food. So you are as healthy as you can be, and so is nature.

To do this requires an understanding of each and every food source, because preparation techniques for each vary. We will guide you through them with simple, everyday ways to traditionally prepare your wholefood ingredients.

See pages 138–49 for our guide to the preparation of whole grains, pulses, nuts and seeds; and pages 185–239 for information on preserving, which includes fermenting, bottling and jarring, drying and curing, and how to store your harvest.

Our 15 food 'rules'.

1. **Don't have rules.** As much as these are 'rules', do what feels right for you. Throw it all out sometimes and come back to it later. The key is balance, and everything in moderation. Having a little bit of something here and there, like refined white flour, is okay. As a foundation, try to eat a natural diet, 90% plants, 95% local, properly prepared, *most* of the time.

2. **Start small and make the best choices you can.** Change your routines slowly. Do what you can, and don't feel guilty if you slip up – be kind and don't judge yourself. Just take your time and do what feels right for you. If you crave something, eat it – it will probably remind you of why you don't eat it anymore. Give yourself time to learn, time for your tastebuds to adjust, and to see how you feel – it is all part of the process.

3. **Food should taste good.** If it doesn't taste good, it probably isn't that good for you. Well-produced food tastes so good that you don't even have to do anything to it. You have never tasted a tomato until you have tasted an heirloom tomato grown in amazing soil, in the sunshine, in its natural growing season, plucked fully ripe straight from the vine. Most tomatoes purchased from our supermarkets or even from local producers – and sometimes even at farmer's markets – can be grown out of season in plastic hothouses; or be genetically modified or a modern hybridised variety; or be grown in sand and fed a cocktail of synthetic fertilisers; or be picked green to ripen later; or all of the above. This is not a natural way to grow food, and it is questionable whether these foods give any real nutrition at all. Additionally, they are absolutely incomparable in terms of flavour, and your body doesn't really recognise them or want to eat more. And understandably so.

4. **Eat like every day is a celebration!** The experiences, the mindfulness and the human interactions that come with eating as if every day is a celebration bring you happiness, make you choose better ingredients, and make you enjoy cooking all the more. Food is meant to be fun.

5. **Share meals.** Every recipe in this book is designed to be shared. There is something so special and natural about sharing meals. You appreciate food more, eat more consciously, and you are more inclined to cook from scratch. We feel that sharing mealtimes is innate; it's how we are meant to eat. You see it in children. They not only reach developmental eating milestones by sharing mealtimes, but they also learn communication skills through the experience of mealtime routines, watching others eat and sharing food.

6. **Grow at least one ingredient.** Touching soil and growing even just one thing will connect you to how things are grown and forever change the way you see food.

7. **Experience your food, or get close to someone who does.** Observe the seasons and grow, gather and nurture what you can. If you don't, be sure to source produce as close to where you live as possible and as directly as you can. You don't have to buy directly from a farmer *every* time, but if you can, do – and better yet, trade.

8. **Cook from scratch as much as possible.** Try to avoid packaged foods and cook from scratch when you can – it's always better for you. You will be cooking using wholefood ingredients, and you will start to understand food better.

9. **Routines make food quick and easy.** Everyone is searching for the ultimate quick-and-easy meal. This is it. If throughout the week you soak some beans and grains, such as chickpeas, lentils or brown rice, and make a staple food (e.g. pizza bases), your kitchen will soon be full of quick-and-easy meals, and your diet will be full of nutrient-rich, well-prepared foods.

10. **Buy it unrefined.** What does it look like when it comes straight from nature? If you look at a product and can't make a connection with the original food, you probably shouldn't eat it. Glossy white sugar is worlds away from the dark green juice that comes out of sugarcane, and we've never seen a white field of wheat. Keep these as 'sometimes foods'.

11. **Buy local, seasonal produce that has been grown in the sunshine.** Just because it's local doesn't always mean it's seasonal, and just because it's seasonal doesn't always mean it's local. You can buy things grown locally in hothouses that are way out of season, and you can also buy things that are in season but may be imported from far away. Be aware of both.

12. **Buy well-produced food.** Not everything has to be certified. We've found that many natural, organic farmers aren't. Either because they can't afford it, or because they don't believe in a certification that allow all kinds of things they would *never* use on their farms. Get to know your farmers and find out what they use – a conversation is better than any certification. If you can't talk to them, look for words like pastured, local, chemical-free, organic and biodynamic.

13. **If something seems unnatural, it probably is.** For example, if buying cheese or milk off the shelf (rather than the refrigerated section) seems unnatural, that's because it is.

14. **No GMO.** Stay away from genetically modified foods; we just don't know what they do to our bodies. Our ancestors didn't eat them, and our bodies just don't know them.

15. **Don't be scared of natural animal fats.** Fats from pastured animals – butter, ghee and lard, as well as in meat and whole dairy – are very stable forms of saturated and unsaturated fats, with vitamins and minerals that you can't get anywhere else. These fats weren't feared in traditional diets, and things like heart disease were very rare. Diets with a balanced amount of animal fat are key to some of the longest-lived populations, such as in Japan, Switzerland, Austria, Greece and France. They help to maintain the proper function of cell membranes and our immune systems, they protect our organs, and allow us to absorb nutrients and minerals that cannot otherwise be absorbed. Steer clear of 'fat-free' products, as they have been heavily processed and the nutrients have been removed. Additionally, avoid unnatural fats, like refined vegetable oils (canola, soybean, safflower etc.) and margarine. These polyunsaturated and trans fats are totally different fats that our bodies don't recognise and can't process. They are highly processed and heat-treated and are generally closer to plastics than they are to food.

GUIDE TO CATEGORIES

GF   gluten free
DF   dairy free
V   vegetarian
VG   vegan

Grown.

Contains key ingredients of plant origin that we can and do grow ourselves.

Gathered.

Contains key ingredients that we can and do gather from the wild.

Nurtured.

Contains key ingredients of animal origin that we can and do raise ourselves.

Su.   summer
A.   autumn
W.   winter
Sp.   spring

Please note that the abbreviations for summer, autumn, winter and spring that appear above our recipes are a general guide to what is available in our temperate climate. Actual availability will depend on seasonal shifts. Summer may start earlier or finish later, winter may be longer or shorter, and these variations are always different from one year to the next (see the *Observe* chapter for more details).

Staples.

The basis of many easy meals – just add fresh vegetables
and a pickle. Most are prepared using traditional techniques,
to make the most nutrient-rich foods.

Traditional preparation guides for whole grains, pulses, nuts & seeds.

These preparation guides are the foundation for so much of what we eat. If we had to pick one thing as the most important practical thing that we have learnt in our lives, this set of techniques would be it – even more than growing food! Preparing these foods in this way has made us feel so good, and has given us so much energy to work as hard as we do – and our guts and minds are healthier than ever.

We know that freshly milling and fermenting grains, soaking beans and sprouting seeds may be new to many people, but this is how it was always done. Modern society has just lost many of these techniques along the way to industrialised food processing and packaging. Our ancestors used these techniques to turn the most basic and unrefined wholefood ingredients – grains, pulses, nuts and seeds – into the highest quality, nutrient-dense foods there are, allowing them to thrive even during times of scarcity.

Preparing grains, pulses, nuts and seeds correctly is one of the true keys to health, and is absolutely necessary if you want to thrive on a diet based predominantly on plants. Additionally, we have found that people who experience unpleasant symptoms after eating certain grains or pulses almost always find that they have no reaction if they are properly prepared.

The structure of grains is a little different to the structure of pulses (beans, peas and lentils), which is different again to the structure of nuts and seeds, so they all behave a little differently in our digestive systems. In response, our ancestors developed appropriate preparations for each. We now understand that whole grains, pulses, nuts and seeds contain enzyme inhibitors – to protect their stability – and other complex compounds, which can wreak havoc in our digestive systems if not deactivated before cooking. Left active, they block the good bacteria and enzymes in our digestive tract from doing their job. That is, they will stop us from being able to properly digest our meal. Each preparation technique that we show you here evolved through trial and error over thousands of years to deactivate these harmful components in each type of food, rendering them not only more nutritious, but also more delicious.

A LITTLE WHOLEGRAIN THEORY

We love whole grains. They form a major part of our natural, regional diet. Whole grains are the edible seeds of a plant in their most complete state. Apart from removing their inedible hulls, whole grains remain intact and are totally shelf stable until ground into flour or rolled (as for oats). They consist of three parts:

- **The bran** is the outer layer, and it contains B vitamins, protective antioxidants and dietary fibre.

- **The germ** contains all of the information the seed needs to grow into a plant. It's loaded with B vitamins, minerals, about 25% of the grain's protein and all of the healthy fats. The germ is the key to a grain's nutrition.

- **The endosperm** is the germ's food supply, where all of the energy is. It contains 75% of the grain's protein but very few vitamins and minerals. It is predominantly comprised of starchy carbohydrate.

Most grains come from a family of grasses commonly known as cereal grasses. Wheat, maize and rice are from this family and currently account for nearly 90% of global cereal production. But there are many other cereals to choose from: wild rice, rye, oats, barley, millet, teff and sorghum. There are also ancient wheat varieties: einkorn, emmer, durum, khorasan and spelt. And finally, there are pseudo-cereals (seeds that are like cereals but don't belong to the cereal family): amaranth, buckwheat and quinoa.

A note on gluten and oats. If you are avoiding gluten, only rye, barley and the wheat varieties contain any. All of the rest are totally gluten free. Contrary to popular belief, oats contain no gluten and only acquire traces of it through processing. They do contain avenin, a protein similar to gluten, but research has shown that many people who are sensitive to gluten have no problem with avenin. Everyone is different; see what works for you.

Why whole grains over 'white' grains?

White rice or flour isn't bad for you. It's just not that good for you either. This is because it consists purely of starchy carbohydrates (the endosperm only), having had all of the bran and germ removed.

As such, it contains none of the B vitamins, dietary fibre and antioxidants of the bran, and none of the vitamins, minerals and fats of the germ. Also, because grain polishing and flour refining are such recent practices, our bodies haven't had time to catch up. As a result, we absorb the pure carbohydrate energy of white grains and flours much faster than the even, steady absorption of the complex carbohydrates in whole grains. This causes short-lived satiation and can lead to chronic blood sugar imbalances. In short, we are just better suited to well-prepared whole grains.

Why freshly milled?

If we want to eat our grains (or indeed our pulses, nuts and seeds) as flour, it is important that we mill them fresh. When we mill grains, we expose the healthy fats in the germ to the air, and they begin to oxidise immediately. Initially, the oxidation just degrades the nutrient value of the grain, but left unchecked, it destroys it entirely, making the grain potentially harmful. Multiple studies have pointed to the importance of milling fresh. One found that rancidity can occur as early as 2–14 days after milling. Another found that after only four generations, a group of rats fed freshly ground wholegrain flour were the only group to remain fertile, compared to one group fed rancid wholegrain flour (15 days after milling), and another fed white flour.

Why stone-milled?

It is also important to use a stone mill, because modern steel-burr milling is a very high-heat process that effectively part-cooks the flour, rapidly increasing the rate of decay. Traditional stone milling is a far gentler and cooler process than steel-burr milling, and it is the only way to ensure the fats and vitamins remain intact in the flour for any length of time.

If you can, get yourself a grain mill and an oat roller. It's a small investment for a huge reward. If you don't have a mill or roller, only buy flour or rolled grains with a 'milled on' date and select the most recently milled, ideally less than two weeks old. Or for small amounts of flour, or grains that are rarely sold as flour, such as millet, you can use a spice or coffee grinder to mill them. Additionally, store them in the fridge or freezer to delay rancidity.

Basic soured grains.

To us, a simple bowl of steaming grains symbolises absolute nourishment. They are so flexible and can be accompanied by whichever vegetables are available and, if you desire, just a little meat, eggs and/or dairy.

Soaking grains in water acidified with apple cider vinegar for at least 12 hours in a warm room deactivates the enzyme inhibitors by simulating germination conditions in the seeds. Apple cider vinegar is our go-to, but you can use any other vinegar, lemon juice, yoghurt or whey to acidulate the water. Grains cooked after being soaked in this way taste sweeter, are more easily digested and contain a world of otherwise unavailable nutrients.

MAKES 3–4 CUPS COOKED GRAINS
TIME: 12–24 HOURS SOAKING
+ 15–90 MINUTES COOKING (DEPENDING ON THE GRAIN)

2 cups whole grain of your choice

1 tablespoon apple cider vinegar (or other vinegar or lemon juice)

Day 1. Add the grain to a jar or saucepan and cover with the appropriate amount of water according to the table opposite. Add the vinegar and set aside to soak for 12–24 hours at room temperature (or even better, in a warm place like on top of a coffee machine).

Day 2. Tip both the soaked grain and the soaking water into a saucepan (or if you've soaked in a saucepan, just place the whole thing on the stove), cover and bring to the boil. Reduce to the barest simmer and cook for the appropriate time according to the table opposite, or until all of the water is absorbed and the grains are tender. The cooked grain can be eaten right away or, for best results, set aside off the heat, covered, for a further 15 minutes to steam before serving.

A note on whey. When using whey to soak grains, please note that it is not as acidic as the other options mentioned above, so it's better to replace the water content entirely with whey.

A note on yoghurt. You can also sour grains in straight yoghurt rather than just adding a tablespoon, as in our traditional bircher (see page 250) and soured doughnuts (see page 340), but use this for baking or eating grains uncooked, not for the above method.

Notes.

When cooking grains in liquid, never add salt until after they're cooked. The salt hardens the carbohydrates in the endosperm, stopping the grain from fully softening.

For an even richer flavour, drain your grains after soaking and measure the liquid. Replace the liquid with the same amount of stock and cook as above.

Measures and cooking times for whole grains.
Cooking times and water absorbency do vary a little from harvest to harvest, but follow this guide and you can't go too wrong.

1 cup of grain	Cups of water	Cooking time
Amaranth	1½	20 minutes
Barley, hulled (pot barley)	2	50 minutes
Buckwheat	1½	20 minutes
Bulgur (burghul/cracked durum)	2	15 minutes
Einkorn (farro piccolo)	1½	30 minutes
Emmer (farro medio)	1¾	40 minutes
Freekeh (green harvested durum)	2½	60 minutes
Khorasan	2½	50 minutes
Millet, hulled	1½	20 minutes
Oats (freshly rolled)	3	30 minutes
Quinoa (washed)	1½	15 minutes
Rice, black	1¾	30 minutes
Rice, brown	1¾	30 minutes
Rice, red	2½	50 minutes
Rye	2½	90 minutes
Sorghum	2½	30 minutes
Spelt (farro grande)	2	50 minutes
Teff	2	20 minutes
Whole wheat	2½	90 minutes
Wild rice	2	50 minutes

Key points.
- Keep grains warm during soaking (25–38°C).
- Sour grains using an acid.
- Don't add salt before or during cooking.
- Cook in the water you used for soaking.

Sourdough culture.

Fermenting grains with a sourdough culture takes them to the next level. Not only does fermenting achieve all of the benefits of soaking with an acid, it also begins to break down the hard-to-digest proteins often blamed for coeliac reactions. In a nutshell, sourdough culture is a living culture full of good bacteria (lactobacilli) in a symbiotic relationship with wild yeasts, which adds a sour taste to your freshly milled flour by producing lactic acid as it digests the carbohydrates. The longer the ferment, the better (within reason!), but even overnight has a big effect. Sourdough culture is alive. You have to feed it, give it love and care for it or it will begin to lose its magical activity and eventually die.

Starting a new culture is simple; it just takes time and patience. It's a really fun process to watch it grow over about a week. Whether you want a gluten-free, whole-wheat or any other kind of culture, always start it with rye flour. Rye has that special something that makes the good things happen. After your culture is very alive, it can be converted to any flour you desire.

MAKES 1 'IMMORTAL' BATCH OF SOURDOUGH CULTURE
TIME: 7 DAYS

400 g rye flour

400 ml unchlorinated water (it must be unchlorinated to allow the wild bacteria and yeasts to grow)

Day 1. Add 50 g of rye flour and 50 ml of water to a 300–500 ml jar and mix well. Set aside in a warm place, about 25–38°C (we leave ours on top of the coffee machine), with the lid in place but not tightened.

Day 2. After 24 hours, discard all but about 2 tablespoons of the mix, then add the same amounts of flour and water to the jar and mix thoroughly before returning it to its warm place.

Days 3–5. Repeat day-2 instructions each day.

Day 6. By now your culture should really be bubbling between feeds. Repeat day-2 instructions twice (12 hours after the last feed, then again 12 hours later).

Day 7. Repeat day-2 instructions 12 hours after the last feed. Twelve hours later your culture should be forming big bubbles and be ready for making bread (see page 152).

Note. A healthy culture smells a little acidic, like vinegar, a little yeasty, like beer, and also a little sweet and fruity, like banana or pineapple. There is quite a lot of variation, but no matter what, it will smell pleasant. If your culture begins to smell like nail polish remover, takes on funny colours, or just doesn't smell right, it's probably not. Best to discard it and start again!

Maintaining your culture. Repeat the process of discarding and feeding daily for at least another week to get your culture really alive, and then freeze about 2 tablespoons for a backup just in case your culture spoils down the track. From this point, you can feed it any wholegrain flour you'd like, be it millet, wheat, brown rice, whatever.

We usually bake 3 kg of bread at a time, and keep our culture in the fridge in between. It's not considered the done thing to refrigerate your culture, but we've never had a problem managing it this way. Plus, we always have a backup in the freezer just in case, which we can simply bring out and feed to make it come alive again.

To use your culture. Two days before you plan on baking, combine 150 g of flour, 150 ml of water and at least 2 tablespoons of sourdough culture in a 1 litre jar and leave in a warm place. That's enough to culture a 3 kg batch of bread (10% by weight). If you want to bake more or less, feed it appropriately.

Twenty-four hours later, your culture will be ready to use. Never put anything in your starter jar but flour and water (especially don't contaminate it with salt, because it will wreak havoc with your culture) and always leave at least 2 tablespoons of starter in the jar. As soon as you are finished, seal the jar and pop it back in the fridge.

To convert to a gluten-free culture. To convert to a gluten-free culture and ensure no cross-contamination with the rye, place 1 cm of active starter in the bottom of a jar. Mix up 100 g of gluten-free flour with 100 ml of water in a separate bowl and add to the jar without stirring. Leave in a warm place for 12–24 hours until bubbles have formed throughout. Take a few tablespoons of the new culture from the top of the jar and place it in a new jar. Add another 100 g of gluten-free flour to the new jar and another 100 ml of water and mix well. Leave in a warm place for 12–24 hours. Your starter is now 100% gluten free.

> **Key points.**
> - A new culture is made from just whole rye flour and water.
> - Sourdough culture is alive! Unless dormant in the fridge or freezer, it must constantly be kept warm (25–38°C) and fed every day.

Eat — Staples. 143

Nixtamalised maize.

MAKES 1 KG NIXTAMAL (ENOUGH TO MAKE 100 TORTILLAS!)
TIME: 10 MINUTES PREPARATION
+ 8 HOURS OR OVERNIGHT STEEPING

1 kg whole dried maize

3 heaped tablespoons hardwood ash

In Nahuatl, the ancient language of the Aztecs, *nixta* means 'ashes', and *tamalli* means 'corn dough'. Nixtamalisation, then, is the traditional Aztec process of cooking whole dried maize in water with hardwood ash and leaving it to steep overnight. When maize was introduced to Europe from the Americas in the late 15th century the wisdom of its proper preparation was not brought with it, with disastrous results. Maize became the staple diet of huge swathes of the European and subsequently African and US populations, especially in poorer communities. Improperly prepared, maize lacked quality protein and B vitamins, and what followed was over three centuries of pellagra epidemics – a cripplingly painful disorder caused by chronic dietary deficiencies. The spread was only stopped well into the 20th century when it was finally realised that in South America no cases of pellagra were to be found, despite widespread consumption of maize. Western scientists finally acknowledged what Native Americans had been passing down through the generations for millennia: nixtamalisation.

During nixtamalisation, the hardwood ashes react with the water to form a super-alkaline environment. On a practical level, the alkalinity allows the maize proteins to bind once ground to form workable tortilla dough (the dough simply crumbles when made with maize flour that hasn't been nixtamalised). But more importantly, on a nutritional level, the process releases maize's rich stores of protein and B vitamins.

Traditionally, nixtamal was either eaten boiled (called hominy) or ground to make a moist dough for tortillas. Grinding it wet, however, requires a special mill called a *molino*. Because our grain mill requires grains to be dry, we have added a drying step into the recipe as an option.

It's also worth noting that you can buy nixtamalised maize flour in select stores (usually wholefood, health or organic type stores). It is called *masa harina* and is literally nixtamal that has been dried and ground into flour. Like other wholegrain flours, it's prone to rancidity, but if you can find some with a recent milling date, it's exactly what you need to make the best tasting tortillas you've ever eaten!

The hardwood ash thing can be a funny one to get your head around, but when we say hardwood ash, we literally mean hardwood ash. Simply collect the ashes from a fireplace or campfire. Softwood ashes, like pine, aren't suitable because of their high resin content. Also be careful that only wood has burned in your fire and not firelighters or anything printed with potentially harmful inks.

Day 1. Place the maize and ash in a pot and cover generously with water. Bring to a simmer and cook for 5 minutes, then set aside for 8 hours or overnight.

Day 2. Drain the maize and wash thoroughly under cold water, rubbing the kernels together between your hands to remove the outer skins and ash. (You don't have to remove all of the skins, just do your best.) You have now made nixtamal and have two choices:

To make hominy. Nixtamal, cooked in water and eaten whole, is called hominy. Simply cover with fresh water to a couple of centimetres above the nixtamal and bring to a simmer. Cover and cook for about 2 hours until the kernels are soft and a little chewy but not at all crunchy.

To make maize flour or polenta. If you have a grain mill, nixtamal can be dried in the sunshine and ground into tortilla flour or polenta (or stored to cook later). Because the outer layer has been compromised, it isn't as stable as non-nixtamalised maize, so we never store it for more than two weeks (read more on drying on page 229). To make tortilla dough, grind dried nixtamal very finely and add a little salt and water. To make polenta, grind dried nixtamal a little more coarsely and follow the basic polenta recipe, opposite.

Key points.
- Use hardwood ash to nixtamalise maize, not softwood ash, like pine.
- Boil and then soak overnight.

Basic soured polenta.

Provided it is only a part of a diverse diet and not a major staple, eating this un-nixtamalised polenta won't cause any problems. Pre-ground polenta is impossible to nixtamalise because the method requires the maize to be whole, but this recipe of soaking and cooking is a pretty great substitute. In fact, even though we have whole maize, we still just usually grind it fresh and follow this method, rather than going next level and nixtamalising, because this recipe just tastes so good!

If you have a grain mill, get your hands on some whole maize (make sure it's not a popcorn variety, as the kernels are too hard and will jam your grain mill – trust us!) and mill your own polenta. If you don't have a grain mill, remember that polenta is as prone to rancidity as any other wholegrain flour. So while it seems counter-intuitive to a healthy planet, steer clear of the bulk bins and try to buy it from the refrigerated section. Otherwise, always try to look for the most recent milling date, and don't buy anything more than two weeks old. Importantly, if maize *is* a major part of your diet, definitely get to know the nixtamalisation process (see opposite).

MAKES ABOUT 4 CUPS COOKED POLENTA
TIME: 12–24 HOURS SOAKING
+ 30 MINUTES COOKING

2 cups polenta

1 tablespoon apple cider vinegar (or other vinegar or lemon juice)

½ teaspoon unrefined salt

a knob of butter (optional)

Day 1. Place the polenta in a jar or saucepan and cover with 2 cups of water. Add the vinegar (we don't usually measure, just splash some in there), stir thoroughly and leave to soak for 12–24 hours at room temperature (or even better, in a warm place like on top of a coffee machine).

Day 2. Place the soaked polenta, soaking water, salt and butter (if using) in a saucepan (or if you've soaked in a saucepan, just place the whole thing on the stove), cover and bring to the boil. Reduce to the barest simmer and cook for about 30 minutes until a wooden spoon stands up in the pot. Serve immediately and keep the leftovers for polenta crisps (see page 275).

> **Key points.**
> - Use an acid to sour polenta.
> - Keep warm during soaking (25–38°C).
> - Cook in the water you used for soaking.

Basic pulses (dried beans, peas and lentils).

Beans, peas and lentils (or 'pulses'), like grains, have enzyme inhibitors that require deactivating. But they also contain oligosaccharides (difficult to digest carbohydrates that are responsible for beans' gassy reputation) and lectins (carbohydrate-binding proteins that render raw pulses absolutely toxic) and removing these enzyme inhibitors, oligosaccharides and lectins is key. Properly prepared, pulses are absolutely awesome foods. They are excellent sources of protein and are packed with minerals – especially iron – vitamins, fibre and healthy fats. As such, they have been a mainstay of traditional diets for as long as humans have tilled the land, and we eat them often.

To draw out the enzyme inhibitors, oligosaccharides and lectins, we soak pulses in *salted* water. It's important not to use an acid here (as you would for whole grains) because acids cause the proteins in pulses to constrict, preventing them from fully softening. We also never cook pulses in the liquid we soak them in, as that's where all of the oligosaccharides and lectins now are!

We always have some pulses sitting cooked and ready in the fridge for whatever dish calls for them, like our mustard, carrots, cauliflower and lentils (see page 297) or chickpea and cauliflower bowls (see page 302).

MAKES 2-3 CUPS COOKED PULSES
TIME: 12-24 HOURS SOAKING + 20 MINUTES TO 4 HOURS COOKING (DEPENDING ON THE PULSE)

1 cup dried beans, peas or lentils of your choice

1 teaspoon unrefined salt

Day 1. Place the pulses in a jar and cover with at least 3 cups of water. Add the salt and set aside to soak for 12–24 hours at room temperature (or even better, in a warm place like on top of a coffee machine).

Day 2. Drain the pulses and wash thoroughly under cold running water. Place them in a saucepan (we prefer a really heavy cast-iron pot for all pulses, as an even distribution of heat gives maximum butter-softness) with enough water to just cover and bring to the boil. Skim off any foam that forms on the surface (that's where any remaining oligosaccharides

are hiding) and reduce to the barest simmer. Cook for the appropriate time as per the table below, topping up the water if necessary, until butter soft.

There should be barely any water remaining when the pulses are ready. Otherwise, strain the liquid (it is delicious to drink), season the pulses well (the salt makes them even more digestible) and serve immediately, or store in the fridge for up to a week.

Note. As with grains, you can substitute the cooking water with stock for a richer flavour.

Table of cooking times for pulses.
Cooking times vary a little from harvest to harvest, but follow this guide and you can't go too wrong. Cooking times are largely based on the size of the seed (with some exceptions), so that's how we've grouped them.

The below cooking times may seem long, however this is to maximise the digestibility of the pulses and to achieve butter-soft results. Long, slow, even cooking over the fire was how pulses were cooked traditionally, and that is what we are trying to replicate.

Pulse	Cooking time
Beluga lentils	20 minutes
Other whole lentils (puy, brown etc.) and small beans (adzuki, mung etc.)	30 minutes
Cowpeas (black-eyed peas), lima beans	50 minutes
Dried whole peas	70 minutes
Cannellini beans, black beans, borlotti beans, fava beans (dried broad beans), kidney beans, pink beans, pinto beans	2½ hours
Great northern beans	3 hours
Navy (haricot) beans	3½ hours
Black pinto beans, chickpeas	4 hours

Key points.
- Soak pulses in water and salt.
- Don't add any acids, like tomatoes, vinegar, yoghurt or lemon juice, until the pulses are cooked.
- Cook in fresh water, not the water you used for soaking.
- Keep warm during soaking (25–38°C).

Sprouts.

Sprouting germinates grains, pulses and other seeds completely, turning them into vitamin-rich, super-digestible baby plants. The sprouting process alters the protein structure of the grain, pulse or seed to make it more digestible, releases a world of vitamins not previously accessible, and completely alters the structure of any remaining oligosaccharides and lectins into easily digestible simple carbohydrates. Sprouts are crunchy and delicious, and can be eaten raw or cooked. You can sprout many seeds, but some are tastier than others. Our favourite by far are puy lentils – they taste so fresh and minerally. We also *love* wheat, rye, mung bean and alfalfa. Enjoy sprouts in curries, stir-fries and salads (like our mixed grain and sprout pilaf on page 294 or sprouted mung daal on page 310), or just on their own.

MAKES 3+ CUPS SPROUTS
TIME: 3+ DAYS TO GROW SPROUTS TO DESIRED SIZE

1 cup grains, pulses or other seeds
(e.g. wheat, lentils, mung beans, fenugreek etc.)

Day 1. Place the seeds in a 2 litre jar and fill with water. Shake the jar in a circular motion over the sink, and then pour the water out. (This washes away any dirt or grime.) Fill the jar with water again and leave to soak overnight.

Day 2. Drain the water but leave the seeds in the jar. Fill with water and drain again. Place some muslin on top, fasten with a rubber band and leave for 24 hours with the opening facing down at a 30–45° angle, allowing any excess water to drain away – on a dish rack over the sink, or in a bowl both work well.

Day 3. Refresh by filling with water and draining again. Leave for another 24 hours the same way – your sprouts should now be growing!

Days 4–6. Repeat the filling and draining for at least 3 days until you have sprouts the size that you want them – we usually let them go until the first tiny green leaves appear!

Store the sprouts in the fridge for over 2 weeks in a fresh jar with no lid. Not using a lid ensures airflow, preventing mould and keeping the sprouts crisp!

Key points.
- Soak in water only (no salt).
- Keep sprouts warm while growing.
- Allow to drain freely while growing.

Nuts and seeds.

Activating nuts and seeds.

Nuts and seeds are an awesome addition to any diet, and they have been part of traditional nutrition forever. They are wonderful sources of minerals, fat-soluble vitamins and healthy fats.

Nuts and seeds all have, in varying degrees, the same enzyme inhibiting mechanisms we've discussed so far, and the soaking process below breaks down these inhibitors and makes nuts and seeds far more digestible and nutritious. The most common term used for this process is 'activation'. Of all the traditional preparation methods, this is the one we don't always use, as it is often difficult to integrate into a baking recipe. Additionally, compared to grains and pulses, we eat very little of these, therefore they aren't putting much strain on our digestive systems.

MAKES 1 CUP 'ACTIVATED' NUTS OR SEEDS
TIME: 12 HOURS SOAKING + 24+ HOURS DRYING

1 cup nuts or seeds

½ teaspoon unrefined salt

Day 1. Add the nuts or seeds and salt to a 1 litre jar or a bowl. Fill with water and set aside to soak for 12 hours in a warm place (we leave ours on top of the coffee machine).

Day 2. Drain the nuts or seeds and wash thoroughly. Use as is for cooking, or spread out in a single layer on a fine mesh rack (to ensure even airflow) and place in the sunshine, on the kitchen bench or in a low oven until totally dry and brittle – make sure they are totally dry or they will likely spoil in just a matter of days. Store in airtight jars in a cool pantry or, ideally, in the fridge for up to 12 months. Eat as a snack or mill into flour.

Note. The cashew is an interesting nut. No cashews are sold totally raw because they must go through a heat-processing step to remove the toxic oil cardol. As such, they tend to go slimy when soaked for long periods. We recommend only soaking them for a maximum of 6 hours to avoid this.

Key points.
- Soak nuts and seeds in water and salt to activate.
- Keep warm during the soaking process (25–38°C).

Making your own nut and seed flours and LSA.
Pre-ground nut and seed meals (like almond flour) and LSA mix (a combination of linseed meal, sunflower meal and almond meal) are *very* prone to oxidation (rancidity). If you have a high-powered blender, we highly recommend making your own versions fresh. Simply put the whole nuts or seeds in the blender and blend on high. This will ensure the nutrients are much more available to your body, and there will be minimal oxidation.

Long-ferment, no-knead sourdough breads.

MAKES 1.7 KG BREAD (1 LARGE LOAF)
TIME: 1 HOUR
+ 24 HOURS FERMENTING

Gluten-free loaf

305 g brown rice flour

305 g gluten-free oat flour (see note on page 140) or buckwheat flour

305 g millet flour or whole-maize flour

85 g psyllium husk

15 g unrefined salt

1.2 litres unchlorinated water (unchlorinated water is essential for the fermentation to work)

100 g gluten-free sourdough culture (see page 142)

Whole-wheat loaf

915 g whole-wheat flour

85 g psyllium husk

15 g unrefined salt

1.1 litres unchlorinated water (unchlorinated water is essential for the fermentation to work)

100 g sourdough culture
(see page 142)

These freshly milled wholegrain, long-ferment, sourdough, no-knead breads are our absolute staples. Matt is the head bread baker in our house. He spent years perfecting his whole-wheat bread recipe only to marry someone who couldn't eat wheat! So it was his mission to perfect a gluten-free version. Along the way we realised that actually I could eat both – the fresh milling of grains and the long fermentation made the wheat easily digestible and stopped any reactions (see pages 140–42 for more information). So now we love both, and eat both! Having well-prepared bread makes everything seem easier – just add some fresh vegetables, a pickle and some homemade mayonnaise and you have a nourishing meal. We make at least a loaf every week and always have some in the freezer as a backup. – LENTIL

Day 1. For either bread, add the flour(s), psyllium husk and salt to a large bowl and combine (we weigh out and mix together the whole grain(s), salt and psyllium husk, and then put them through our grain mill together to form a lovely even flour mix!).

Add the water to another large mixing bowl and stir in the sourdough culture.

Add the dry ingredients to the sourdough mix (not the other way around). Using one hand, quickly begin to mix by scooping your hand deep into the mix, pulling up a handful of ingredients, folding them back on top of the rest and pushing down into the centre of the bowl. Use your other hand to rotate the bowl, repeating the action until all of the ingredients have come together evenly. The mix will seem *very* wet at first, but don't be fooled – you'll need to act fast because the psyllium husk will quickly absorb all that excess water, making the dough much harder to work with.

When you've formed a nice, soft dough, place a damp towel over the bowl, or cover with a close fitting bowl, and leave the mixture in a warm place for at least 24 hours (we've even pushed it to 72 hours, and it was still great!). We actually put ours in a bucket with a loose-fitting lid and wrap it all up in an electric blanket. This technique ensures a strong fermentation, especially in winter! The dough should expand up to triple its size during fermentation, so make sure your vessel is big enough!

Day 2. You are ready to bake when the ferment smells fruity and sour and has at least doubled (but almost tripled) in size.

Preheat the oven to its maximum setting – for us 250°C – and grease a baking tray with butter or line it with a sheet of baking paper. (For old ovens – especially gas ones – a great trick is to place three house bricks under the bottom rack. This really helps to maintain the temperature when you open the door to place your loaves inside.)

Scoop or gently turn the dough out of the bowl and onto your tray. If you'd like, now is the time to score lines on the top with a sharp, wet knife. Bake for 1 hour, checking the bread after 50 minutes in case it is overcooking. Your loaf is ready if it sounds slightly hollow when tapped on the underside.

Remove from the oven and place on a cooling rack until fully cooled. We know it's so hard not to eat it straight away (and sometimes we can't help ourselves!), but allowing the bread to completely cool – known as 'curing' – greatly improves the texture and longevity of the loaf. The gluten-free loaf is particularly sticky until it has cured. Once cured, your loaf will keep well on the kitchen bench for 1–2 weeks, but is best placed up on a rack for even air circulation. Or cut into slices and freeze.

Notes.

All ovens are different and dough is an unpredictable living thing. We like quite a hard-baked loaf that's beautifully soft on the inside but crisp and sometimes even a little dark on the outside. You will learn over time exactly what works for you.

Using buckwheat instead of oats in the gluten-free variation will form a very moist loaf. In that case we usually cure ours for an additional 12 hours before we eat it, otherwise it can be a bit too sticky.

If you can't find millet flour, and don't have a grain mill, try grinding whole millet in a spice grinder.

We usually make a triple batch and divide it into three loaves before baking.

FIELD NOTES

On wheat. Wheat has become such a sensitive subject in the health world. But it has been sustaining generations of humans all over the world for thousands of years. Only recently has it caused widespread health problems, which we believe can be solely attributed to the highly refined and rancid forms it is so often served in these days. Certainly the ancient wheats – emmer, spelt and einkorn – seem to be less contentious, but even the common wheat grown today is a delicious and nutritious food when prepared properly, the traditional way, through fermentation and souring (see pages 138–42 for more information).

On psyllium husk. We are very sceptical about the edibility of all the gums, binders and rising agents most pre-made, gluten-free breads contain, so we spent many hours testing and trialling natural alternatives. Psyllium husk has proven to be an absolute powerhouse in our gluten-free flour blends. It is just so water absorbent, it makes our breads consistently moist and light, and gives the digestive system a deep cleanse. Psyllium does come from far away – India for us – but a little bit goes a long way, and it is an exceptionally well-grown crop. We've come to love it so much that we even use it in our whole-wheat bread now too!

Soured wholegrain pizza bases.

This recipe is magic. It makes perfectly textured, elastic pizza bases, is super easy, and it still prepares your grains well – using an acid to sour them. Please try it; it might just change your life. You can throw everything in a bowl, leave it overnight and roll it out when you're ready to cook. You can also leave the dough in the fridge to use throughout the week, or put the pre-made bases in the freezer for an easy meal later.

Day 1. Combine all of the ingredients except the water in a large bowl and mix well with your hands. Gradually add the water and knead until the mixture comes together. Continue to knead for about 5 minutes until you have an even dough that forms a ball. Cover the bowl and leave to sit for 12–24 hours.

Day 2. Preheat the oven to 250°C fan-forced. Line baking tray(s) with silicone baking mats or baking paper.

Divide the mixture into eight equal pieces. Flour your bench and roll the dough into thin pizza bases.

Top the bases with your favourite ingredients and cook for about 12 minutes until everything is just starting to brown. Alternatively, cook for just 3–4 minutes, cool and freeze for later.

MAKES 8 MEDIUM PIZZA BASES
TIME: 20 MINUTES
+ 12-24 HOURS SOURING

200 g brown rice flour

200 g gluten-free oat flour (see note on page 140)

200 g buckwheat flour

50 g psyllium husk

3 tablespoons extra-virgin olive oil

3 tablespoons apple cider vinegar

a pinch of unrefined salt

800–900 ml unchlorinated water (unchlorinated water is essential for the souring to work)

Soured buckwheat pancakes.

You can make these buckwheat pancakes either sweet or savoury or turn them into little pikelets and store them in the fridge to put in the toaster for an easy breakfast during the week.

MAKES ABOUT 8 PANCAKES
TIME: 30 MINUTES + 12-24 HOURS SOURING

350 g (2½ cups) buckwheat flour

2 tablespoons apple cider vinegar

250 ml (1 cup) unchlorinated water
(unchlorinated water is essential for the souring to work)

125 ml (½ cup) milk of your choice

2 eggs, whisked

2 tablespoons unrefined sugar (e.g. rapadura)

2 tablespoons butter, melted, plus extra for cooking

2 teaspoons bicarbonate of soda

Day 1. Place the flour, vinegar and water in a bowl and stir until it forms a thick paste. Cover and set aside in a warm place for 12–24 hours to sour.

Day 2. Add the remaining ingredients to the bowl and whisk together to form a smooth batter.

Heat a frying pan until medium–hot (it will sizzle when you put a little splash of water in it). Melt a knob of butter in the pan and, using a ladle, pour in a small amount of batter – make these as big or small as you like.

Allow the pancake to cook until it's bubbly and doesn't stick to the bottom of the pan – you should be able to flip it easily! Flip and fry it on the other side until golden brown. Place the pancakes in a tea towel or cover with a plate to keep them warm while the rest are cooking.

Serve warm or refrigerate for easy breakfasts during the week (see our greens and kimchi pancakes on page 254).

Note. If you want a sweeter batter, just increase the sugar to taste.

Soured buckwheat crepes.

This is super similar to the buckwheat pancakes and are great either sweet or savoury. Wrap anything in a crepe and it's always good.

MAKES ABOUT 15 CREPES
TIME: 30 MINUTES + 12-24 HOURS SOURING

280 g (2 cups) buckwheat flour

2 tablespoons apple cider vinegar

250 ml (1 cup) unchlorinated water
(unchlorinated water is essential for the souring to work)

375 ml (1½ cups) milk of your choice

4 eggs, whisked

2 tablespoons butter, melted, plus extra for cooking

2 tablespoons unrefined sugar (e.g. rapadura)

a big pinch of unrefined salt

Day 1. Place the flour, vinegar and water in a bowl and stir until it forms a thick paste. Cover and set aside in a warm place for 12–24 hours to sour.

Day 2. Add the remaining ingredients to the bowl and whisk together to form a smooth batter.

Heat a frying pan until medium–hot (it will sizzle when you put a little splash of water in it). Melt a knob of butter in the pan and, using a ladle, pour in a small amount of batter. Quickly roll the pan so that you end up with a thin layer of batter – this should be one quick movement!

Allow the crepe to cook until it's bubbly and doesn't stick to the bottom of the pan – you should be able to flip it easily! Flip and fry it on the other side until brown. All up, this process should take around 1–2 minutes per crepe. To keep the crepes warm and prevent them drying out, place them in a tea towel or cover with a plate while the rest are cooking.

Serve warm with your favourite filling (see recipes on pages 322 and 336).

FIELD NOTES

On skipping souring in this recipe. Pancakes and crepes conjure up childhood memories and make some of the best spontaneous weekend meals. So, if you had to skip souring grains in any recipe, we would give you permission to do so in this one. Replace the buckwheat flour with rice flour (it must be very finely ground or it will be grainy), omit the vinegar, add just a ½ cup of water and simply whisk together and cook.

Gluten-free shortcrust pastry – sweet or savoury.

This pastry is delicious. And easy. Life changing. You must dance with your pastry for it to work – really work it, feel it and love it. It will always turn out better this way. It's just the way it is.

Place all of the dry ingredients in a blender and blend until fine. Transfer to a large bowl with the remaining ingredients and massage well with your hands. Really work the dough, kneading it firmly for 5–10 minutes until it comes together. If it's a little too dry, gradually add water in tiny amounts until it comes together. Refrigerate the dough covered or wrapped in baking paper for a few hours until it's really cold and firm.

Once chilled, the pastry can be rolled out on a floured bench to fit any tin.

To pre-bake the pastry before adding the filling, bake at 180°C fan-forced for 5–10 minutes – you can use pastry weights (we just use dried beans), though it's not crucial. To fully cook the pastry, bake for 15 minutes.

Alternatively, the uncooked pastry will keep in the fridge for around a week, and any excess can be frozen.

Notes.

Because this recipe is gluten free, make sure you knead it well to ensure the ingredients bind together.

It is really key that the dough is cold before rolling it out, otherwise it won't roll well.

This pastry works best when it's baked and served in a pie tin, as the pastry won't hold together well if you remove it from the tin, fill it and then bake again.

MAKES 650 G
TIME: 15 MINUTES
+ COOLING TIME

Sweet version

180 g white rice flour, plus extra for rolling (or extra buckwheat flour)

180 g buckwheat flour

65 g tapioca flour

3 tablespoons unrefined sugar (e.g. rapadura)

a pinch of unrefined salt

120 g cold unsalted butter, cut into small cubes

1 egg

1 egg yolk

1 tablespoon cold water

Savoury version

180 g white rice flour, plus extra for rolling (or extra buckwheat flour)

180 g buckwheat flour

65 g tapioca flour

½ teaspoon unrefined salt

120 g cold unsalted butter, cut into small cubes

1 egg

1 egg yolk

3 tablespoons cold water

Sourdough pastas.

MAKES 1.2 KG (WET WEIGHT)
TIME: 45 MINUTES
+ 24 HOURS FERMENTING

Gluten-free pasta

200 g millet flour (if you can't find millet flour, grind whole millet in a spice grinder)

200 g brown rice flour

200 g buckwheat flour

50 g psyllium husk

¼ teaspoon unrefined salt

375 g gluten-free sourdough culture (see page 142)

250 ml (1 cup) unchlorinated water (unchlorinated water is essential for the fermentation to work)

2 tablespoons extra-virgin olive oil

3 eggs

3 egg yolks

200 g white rice flour, for rolling

Whole-wheat pasta

600 g whole-wheat flour

50 g psyllium husk

¼ teaspoon unrefined salt

375 g sourdough culture (see page 142)

250 ml (1 cup) unchlorinated water (unchlorinated water is essential for the fermentation to work)

2 tablespoons extra-virgin olive oil

3 eggs

3 egg yolks

200 g whole-wheat flour, for rolling

Special equipment

pasta machine

This recipe is one that has developed as a result of a huge amount of trial and error, and lots of love. It was our mission to make both a gluten-free and a whole-wheat sourdough pasta that actually held together. We still remember some of the trial versions, sharing them with friends and laughing at their poor attempt to be pasta. But we finally nailed it. This pasta is truly delicious. It's slightly different in flavour to 'standard' pasta, being both sweet and savoury at the same time, with the most perfect tang from the fermenting process. This is definitely one of our more involved recipes, but it's so worth it and it gets easier and easier the more you make it. You have to start this recipe at least one day before you need it, but you can store the dough in the fridge for up to a week and cook it fresh throughout the week. Alternatively, dry it or freeze it for easy meals later.

Day 1. For either dough, mix the flour(s), psyllium and salt in one bowl and the culture, water and oil in another. Add the dry ingredients to the wet ingredients (not the other way around) and, using the tips of your fingers, bring the two together in a circular motion until a crumb is formed. Now continue to mix with your hands, bringing together the crumb into a firm ball of dough. It will be drier than your average dough at this stage, but it should just hold together in one cohesive mass. If it's too dry to even hold together, work in 1 tablespoon of water at a time until it does. Place the dough in an airtight container and leave at room temperature for 24 hours.

Day 2. Pull apart your dough in a mixing bowl and add the eggs and egg yolks. Combine with your hands and knead to bring it all back together. Initially the yolks will make the dough very sticky (it's their nature) but just keep kneading and you'll obtain a really nice, workable consistency. If it's too wet, dust with some of the extra flour and continue kneading until your dough is elastic (10–15 minutes kneading is ideal). The Italians say your pasta dough should feel soft but firm, like a young woman's breast. Ha!

You can use the dough immediately, refrigerate in an airtight container for up to a week, or freeze it in an airtight container for later use.

When you're ready to roll the dough out, get yourself a glass of red wine – pasta always turns out better when there is red wine involved! Dust the counter top with extra flour and break off a piece of dough a little smaller than a tennis ball. Give it one final knead in the flour before rolling it flat with a rolling pin. Dust both sides with a little more flour and put through the pasta roller on setting number 3 out of 9, or the equivalent – if your dough falls apart when you do this it is probably too wet, just roll in a little flour and knead some more. Fold the rolled dough in half, flatten together and put it through the roller in the same direction as the first time, so that now both the first bit to come out last time *and* the last bit to come out last time go through first – this is very important. Repeat this several times, dusting with flour occasionally after folding, until the pasta is very smooth and a fairly even rectangle.

Now air-dry your pasta for 15–30 minutes over a wooden rail or wire rack until you can gently pinch the two halves together and they don't stick to each other. Don't leave it for too long, or it will begin to crack.

Dust your air-dried pasta on both sides one last time with a little extra flour and run through the pasta roller on setting 3 again (out of 9, or the equivalent), then turn to setting 4 and run the pasta through without folding it, and then turn to setting 5 and run it through again so that you have a long, thin sheet. If you like it even thinner, you can keep going up the numbers, but we find setting 5 or 6 out of 9 ideal.

For lasagne or ravioli (see ravioli recipe on page 306), leave the sheet as is, or for noodles, roll through the linguine setting. You can cook your pasta immediately at this stage, or dry it in a 50°C oven until completely brittle and store in an airtight container in the pantry for later use. You can also freeze linguine or pasta sheets in an airtight container in single layers separated with baking paper. Now take a sip of wine – you have just made sourdough pasta!

Notes.

You must dance with your pasta dough – if you have never made pasta dough before and/or this fails the first time, try again! You will get there, and it will get easier every time.

Remember if you can't prepare it the next day, the dough can be stored in the fridge for up to one week.

If your pasta is falling apart, knead it more and don't be scared of over kneading the dough – this is key.

FIELD NOTES

On cooking fresh pasta. Bring a large saucepan of water to the boil and add a glug of olive oil and a generous pinch of salt. Turn down to a gentle boil and gently place your pasta in the water. Cook for 1–2 minutes until *just* soft. Be careful not to overcook, or it will begin to fall apart. Drain, toss in olive oil and serve.

On cooking dried pasta. Bring a large saucepan of water to the boil and add a glug of olive oil and a generous pinch of salt. Turn down to a gentle boil and gently place your pasta in the water. Cook for 3–4 minutes. Again, don't overcook, or it will begin to fall apart. Drain, toss in olive oil and serve.

Ghee.

MAKES 400 G
TIME: 20–30 MINUTES

500 g unsalted butter,
coarsely chopped

Special equipment

filter paper or muslin cloth

500 ml dark-coloured glass jar
with lid

Ghee is the pure fat component of butter. It's a way to preserve butter fat by removing the milk solids, so that it becomes stable and is able to sit out on the shelf for many months. Ghee is a very traditional and nourishing food. In ancient Indian Ayurvedic medicine, ghee is considered the source of the deepest wellbeing. And we get it. Ghee is rich and sweet and adds so much depth to dishes. It has an especially high smoke point (around 250°C), so is great for frying or cooking on high heat (try our cardoon chips on page 276), and we love the flavour it adds to curries (see page 310 for our daal recipe) and roast vegetables.

Slowly melt the butter in a saucepan over a medium heat. When the butter begins to simmer, reduce the heat to low and continue to simmer very gently for 10–15 minutes, watching carefully. Foam will rise and then subside. Then the golden liquid will bubble, before easing and finally foaming again. As soon as the second foaming begins, immediately remove the pan from the heat or you will burn the milk solids that have settled on the bottom of the pan and spoil the ghee.

Strain the liquid while it's still hot through a funnel or colander lined with filter paper or muslin (or paper towel). If using a funnel, you can pour directly into the storage jar, otherwise transfer once strained. Sometimes the filter can block a little, but eventually all of the ghee will drip through, leaving just oily milk solids on top and pure ghee below.

Ghee will keep longest and freshest when stored in the fridge. That said, throughout tropical India it is never stored anywhere except on a kitchen shelf. So long as all of the milk solids have been removed, ghee is very stable. Storing it away from light will help it retain its bright colour, flavour and nutrients – hence the dark jar.

FIELD NOTES

On the nutrition of ghee, butter and cream. Butter and cream are full of vitamin A, vitamin E and selenium, which protect against disease and promote a healthy immune system and calcium absorption. Additionally, butter contains vitamin K2, which is only present in butter fat from cows raised on green pasture. Vitamin K2 is a very special vitamin, responsible for the distribution of calcium in the body and when combined with vitamins A and D massively reduces the effects of ageing and the development of degenerative diseases. Contrary to commercial marketing messages, margarine, on the other hand, is made from highly heated and processed solidified fats – vegetable oils, such as corn and soy. This process removes all vitamins and creates a non-absorbable form of fat that has to be bleached and coloured to remove the grey colour. This process is, in fact, very similar to how plastic is made. Don't eat margarine.

Sour cream & cultured butter.

Sour cream, also known as cultured cream, and cultured butter are, well, just delicious. This recipe is about making the best cream and butter there is.

When our cow is in milk, we hand-milk her every night. We leave the milk to sit until the cream settles on top, and then skim it off. Butter and cream are some of the most traditional foods there are, and are so good for you. In particular butter, as the nutrients are more concentrated (see field notes on opposite page). If you just want to make 'uncultured' butter, you can skip the sour cream step, or if you just want sour cream, stop there and don't go on to making butter.

To make sour cream. Place the cream and yoghurt in a jar, stir well and leave in a warm spot at room temperature for 12–24 hours, depending on how sour you want it to taste. If you just want sour cream (not cultured butter), simply place the jar in the fridge. Otherwise continue to follow the next steps to make cultured butter.

To make cultured butter. To make this process faster, make sure that the sour cream is at room temperature and the jar is only a third to half full. Place a lid on the jar and shake. It will get thicker. Keep shaking. Eventually it will get so thick it will fill the jar and become really hard to shake. Keep shaking. All of a sudden you will notice that it separates into two distinct parts and solids are splashing around in the liquid. Stop shaking.

Using a strainer, separate the liquid (buttermilk) from the solids (butter). Form the butter solids into a ball in the strainer, and then place the ball into a bowl of iced water. Repeatedly squeeze and shape the butter in the iced water to squeeze out any excess buttermilk. The butter is ready when you squeeze it and the only liquid that runs out is totally clear. This is a super-important step, as it will stop the butter from going prematurely rancid. Take it out of the iced water and squeeze out any remaining liquid. Massage the salt into the butter with your hands. You've made butter!

Store the butter in the fridge for 3–4 months, or freeze for 1–1½ years.

MAKES 500 ML SOUR CREAM
OR ABOUT 200-250 G
CULTURED BUTTER
TIME: SOUR CREAM, 2 MINUTES
+ 12-24 HOURS CULTURING;
CULTURED BUTTER, 5-15 MINUTES
(DEPENDING ON WHO IS
SHAKING THE JAR!)

500 ml (2 cups) cream

2 tablespoons natural yoghurt (it must have live cultures – see our recipe on page 170)

1 teaspoon unrefined salt

FIELD NOTES

On buttermilk. When making cultured butter, the cream separates into butter (the solids) and buttermilk (the liquid). Buttermilk made from sour cream is full of good bacteria and is high in calcium. Don't discard the buttermilk, as it can be used as a replacement for milk in many recipes, such as in pancakes (see page 158).

Natural yoghurt.

MAKES 1.1 LITRES
TIME: 10 MINUTES
+ 10-24 HOURS COOLING
AND CULTURING

1 litre (4 cups) milk
(cow's, goat's or sheep's)

100 g natural yoghurt
(it must have live cultures)

Special equipment

thermometer

Real yoghurt contains milk and good bacteria. That's it. And it's so good for you. Even if you only make yoghurt once, it's an empowering thing to know how to make. It's nice to know how to control its taste, flavour and thickness, and to know exactly what is involved in making something that is, for most of us, a weekly staple. The key to making yoghurt is getting the temperature right and starting with a good yoghurt culture. We make it in big batches, as it lasts about a month in the fridge. This recipe depends on your taste preferences: whether you like your yoghurt thin or thick, sour or less sour.

Day 1. Heat the milk to 35–40°C and pour into a 1.5–2 litre jar. Add the yoghurt to the jar, seal and shake! Set the sealed jar aside in a warm place to maintain 35–40°C for 10–24 hours. We put it on top of our coffee machine to maintain the temperature. Other ideas to keep it warm are wrapping it in an electric blanket, placing it near a wood stove or near a fire, or wrapping it in a blanket somewhere warm.

Day 2. The yoghurt is ready once it has thickened. Play with how long you leave the yoghurt to culture – everyone has different tastes and likes it at different stages, thicknesses and sourness. Experiment! Once you're happy with it, seal the jar and store it in the fridge for up to 1 month.

To make a sour yoghurt. The longer you leave the yoghurt at 35–40°C before putting it in the fridge, the more cultured (more populated with live bacteria) it will become and the more tart it will taste.

To make a thick yoghurt. Line a colander with a double layer of muslin and place it over a bowl. Pour the yoghurt into the muslin and leave it in the fridge to strain overnight, or until the desired thickness is achieved. This is the real way to make Greek yoghurt, rather than by adding milk solids.

Note. Don't forget to save some yoghurt each week to make the next batch!

Labne (yoghurt cheese).

This is the easiest cheese in this book. Simply press out yoghurt, mix in herbs and coat in olive oil to make a delicious cheese. One of our all-time favourite flavour combinations is this labne with mustard (see page 182) and mayonnaise (see page 182) on fresh sourdough bread (see page 152). For a sweet variation of labne, omit the salt and herbs and use it fresh (as in our carrot crepes with burnt oranges on page 336).

Day 1. Combine the yoghurt, herbs and salt in a large bowl.

Line a colander with a double layer of muslin and sit over a bowl. Pour the yoghurt into the muslin and leave it in the fridge to strain for 12 hours.

After 12 hours you will have made lovely, thick Greek-style yoghurt. To continue to make labne, fold the muslin over the yoghurt, return it to the colander and place a 1–2 kg weight (a stack of small plates will do) on top and leave for a further 12 hours in the fridge.

Day 2. Roll the labne into balls and place them in a jar, covering with olive oil as you go. The labne will keep in the fridge for at least a month.

Note. Use the leftover whey to make ricotta (see page 176).

MAKES 230 G
TIME: 10 MINUTES
+ 24 HOURS PRESSING

500 g natural yoghurt
(see opposite)

1 teaspoon dried herbs (we used oregano, za'atar and marjoram)

¼ teaspoon unrefined salt

extra-virgin olive oil

Special equipment

muslin cloth or nut bag

Feta, our way.

MAKES 250–300 G
TIME: 30 MINUTES
+ 24 HOURS SITTING
AND PRESSING

Feta

2 litres milk (cow's, goat's or sheep's)

1 heaped tablespoon natural yoghurt (it must have live cultures – see our recipe on page 170)

90 ml unchlorinated water (this is essential to properly preserve the feta)

¼ teaspoon liquid vegetable rennet (chymosin)

¼ teaspoon unrefined salt

Brine (10%)

600 ml unchlorinated water (this is essential to properly preserve the feta)

60 g unrefined salt

Special equipment

thermometer

cheesecloth or muslin cloth

cheese mould (this has to have holes in it, you can use an old bucket and put small holes in it)

This is a mild feta, crumbly but still creamy. We have tried to make this recipe as simple and as foolproof as possible. Sometimes cheese recipes can look so overwhelming and complicated that you are too paralysed to even start. This is our method of making feta, which cuts out some of the 'standard' steps and makes it easy to fit into your daily routine. Feta is a great way to use up excess milk and preserve it for 3–6 months.

Day 1. If you have your own cow, the milk will be the ideal temperature straight from the udder, but if you don't have fresh milk, gently heat your refrigerated milk to 38–40°C in a large saucepan, stirring constantly so it doesn't burn. Add the yoghurt and mix well. Set aside for 1 hour.

Place the water and rennet in a small bowl and mix well. Stir the milk vigorously and slowly add the rennet mixture. Stop stirring as soon as it has all been added. Cover the mixture and set aside somewhere where it won't be touched, but don't refrigerate. Don't move or stir the mixture at all – this is essential. Leave untouched overnight or for 8–12 hours.

Day 2. In the morning, press the top of the curds with your finger – you should see a 'clean break' where the curds break apart with 'sharp' edges and the whey will start to fill the break.

Using a long knife, deep enough to reach the bottom of the pan, cut the curds vertically in lines 1 cm apart, then turn the pot 90° and repeat to make a checkerboard pattern. Cut the curds at a 45° angle to the left and finally at a 45° angle to the right – we're aiming for about centimetre cube-ish sized pieces (they don't have to be perfect, just as even as possible).

Make yourself a coffee and leave the feta to sit for 5 minutes.

With a slotted spoon, gently lift the curds from the bottom of the pot to the top, which helps to evenly release the whey from the set curds. Catch up on some reading and leave the curds to sit for another 5 minutes, then gently lift the curds again. Take another 5 minutes to finish your coffee.

When you're done, pour the curds and whey into the cheesecloth. Tie the cloth up and suspend it over a saucepan or bucket and leave it at room temperature for 4 hours.

Turn the feta out of the cheesecloth into a bowl and sprinkle over the salt. Mix until well combined. Place the salted curds back into the cheesecloth and sit in the cheese mould. Place a 3–4 kg weight on top (a stack of small plates will do) and set aside overnight at room temperature.

Day 3. In the morning, your feta should now be hard and set. Cut into 2–3 cm pieces and place in a large jar.

Now make the brine. Vigorously combine the water and salt in a jug and stir until all of the salt has dissolved. Pour the brine into the jar, making

sure it covers the feta. Put the lid on and store in the fridge for at least 2 weeks to cure before eating. This curing period is what will give your feta its distinctive salty sharpness. Store in the fridge for 3–6 months.

Notes.

You can also preserve the feta in salted whey, but it only lasts up to about a month preserved this way.

You can also use vegetable-derived rennet, though it will add a bitterness to the cheese. This is why chymosin-derived vegetarian rennet is a much better option.

FIELD NOTES

On leftover milk products. When making cheese, you are often left with whey – the watery part of milk that is left after the cheese curds have formed. Whey can be great for fermenting grains, using in breads or cakes and making ricotta (see page 176). Just be aware that in some recipes, the leftover whey may contain salt. You can't use salted whey to sour whole grains, as the salt will prevent the grains from cooking properly. But you can still use it for ricotta, breads and cakes.

Cheat's ricotta.

A super-quick and easy, mild and soft cheese that's good on everything – sweet or savoury! Ricotta was traditionally made using whey that was left over from making other cheeses and was called *ricottone* – this is our cheat's version, using whole milk. You can, of course, use whey if you do have some, just remember that you'll have a much smaller yield.

MAKES 300–400 G (LESS IF USING WHEY INSTEAD OF MILK)
TIME: 30 MINUTES + 1 HOUR STRAINING

2 litres cow's milk (or whey)

½ teaspoon unrefined salt, plus extra

3 tablespoons lemon juice

Special equipment

thermometer

muslin cloth, cheesecloth or nut bag

Place the milk and ½ teaspoon of salt in a large saucepan and warm over a medium heat until it reaches 80°C, stirring often to make sure it doesn't stick to the bottom. Keep the milk at 80°C for a few minutes over a low heat.

Turn off the heat and gently stir the milk in a circular motion with a wooden spoon while slowly adding the lemon juice. Stop stirring as soon as it's all added. The milk should coagulate and form curds (it will look all lumpy). Set the mixture aside for 15 minutes or so to let the curds come together.

Line a colander with a double layer of muslin and place it over a bowl. Pour the mixture into the cloth and allow it to drain for an hour or so until it becomes thick and solid.

Massage in salt to taste and store in an airtight container in the fridge for up to 1 week. Eat it on everything, hot or cold.

Paneer.

Paneer is like haloumi, but easier to make for just as good a result. Traditionally, this simple curd cheese was considered the most assimilable and digestible protein you could eat. Serve hot with bright vegetables (like our fried paneer and summer squash on page 298), in curries in place of meat, or as a replacement for haloumi in any recipe.

MAKES 150–250 G
TIME: 10 MINUTES + 4–12 HOURS PRESSING

300–400 g ricotta (see opposite)

½ teaspoon unrefined salt

½ teaspoon nigella seeds (optional)

Special equipment

muslin cloth, cheesecloth or nut bag

Place the ricotta, salt and nigella seeds (if using) in a bowl and mix to combine.

Line a colander with a double layer of muslin and add the salted ricotta. Place over a bowl and fold the cloth back over the ricotta. Place a 1–2 kg weight on top (a stack of small plates will do) and leave to press in the fridge for 4–12 hours. The longer the press, the firmer and drier the texture will be. Experiment to see what you like best.

Paneer can be sliced and fried immediately, kept in the fridge for up to a week, or stored in a 5% brine solution (see field notes on page 198) in the fridge for up to a month (though the longer you store it the saltier it will get!).

Rendering fat (e.g. lard).

Animal fats have been used in cooking forever. These fats get a lot of bad press these days because of their apparently high levels of saturated fat, but actually they contain much less saturated fat than coconut oil, are a wonderful source of energy, and are rich in fat-soluble vitamins. We love cooking in lard (pig fat), duck fat, chicken fat or tallow (lamb or beef fat) just as much as we love cooking in olive oil or butter. Like all things, it's all about balance and diversity.

Preheat the oven to 100°C fan-forced.

Chop the fat into small cubes and spread out in a large baking dish. Place the dish in the oven and cook, uncovered, until the fat is melted and clear and there are crispy bits floating on the surface (around 4–5 hours).

Strain the fat while it's still hot through a funnel or colander lined with filter paper or several layers of muslin. If using a funnel, you can pour directly into the storage jars, otherwise transfer once strained. Sometimes the filter can block a little, but eventually all of the fat will drip through leaving just the oily crispy bits on top and pure fat below.

Due to their high levels of less stable unsaturated fats, rendered fats should be stored in the fridge where they will keep for months. Storing them away from light will help to retain their colour, flavour and nutrients – hence the dark jar.

Note. You can also use the fat that settles on the top of your waste bone stock (see page 180). Just refrigerate the stock so that the fat solidifies in a layer on top. Skim this layer off and gently heat in a small pan. Pour into a jar to store, being careful not to pour in any of the stock liquid that may have sneaked into your pan with it.

MAKES 700–800 G
TIME: 4–5 HOURS

1 kg well-sourced animal fat (or tails or skin), available from any good butcher

Special equipment

filter paper or muslin cloth

2 x 500 ml dark-coloured glass jars with lids

FIELD NOTES

On types of fat. Fat can be rendered from many different parts of an animal. Suet, the fat around the kidneys of mutton or beef has long been prized, so too the tails of ducks, geese and chickens. But even just the skin of poultry can produce a surprising quantity of fat once rendered. Some fats are white, some more yellow. The yellow colour is usually due to a higher concentration of vitamin A, indicating a more nutrient-dense fat.

Vegetable stock.

Stocks are gateways to easy meals. They have heaps of flavour and are full of nutrients, simply add some vegetables, meat, grains and spices and you have an easy 'one pot wonder'. You can use any old vegetables you have left over from the week, oversized vegetables (they're past their best) from the garden, or if you have an overabundance of one vegetable (because you overplanted it in the excitement of planting). Vegetable stock is so easy: throw it all in a pot and leave it for 8–12 hours to cook down, then freeze it for easy meals later.

MAKES ABOUT 2 LITRES
TIME: 8–12 HOURS

1 kg mixed vegetables (try to include some root vegetables for the best flavour), cut into large chunks

2 carrots, halved

4 celery stalks, cut into 20 cm lengths

1 onion, halved

3 litres unchlorinated spring water

1 bunch of parsley (or any other herbs), tied together with twine

5–10 black peppercorns

Preheat the oven to 220°C fan-forced.

Place the vegetables on a baking tray and roast for 10–15 minutes until browned.

Tip the vegetables into a stockpot and cover with the water. Add the parsley and peppercorns and bring to the boil. Turn the heat right down and simmer for 8–12 hours with the lid on.

Strain, discarding the vegetables (they will be tasteless as they've given up all their nutrients to the water). Refrigerate or freeze the stock in airtight containers.

Notes. For a stronger flavoured and more concentrated stock, take the lid off towards the end and reduce the liquid.

It's important not to add salt to your stock if you intend to soak grains with it or make something like risotto, as it will prevent your grains from cooking (see page 141).

Waste bone stock.

When meat is processed, so many people these days throw away the bones. This is one of the most nutritious parts of the animal and we think it's crazy to ever throw these away. Traditionally, making stock was always a key component of processing any animal, so that all parts of the animal were used. If you don't raise or hunt your own animals, go to a butcher who stocks meat from well-sourced, pasture-raised animals and get some bones or carcasses that would otherwise go to waste.

MAKES ABOUT 6 LITRES
TIME: 12–24 HOURS

4 kg bones (meat, chicken, fish, shellfish or game)

8 litres unchlorinated spring water

Preheat the oven to 220°C fan-forced.

Place the bones on a baking tray and roast for 10–15 minutes until browned.

Tip the bones into a stockpot and cover with the water, leaving at least a few centimetres of space at the top. Bring to the boil very slowly over a low heat, skimming off any foam as it rises to the top. Turn the heat down and simmer very gently for 12–24 hours with the lid on. (Some say that slowly bringing half of the water to the boil first, then adding the other half cold and bringing it back to the boil causes the meat and bones to contract and release even more goodness. Sometimes we do this, and sometimes we just add it all at once.)

Strain the stock and pick the meat off the bones to eat, or add to a recipe, such as spring chicken soup (see page 312) or wild duck ramen (see page 321). Refrigerate or freeze the stock in airtight containers.

FIELD NOTES

On the nutrition of bone stocks. Bone stocks are full of amazing vitamins and minerals that you can't get anywhere else. They support proper functioning of the brain and nervous system and are 'protein sparing' – so the more you eat (drink) them, the less protein you need in your diet to maintain healthy all-round body function. Traditionally, they have been revered as powerful cure-alls and that's exactly how we see them in our house. If your stomach is feeling a bit 'off', or your body is feeling run down, have a hot cup of this with a squeeze of lemon juice and a pinch of salt and we promise all things will be better.

Mayonnaise.

This goes on everything. It makes even a humble bowl of steamed vegetables and rice taste amazing. Mayonnaise was a mystery to us for so long. We just went without. But it turns out it's super easy. The thing that put us off was the vegetable oils, which we aren't fans of because they are so highly processed. Olive oil becomes bitter when blended, and sesame oil can taste too strong, but finally we hit upon cold-pressed sunflower oil – locally grown and wonderfully neutral, making it the perfect candidate for classic mayonnaise without all of the processed oils!

The secret to this recipe is adding the oil slowly. And sometimes, even though you follow all of the steps, mayonnaise just goes wrong and splits. Don't beat yourself up – go again, and we promise it will work!

MAKES 300 ML
TIME: 10 MINUTES

3 egg yolks

1 tablespoon apple cider vinegar

250 ml (1 cup) cold-pressed sunflower oil

juice of ½ lemon

1 teaspoon unrefined sugar (e.g. rapadura), dissolved in a splash of hot water

¼ teaspoon unrefined salt

Place the yolks and vinegar in a blender (or in a jar if you prefer to use a hand-held blender) and blend while very slowly adding the oil – this is key to stop it splitting. The mixture should start to look creamy once you have added about half of the oil. Add the lemon juice and keep blending while slowly adding the rest of the oil. It should now be thick and creamy. If it's not super creamy, add more oil a little bit at a time until it is. Add the sugar and salt and blend again to combine. This will store for up to a week in the fridge.

Note. If you don't mind a mildly bitter flavour from olive oil, you can use half sunflower oil and half olive oil – add the olive oil at the end of the blending process to reduce the bitterness.

Mustard.

Fresh mustard is so easy to make – who knew?! Now we can't imagine ever buying it, the flavour of homemade mustard is incomparable. A simple, classic staple. So good paired with mayonnaise.

MAKES 250 G
TIME: 5 MINUTES

50 g (⅓ cup) yellow mustard seeds

50 g (⅓ cup) black mustard seeds

2 teaspoons unrefined salt

2 teaspoons ground turmeric

125 ml (½ cup) water

3 tablespoons apple cider vinegar

1 teaspoon unprocessed honey

Combine all of the ingredients in a blender and blend until it forms a smooth paste. This will keep for up to a year in the fridge.

Note. To make a vegan version of this recipe, replace the honey with unrefined sugar.

Preserves.

Preserving abundance throughout the season,
for the next one. Fermenting for health.

Preservation guide: introduction

People have been preserving food forever. Before the invention of fridges, knowing how to preserve your harvest by salting and drying meats or fermenting vegetables was an absolute necessity. These days, the need for preserving may seem to have disappeared, but we feel it's as important as ever. We *still* see preserving your harvest as a fundamental part of living a full life. It's in our blood, so to speak, and there remains a deep satisfaction in preparing a larder so that you can enjoy foods that are out of season year-round.

WHAT IS PRESERVING?

When we preserve, what we are doing is putting a stop to:

- **'Bad' bacteria.** Bacteria, yeasts and moulds exist naturally to ensure things decay from the outside in (a good thing really, imagine if nothing decayed!). The three are actually one and the same – different stages of the one phenomenon. Bacteria develop into yeasts, which develop into moulds, and all stages will rapidly spoil your food. To preserve, we must stop them from doing this, and there are different methods that make this possible. One family of bacteria, though, are 'good'. Lactic-acid producing bacteria actually stop bad bacteria from doing their thing. These good bacteria are very helpful to us when preserving fermented foods, and are also very important for the health of our digestive system.

- **Enzymes.** Natural enzymes are present in all raw foods, breaking them down from the inside out. Enzymes are like self-destruct mechanisms that are present in all organisms. While an organism is alive, enzymes are there to digest all kinds of things as part of the natural functioning of the plant or animal. But as soon as that plant or animal dies, they get to work digesting the plant or animal itself from the inside out, and that means spoilage. These natural enzymes are really great for our health, but in order to preserve them and the food they are a part of, we have to make sure they remain stable and don't enter the 'self-digesting' mode.

HOW DO WE DO IT?

To counter the bad bacteria, yeasts, moulds and naturally occurring enzymes, we utilise one or more of the following conditions:

Temperature.

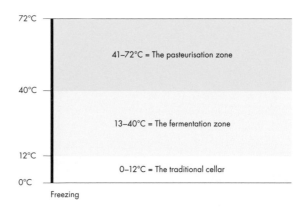

72°C	
	41–72°C = The pasteurisation zone
40°C	
	13–40°C = The fermentation zone
12°C	
	0–12°C = The traditional cellar
0°C	

Freezing

Freezing. Freezing forces bacteria and enzymes into a dormant state, keeping things stable for as long as the conditions persist.

Cellar conditions. Traditional cellar temperatures hold bacteria and enzymes in a near dormant state where they can move only very slowly (the lower the temperature, the slower the movement). The preserved foods we talk about in this book will remain totally stable under these conditions.

The fermentation zone. This is the ideal temperature range for the health and activity of bacteria (both good and bad) and enzymes. If bad bacteria predominate, food will spoil rapidly in this zone. If good bacteria predominate, fermentation will begin to occur between 12°C and 25°C, but quite slowly, and between 25°C and 40°C, most vigorously. We always recommend aiming between 25°C and 38°C because most domestic thermometers aren't super accurate, and you don't want to enter the pasteurisation zone.

The pasteurisation zone. Pasteurisation means the complete destruction of most enzymes and the reduction of bacterial populations to completely harmless levels. From 41°C, bacteria and enzymes begin to die. The longer you hold foods in the lower range of the zone, the more bacteria and enzymes will die, but at this lower end of the scale, pasteurisation can take many hours, even weeks. If foods are held at 72°C for just 15 seconds, though, instant pasteurisation occurs.

Salt and sugar levels.

Bad bacteria require moisture to live, and salt and sugar take the moisture out of foods, which means bacteria can no longer grow in them. This happens through a process called osmosis, where moisture molecules in the foods' cells are replaced with salt or sugar molecules, effectively dehydrating the food on a cellular level, locking out 'bad' bacteria and forcing enzymes into a dormant state. If any bad bacteria come into direct contact with salt, they are dehydrated and killed (such as when we cure foods, see page 228). Also, fortunately, good bacteria are more tolerant of salty environments, so when we salt foods (for example, through fermentation, see page 188), we give them a head start and allow them to outbreed the bad bacteria.

Acidity.

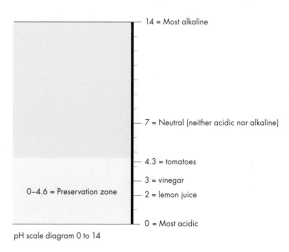

pH scale diagram 0 to 14

The pH scale is used to measure how acidic or alkaline a substance is. It is a logarithmic scale, which means that a change of one unit of pH equals a tenfold increase or decrease in acidity: 7 is neutral (neither acidic nor alkaline), 6 is a little acidic, 5 is ten times more acidic than 6, 4 is ten times more acidic again than 5 and so on in both directions. Bad bacteria cannot grow in an environment with a pH of 4.6 or below, and we can create such an environment with things like vinegar or good bacteria (which create lactic acid, low pH).

Note. This is a very different line of thinking to how various foods affect the acidity or alkalinity of your body when consumed. That is measured *after* a food has been digested (not, as above, *before* it has been digested) and even a very acidic food, like lemons, can have a very alkalising (positive) effect on your body.

TECHNIQUES

You can preserve using any of the following techniques, each of which utilises one or more of the above conditions:

- Lacto-fermentation (see page 188)
- Bottling (see page 214)
- Drying and curing (see page 228)
- Preservation under oil, like tuna (see page 233) (requires pasteurisation and/or fermentation first)
- Wild yeast fermentation, like wine (see page 190) and sourdough culture (see page 142)
- Good storage (see page 238)
- Freezing

Preservation guide 1: lacto-fermentation

Fermentation is a very ancient technique and has been keeping humans healthy and fed for thousands of years. Lacto-fermentation preserves by helping the good bacteria (lactobacilli) overpower the bad. *Everything* is preserved in the process, including all of the original vitamins and minerals, plus the natural enzymes, and, as an added bonus, the bioavailability of most of the vitamins and minerals is actually enhanced due to the pre-digestion performed by the good bacteria and enzymes. As a result, the taste of the food is enhanced, differing almost totally from its raw, unpreserved state. When we consume the good bacteria present in fermented foods, we are also maintaining the balance of good to bad bacteria in our digestive systems, and happy digestion equals lots of energy for our bodies.

Lactobacilli (the good bacteria).

Lactobacilli are everywhere, especially in our guts and on plants that grow in or close to the soil (but not when grown using hydroponics or the like). They live by digesting carbohydrates (sugars and starches), and produce lactic acid as a by-product. The lactic acid they produce is responsible for the sharp taste of traditional pickled vegetables, like sauerkraut and kimchi (these good bacteria are also present in other traditional foods, like cultured (sour) cream, yoghurt and sourdough bread), and creates a low pH (acidic) environment that the good bacteria love, but that bad bacteria cannot survive in – hence our food is preserved.

Lactobacilli are incredibly good for your digestive function – when your gut is full of good bacteria, bad bacteria can't take hold. They are also really important for immune function, the development of digestive enzymes and are thought to assist in the prevention of allergies.

Because lactobacilli are naturally occurring bacteria, we don't need to inoculate our ferments with them. We simply have to create an environment conducive to their survival. Basically, we need to make sure that they multiply faster than the bad bacteria.

Unrefined salt.

You *can* lacto-ferment without salt, but the right result is certainly more guaranteed when you use it. As described on page 187, salt dehydrates food through a process called osmosis. Lactobacilli are far more tolerant of salt than bad bacteria, allowing them to get to work digesting the carbohydrates in the fermenting food, producing lactic acid and rapidly multiplying. Soon they have produced so much lactic acid that the environment is so acidic that no new bad bacteria can survive – remember bad bacteria cannot live in a highly acidic environment. You can salt your vegetables dry, or you can soak them in brine. Both have exactly the same effect, it's just that one or the other is usually more appropriate depending on the food.

Over-fermentation.

One thing to understand is that you *can* over-ferment your foods, which is why in the following recipes we say to refrigerate them after 5–7 days fermenting at room temperature. When we say over-ferment, we don't mean they spoil or go bad – in fact, they would technically be even better for your digestion. What it means is that the good bacteria have started to digest the cellular structure of the food you are preserving, and that means it will begin to taste overly sour and eventually become mushy in texture. Again, they're not bad for you; they're just not that pleasant to eat anymore. Stick to the refrigeration steps in the recipes and you'll be fine, although you don't *necessarily* have to refrigerate to slow the ferment. Lactobacilli are extremely sluggish below about 12°C (see the temperature guide on page 186), the average temperature of a traditional cellar. So if you have a cellar, use that. Additionally, it is key to note that if it is winter and constantly below 12°C when you are trying to ferment, it's not going to work very well. You will need to keep the food warm. Try placing it in a heated room, near a fire or on top of a coffee machine, or even wrap it in an electric blanket.

Salt ratios.

We always use a 2–5% brine, or 2–5% salt to raw vegetable weight for dry salting – that is to say, 20–50 g of salt to 1 litre of water or 1 kg of vegetables. If, as with kimchi, you are washing the vegetables after salting, go as high as 10%. In each case, this is plenty of salt to get the lactobacilli off to a great start, without making the ferment too salty to eat. Any higher than 5% salt in the finished product and we promise that you'll want to spit it out! There are exceptions though, generally for things that are bitter or contain tannins. For example, we ferment our olives in a 10% brine. We have tried to ferment olives in a less salty brine but never with as good a result. It's all about the tannins in the olives, and they just taste better when fermented in very salty water, then washed thoroughly before eating.

Natural wine!

We don't think there is ever a time when wine shouldn't be followed by an exclamation mark! For us, wine is the symbol of so many things. It represents celebration and reward after hard work. It represents transformation and the relationship between humans and nature. It represents fun and friends and harvest and laughter. And it represents celebration and magic and science all at the same time. Wine is awesome!

You can harvest grapes off the same vines and use the same winemaking techniques year after year and yet your wine will always be different. The sun and the rain will be different, as will the ferment, the temperature over winter and the secondary fermentation in spring. All you can do is provide the best grapes with the optimum environment to undergo this most magical of transformations. And cross your fingers. All we ever hope for is something drinkable. That is the original point of making wine after all: to preserve the dense calories of grape sugar for a year until the next harvest. But so far, we have been lucky and rewarded with only wonderful, wonderful wine.

Maybe it's because when you make wine the entire experience gets infused into the bottle. All the love, laughter and challenge. All the blood, sweat and tears. It's all in there. Someway, somehow the experience is almost as nourishing as the consumption. Wine is the ultimate example of how important it is to experience your food.

Making our own natural, wild wines means that every other wine tastes different to how it used to. We can feel the soul of another handmade wine. We can feel its nuance and uniqueness. And we celebrate

truly magnificent wines all the more. So it's not just that our experience of winemaking has elevated our enjoyment of only the wines we make; our experience of winemaking has elevated our enjoyment and appreciation of wine and winemaking in general. We don't claim to be winemakers, but we are wine makers, and that's a beautiful thing.

People study for many years to become winemakers, but when it comes down to it, anyone can make wine. You just have to know when to be clean and when to be a bit wild! We make wine like we farm: we observe nature, learn its processes, learn how to provide the best conditions, and then get out of the way. To us, natural winemaking involves no chemicals at any point, from growing the grapes through to bottling the wine. It requires only vines, water and a bit of effort. We will add sulphur if, for one reason or another, our wine won't be stored in stable cellar conditions, but otherwise we feel it's unnecessary.

So here's how we make our wine. All these steps can be replicated whether you have 5 kg of grapes or 5 tonnes. Next autumn, get your hands on some grapes (see the *Trade* chapter for our story of finding our grapes), gather some friends and experience a ritual that's been happening for more than 8,000 years!

Step 1 – Harvest. Hand-harvest the best fruit you can at the right sugar level (11–13% for whites and 12–14% for reds, which we test with a hydrometer or refractometer). All things going well, the percentage of sugar in the grapes equals the percentage of alcohol in the finished wine. We understand that not everyone has access to a vineyard, but any good grocer should be able to order in wine grapes (they are very different to table grapes, so be specific), or find someone with a vineyard – there are lots of them!

Step 2 – De-stemming and crushing. De-stemming is the separation of the grapes from the stalks and leaves, which can impart a bitter taste. Crushing releases the juice from the berries to allow it to ferment. If you have picked with care, there won't be any leaves, but there will be lots of stems, and we prefer most of them removed. On a small scale, simply de-stem by hand, and then crush the berries with your hands, feet, a potato masher, whatever. We pick at least 1 tonne of fruit, making hand de-stemming impossible, so we use a small 'crusher/de-stemmer' that macerates the bunches with rotating arms and drops the berries through a coarse sieve, catching the stems and leaving us with smashed berries floating in juice!

At this point, the process diverges for whites and reds. For white wines, the skins and seeds are usually completely removed by pressing (Step 4) and then the pressed juice is fermented (Step 3) in vats but without plunging. So for whites, you need to complete Step 4 before you move to Step 3, then continue to Step 5 and 6. You can leave white juice with the skins and seeds to ferment, but this makes a white with a *whole* different character than you might be used to!

Step 3 – Primary fermentation and plunging.
We then ferment our red grapes (and white juice) in open-topped 400 litre vats with old bed sheets on top to keep the bugs out. The fermentation occurs through the action of wild yeasts naturally present on the berries, which digest the sugars and produce alcohol and carbon dioxide. The process takes a few days to really get going, and then continues for about 14–21 days, depending on the weather (hotter weather equals faster fermentation). Whites are generally harvested earlier than reds, when the weather is still a bit warmer. Where we live, it *usually* takes closer to 14 days for whites and 21 days for reds.

During fermentation of reds, the carbon dioxide carries the skins and seeds to the surface, forming a solid cap on top of the juice. It's good to have the skins and seeds down in the juice, though, to impart colour, flavour and tannin. So once a day we 'plunge' or 'punch-down' the cap until it is mixed with the juice again. This primary fermentation is complete when the cap sinks – the yeast is no longer producing carbon dioxide to hold the cap up, as it has run out of sugars to eat. As carbon dioxide is heavier than oxygen, it forms a fairly effective barrier on the surface of the juice. When the fermentation has finished, though, that barrier is no longer there, so it's very important to press and move to closed storage as soon as possible to avoid oxidation (which will discolour and alter the flavour of the finished wine).

Step 4 – Pressing. When the cap sinks for our reds, or as soon as we've crushed for our whites, we press. We fill our little wooden press with freshly fermented wine (or crushed white grapes) and the skins and seeds. Most of the wine (or juice) runs freely out. We then stand on top of the press plate to exert just a little pressure, but we believe the best wine doesn't require much force. These last pressings would be best for vinegar!

Step 5 – Bulk ageing and secondary fermentation.
The pressed wine then goes into old oak barrels to chill

out for a while. This is called bulk ageing. We can't bottle it yet because there is still a second fermentation: malolactic fermentation, or simply 'malo'. This is where lactic acid bacteria digest sharp-tasting malic acid (tart like green apples), into softer lactic acid (a more rounded sharpness, like cultured (sour) cream). More carbon dioxide is also created. If we bottle before the malo, the carbon dioxide could cause the bottles to explode! To prevent pressure building up in the barrels, we use a simple airlock that allows air out, but not in.

It is usually quite cool by the time the wine is in barrel (mid to late autumn), and so the wine is usually around 10°C. Lactic acid bacteria are very sluggish below 12°C, so malo typically doesn't happen until spring. (If your wine is inside, though, it may begin right away.) It is important to ensure the barrels are 'topped up' during this period. Alcohol and water will both evaporate through the barrel's timber, and this can leave a significant surface area of wine exposed to air inside the barrel, which means oxidation (i.e. vinegar in the making). So, every few weeks, if the level of wine in the barrels drops, we top it up to the bung with some finished wine (we store any wine that won't fill a barrel in glass demijohns for this purpose).

In spring, we begin to see tiny bubbles of carbon dioxide in the airlocks. Soon there are big bubbles.

Once the malo really gets going it is generally over in about 4 weeks. The bubbles stop and we are ready to bottle.

Step 6 – Bottling. During the winemaking process, we always keep everything clean with filtered water and stay tidy. But for bottling, we make sure we are *extra* clean. You don't want dirt or dust in your bottles, inside your caps or on your corks. We usually bottle with reused screw caps that we drop in boiling water. We clean our bottles with hot soapy water, then rinse and dry them thoroughly. And then we bottle.

During the wine's time in barrel (about 6–7 months at bottling), solids, or 'lees', will have settled to the bottom. If, like us, you'd rather not use any preservatives in your wine, lees are a natural preservative that will keep your wine in perfect condition while it is in contact with them. At bottling, though, it's important to not disturb the lees or the bottles will contain unwanted sediment. We also don't want to expose our wine to any more oxygen than we have to. So we use a siphon and place it into the barrel clear of the lees, then bottle directly. Perfect. Bottling takes time. But when it's done, so is your wine – and that's an *incredible* feeling.

Waste wine vinegar.

If you drink wine, you will never have to buy vinegar again. Have you ever opened a bottle of wine, drunk half of it and gone to drink it a week later, only to find it just doesn't taste that good anymore? That is the wine oxidising and basically turning into vinegar, which is what the acetic acid bacteria – naturally present in your wine – wants to do, but we stop it by bottling and sealing it to lock out the oxygen. This recipe just gives leftover wine that kickstart to make sure it becomes vinegar. Now you know how to make it, you will have more vinegar than you ever need, and will never waste that leftover wine again.

Add the wine to a jar, followed by the vinegar. Place a cloth on top and fasten with a rubber band. This is very important, as it must be exposed to oxygen for it to become vinegar (the cloth just keeps insects out).

Place the jar in a dark, warm place and stir occasionally to help the bacteria along with some extra oxygen. It may take a long 3–6 months to become vinegar if the wine has preservatives in it (it's their job to stop this happening!), but un-sulphured, natural wines (as they were made traditionally) might only take a number of weeks.

You can use this vinegar to make the next batch, and so on.

Note. It is important that the vinegar is kept out of sunlight, as it may kill the vinegar culture.

MAKES 200 ML
(USE THIS AS A GUIDE AND ADJUST USING THE SAME RATIO TO SUIT HOW MUCH VINEGAR YOU NEED)
TIME: 5 MINUTES
+ 3–6 MONTHS CULTURING

100 ml red or white wine

100 ml unpasteurised vinegar (with the cloudy 'mother')

Honey ginger beer.

MAKES 12.5 LITRES
TIME: 3 WEEKS

1 kg unprocessed honey

unchlorinated water
(unchlorinated water is essential
for the fermentation to work)

250 g ginger

250 ml (1 cup) lemon juice

Special equipment

10 x 1.25 litre used plastic bottles,
Champagne bottles or other
high-pressure glassware. Do not
use regular glass bottles, like wine
bottles, as ginger beer is very
bubbly and has a reputation for
blowing them up. Champagne
bottles work great, but do be sure
you wire down the cork or use
a crown sealer.

15 litre food-grade bucket or large
non-reactive stockpot

I swear I used to think mentor #1 (Brian) lived wholly and solely on his homemade ginger beer. Everywhere we went he would bring with him a little cooler full of the chilling bottles, and while I ate lunch, Brian would just sip away. For months, I never once saw him eat food, even though we'd spend all day together.

The day he invited me around for dinner and I learnt that he actually just doesn't eat between breakfast and dinner was a sad moment – a little of the man's mystery was lost. But I must say, he does drink a lot of ginger beer.

So this recipe is inspired by Brian. We have sacrilegiously altered the original recipe here to use just what we grow on the farm – our lemons, ginger from the greenhouse and honey from the hive. It has no refined sugar (only honey), is full of flavour and is much better than any soft drink you will ever buy. – MATT

It takes about 3 weeks from start to finish to make ginger beer and the process has three distinct parts:

Part 1: Preparing the culture – 2 minutes a day for 7–9 days.
Part 2: Mixing the batch – 30 minutes hands-on time.
Part 3: Bottle fermentation – 14 days waiting.

Part 1 – Preparing the culture. Dissolve 2 teaspoons of honey in 125 ml (½ cup) of hot water and add to a 1 litre jar. Peel and chop 35 g of the ginger and then grind using a mortar and pestle. Add the ginger and 250 ml (1 cup) of cool water to the jar, then seal with a lid and shake well. Loosen the lid but leave it on, and set aside at room temperature for 24 hours.

Every day for the next 7 days, feed the mixture with another 35 g of freshly ground ginger (prepared as before) with 2 teaspoons of honey that has been dissolved in a splash of hot water. Leave at room temperature with the lid on but loose.

Part 2 – Mixing the batch. Your culture should now be alive and happening with a layer of bubbles on top – if not, throw it away and start again. It's now time to mix up your brew. In a 15 litre food-grade bucket or large non-reactive stockpot, dissolve the remaining honey in 2 litres of boiling water. Add 10 litres of cold water, then the lemon juice (don't add the lemon juice straight to the boiling water as it ruins its preservation qualities) and culture, reserving some of the ginger chunks and sediment for your next brew. Combine thoroughly and transfer to clean bottles, leaving about 5–6 cm at the top of each. Cap or cork the bottles, ensuring they are securely sealed.

Place the reserved culture in the fridge until you want to make another batch. The next time you want to brew, simply take the jar out of the fridge and repeat the culture preparation steps above, adding it to the sediment.

Part 3 – Bottle fermentation. Now you just have to wait for 14 days. It might take a little longer, or it might take a little less time. When plastic bottles are ready they will be very hard to the touch, but if you've bottled into glassware, you'll just have to test a bottle! When they are ready, transfer to the fridge to stop the fermentation, and enjoy at your leisure.

Note. Pubs will often collect their used 1.25 litres bottles for you if you ask, which is a great way to keep them out of landfill!

Ultimate dill pickles.

MAKES 1 X 1 LITRE JAR
TIME: 10 MINUTES
+ 5–7 DAYS FERMENTING

400 ml pickling brine
(see field notes)

1 garlic clove, halved
(unpeeled is fine if clean)

1 teaspoon mustard seeds

1 teaspoon coriander seeds

1 teaspoon black peppercorns

600 g small cucumbers (you can
pickle any size you like – the only
restriction is the size of the vessel)

2 dill flowers (or replace with dill
fronds if you can't source them)

When it comes to pickles, we think these guys are the undisputed kings. When winter arrives and you have no more fresh cucumbers, you'll be glad you made this. Vary the recipe with whatever herbs and spices you love. Try tarragon instead of dill, or add a hint of chilli. Have a play!

Day 1. Make the pickling brine (see field notes). Add the garlic and spices to a 1 litre jar, and then stuff in the whole cucumbers so that they are all nice and snug. Pour the brine over the cucumbers, filling the jar to the brim. Place the dill flowers on top to make sure the cucumbers stay below the surface of the brine – this is key, otherwise the exposed parts will become soft or mouldy. Put the lid in place but don't fully tighten it. Sit the jar on a plate (liquid will spill over the lip of the jar during the fermentation) and leave to sit for 5–7 days at room temperature.

Days 5–7. The cucumbers should have turned from a bright green to a nice olive colour. They should be crunchy. If any pickles floated above the brine and turned soft or mouldy, just cut off the soft part and discard.

If you're happy with how they have fermented, put them in the fridge. If they're not quite ready, give them a couple more days. If you want your pickles to last the longest and stay the crispest, drain the pickles from the pickling brine (which can be reused for the next batch) and cover in fresh brine before storing in the fridge. When kept in the fridge, pickles have a very long shelf life, well into the following season of cucumbers.

Notes.

You *must* pickle whole cucumbers, otherwise they will go mushy – they can be any size, as long as you have an appropriate vessel.

This recipe is based on summertime pickling. Fermenting takes longer when it's colder (shorter if you're in the tropics!).

See pages 186–87 for more information on preservation, and pages 188–89 for more information on fermentation.

FIELD NOTES

On pickling brine. A pickling brine is a solution of salt dissolved in unchlorinated water. For the fermentation to work the amount of salt needs to be 2–5% of the water volume. So to make 400 ml of brine you need to dissolve 8–20 g of salt in 400 ml of water. You must use unchlorinated water, as chlorine is an antibacterial, meaning it will stop all those wonderful lactic-acid producing (good) bacteria from doing their thing. Rainwater or spring water is best. We always use unrefined salt to make our brines, as we think it not only tastes the best but keeps the pickles extra crisp!

Fermented pickles.

Master recipe.

Follow this recipe with the combinations listed opposite, or refer to our dill pickle recipe (see page 198) for more detailed information.

Make up 2–5% pickling brine
(see field notes on page 198).

Add the spices to the jar(s).

Add the vegetables to the jar(s).

Fill the jar(s) with the pickling brine.

Place a 'sacrificial leaf', such as a cabbage leaf or dill fronds or flowers, on top to keep all of the good stuff submerged.

Put the lid in place but don't fully tighten. Sit the jar on a plate.

Leave to ferment for 5–7 days at room temperature.

Discard the sacrificial 'leaf' and refrigerate.

Green beans.

Sharp, a little sweet and altogether a surprising and intriguing pickle.

MAKES 1 X 1 LITRE JAR
TIME: 10 MINUTES + 5-7 DAYS FERMENTING

Brine
600 ml

Spices
1 teaspoon cloves
5 tarragon sprigs

Vegetables
500 g green beans

Sacrificial 'leaf'
2 dill flowers

Brussels sprouts.

We always make a few jars of these guys every year to enjoy sprouts in peak summer.

MAKES 1 X 1 LITRE JAR
TIME: 10 MINUTES + 5-7 DAYS FERMENTING

Brine
500 ml

Spices
1 teaspoon mustard seeds
1 teaspoon coriander seeds
1 teaspoon black peppercorns
1 garlic clove, halved (unpeeled is fine if clean)

Vegetables
600 g brussels sprouts, trimmed

Sacrificial 'leaf'
2 dill flowers

Radish seed pods.

All your radishes bolted to seed? Pickle the seed pods! A delicious addition to salads.

MAKES 1 X 1 LITRE JAR
TIME: 10 MINUTES + 5–7 DAYS FERMENTING

Brine

700 ml

Spices

2 dried chillies, finely chopped

2 garlic shoots, finely chopped

2 teaspoons sesame seeds

Vegetables

400 g radish seed pods

Sacrificial 'leaf'

2 radish leaves

Hot green chillies.

These chillies are great for spicing up a sandwich, a pizza, anything really.

MAKES 1 X 1 LITRE JAR
TIME: 10 MINUTES + 5–7 DAYS FERMENTING

Brine

500 ml

Spices

1 teaspoon mustard seeds

1 teaspoon coriander seeds

1 teaspoon black peppercorns

1 garlic clove, halved (unpeeled is fine if clean)

Vegetables

600 g whole hot green chillies (jalapeños are our favourite)

Sacrificial 'leaf'

2 dill flowers

Whole cabbage.

This recipe takes brine pickling to the next level and is a super-traditional way to preserve your cabbages. They are the main ingredient for our cabbage rolls (see page 279) and bring a sharpness that boiled cabbage leaves never could. Follow the master recipe but in a small drum or barrel. So much fun.

MAKES 3 WHOLE PICKLED CABBAGES
TIME: 10 MINUTES + 7–10 DAYS FERMENTING

Brine

15 litres

Spices

3 tablespoons mustard seeds

3 tablespoons coriander seeds

1 garlic bulb, halved (unpeeled is fine if clean)

3 tablespoons black peppercorns

1 bunch of dill flowers (about 150 g)

Vegetables

3 large cabbages (about 6 kg total), whole, washed as much as possible

Sacrificial 'leaf'

weigh down with plates

Note. Once fermented, you can separate the individual cabbage leaves, pack them into large jars and cover them with fresh brine to make them easier to store.

green beans.

brussels sprouts.

rad

ed pods.   hot green chillies.   whole cabbage.

Sauerkraut.

MAKES 2 X 1 LITRE JARS
TIME: 20 MINUTES
+ 5–7 DAYS FERMENTING

2 kg white cabbage,
finely sliced on a mandoline,
2 large outer leaves reserved
as 'sacrificial leaves'

2 tablespoons unrefined salt

In our house, it's a constant battle of favourites between sauerkraut and kimchi (see page 206). They share similar techniques, yet couldn't be more different. We have tried so many variations of this recipe – different varieties of cabbages, fennel, apple, spices (you can add all kinds of things to your sauerkraut) – but this couldn't-be-simpler plain white cabbage version remains our favourite! It is mild yet thoroughly pungent in its own cabbagey way. There are so many layers to its flavour that it's almost a meal in itself, and it perfectly accompanies almost anything savoury.

Day 1. Combine the cabbage and salt in a big mixing bowl and massage thoroughly and firmly with your hands for about 5 minutes or until the salt begins to draw out liquid from the cabbage. Stuff into two 1 litre jars, pushing down hard to extract the liquid out of the cabbage.

Stuff a reserved cabbage leaf in the top of each jar to keep the sliced cabbage totally submerged in the extracted liquid. Put the lids in place but don't fully tighten them. Sit the jars on a plate (liquid will spill over the lips of the jars during the fermentation) and leave to sit for 5–7 days at room temperature.

Day 5. Remove the sacrificial leaves and have a taste of the cabbage underneath. When ready, your sauerkraut will be sharply acidic and smell very cabbagey, but it shouldn't smell 'off' at all. The cabbage should still be crunchy.

If your cabbage has turned soft, or black or colourful moulds have developed, something has gone wrong, and the batch should be discarded. If a little white mould develops at the surface, though, that's totally fine, just scrape it away and discard. Once ready, discard the sacrificial leaves and store your sauerkraut in the fridge. It will last for at least a year, but usually much longer.

Notes.

We make a huge batch of this sauerkraut every year – scale the recipe up or down based on how much *you* want to make.

This recipe is based on mid-autumn pickling. Fermenting takes longer when it's colder (shorter if you're in the tropics!).

See pages 186–87 for more information on preservation, and pages 188–89 for more information on fermentation.

Pickle any leftover cabbage cores as per the leftover vegetable pickle recipe on page 219.

Kimchi.

MAKES 2 X 1 LITRE JARS
TIME: 30 MINUTES
+ OVERNIGHT SOAKING
+ 5-7 DAYS FERMENTING

2 kg wombok, coarsely chopped,
2 large outer leaves reserved as
'sacrificial leaves'

500 g carrots, grated or very
finely julienned

250 g unrefined salt
(10% of the fresh vegetable weight)

unchlorinated water
(unchlorinated water is essential
for the fermentation to work)

Paste

200 g unprocessed honey
(or unrefined sugar)

150 g Korean chilli powder
(see note), more if you like
it extra hot

5 large spring onions
(about 150 g in total),
finely chopped

5 cm piece of ginger,
finely chopped

1 garlic bulb, crushed

1 tablespoon responsibly
sourced fish sauce
(more if you like it extra funky)

1 tablespoon unrefined salt

If I had a dollar for every time I've read 'this is *the* traditional kimchi recipe', I'd be a rich man. The truth is, there is no traditional kimchi recipe – every region of Korea has its own unique style, and every household has their own special secrets on top of that! To us, kimchi is pungent but sharp, salty but sweet, with deep umami intensity and yet thoroughly light. Such a beautiful set of contradictions. We use the same kimchi style to ferment all kinds of veggies in our home, but the classic for us will always be with wombok (Chinese cabbage) – we grow a crop every year just for this purpose. This version throws in some carrots too, but otherwise it's pretty old-school. It's refreshing, crisp and great with anything from savoury morning pancakes (see page 254) to a steaming bowl of ramen (see page 321). – MATT

Day 1. Place the wombok, carrot and salt in a very large mixing bowl (or a food-grade bucket) and mix thoroughly with your hands. Add enough water to cover the vegetables, place a plate on top so they are all submerged and leave overnight at room temperature to brine.

Day 2. Drain the vegetables and submerge them in fresh water. Drain, taste and repeat. When ready, the cabbage shouldn't taste at all bitter and be just saltier than seems normal. If too salty or at all bitter, wash, drain and taste again. If not salty enough, add more salt until you hit the spot.

Using a mortar and pestle, thoroughly grind all of the paste ingredients until smooth. Taste. If you want it a little funkier, add more fish sauce. If you want it hotter, add more chilli. More pungent? Add more garlic. Remember, there will be a distinct sourness that will be introduced from the lacto-fermentation – you'll just have to imagine that being there. When you're happy, place the paste in a large mixing bowl with the vegetables and massage thoroughly with your hands – you may want to wear gloves!

Stuff the mixture into two 1 litre jars, pushing down to extract the liquid from the vegetables. Stuff the reserved wombok leaves in the top of each jar to keep the vegetables totally submerged. Put the lids in place but don't fully tighten them. Sit the jars on a plate (liquid will spill over the lips of the jars during the fermentation) and leave to sit for 5–7 days at room temperature.

Day 5. Remove the sacrificial leaves and try the vegetables underneath. When ready, your kimchi will be sharply acidic and smell very strongly pungent, but it shouldn't smell 'off' at all. The vegetables should still be crunchy. If your vegetables have turned soft, or black or colourful moulds have developed, something has gone wrong, and the batch should be discarded. If a little white mould develops at the surface, though, that's totally fine, just scrape it away and discard. Once ready, discard the sacrificial leaves and store your kimchi in the fridge. It will last for at least a year, but usually much longer.

Notes.

Using Korean chilli powder, or 'gochugaru', is key to nailing kimchi. We grow our own Korean chillies (seeds are available online), dry them and blitz them in a high-powered blender, but gochugaru powder is also available in Asian supermarkets.

This recipe is based on summertime pickling. Fermenting takes longer when it's colder (shorter if you're in the tropics!).

See pages 186–87 for more information on preservation, and pages 188–89 for more information on fermentation.

To make a vegetarian version of this recipe, simply omit the fish sauce.

Kimchi fermenting in our traditional clay fermenting pot, which creates a perfect water seal. The pot was made for us by our friend, Sophie Harle.

Fermented hot sauce.

This is not a sauce for the faint hearted (although if you do have a faint heart, you could use the same technique with a milder chilli). It is FIERY hot from the habaneros, fruity from the white wine and just the perfect amount of sweet from the sultanas. What a simple, balanced, knock-your-socks-off condiment! Lentil puts this on *everything* and then complains about how hot it is every time, but then puts more on her plate because it's *that* good. Enjoy! Oh, and maybe wear gloves to process those chillies – our legendary Irish intern, Michael, said his hands burned for three days after he prepped this for us! – MATT

Day 1. Place the chillies, sultanas and salt in a bowl and mix well. Stuff the mixture into a 1 litre jar and fill with wine. If you can, place a smaller glass jar lid inside the jar to keep the chillies submerged, then place the actual lid on but don't fully tighten it.

Sit the jar on a plate (liquid will spill over the lip of the jar during the fermentation) and leave to sit for 7–10 days at room temperature. Keep the jar topped up with wine if the liquid level drops.

Day 7. At about day 7, start to taste it (beware of the fire!). When ready, the pickling liquid should be tangy, fruity and *very* spicy.

When you think it has fermented enough, tip the entire contents into a high-powered blender and blend into a smooth sauce before returning to the jar and storing it in the fridge. Fermented hot sauce will keep in the fridge for at least a year, but usually much longer. We make about 10–15 litres of this every year and decant into small jars as needed!

Notes.

If a fine, white mould forms on the surface of your sauce, this is totally fine – just scrape it off. But if you see any colourful or black mould, discard the batch and start again. It should smell good and taste delicious.

This recipe is based on summertime pickling. Fermenting takes longer when it's colder (shorter if you're in the tropics!).

See pages 186–87 for more information on preservation, and pages 188–89 for more information on fermentation.

The colour of the sauce will vary depending on what kind of chillies you use.

MAKES 1 X 1 LITRE JAR
TIME: 10 MINUTES
+ 7–10 DAYS FERMENTING

750 g habanero chillies, coarsely blitzed in a food processor or coarsely chopped

75 g sultanas

1½ tablespoons unrefined salt

dry white wine

Brined olives.

MAKES 5 X 2 LITRE JARS
TIME: 10 MINUTES
+ 3 DAYS SOAKING
+ 6 MONTHS WAITING!

5 kg freshly picked olives

unchlorinated water
(unchlorinated water is essential
for the fermentation to work)

500 g unrefined salt

10 garlic cloves

5 rosemary sprigs

5 oregano sprigs

5 thyme sprigs

5 dried chillies

1 lemon, sliced

5 fennel flowers (see field notes)

We're very lucky – olives grow wild on the banks of the river where we live. They're everywhere – it's ridiculous – so we don't have to grow them! This recipe works just as well for our little wild olives as for big farmed olives. We pick our olives when they are 'on the turn' (in transition from green to black), so we end up with a mix of green, black and everything in between. Black olives are sweeter after fermenting, green olives a little more piquant – but they're both awesome. These olives are one of our all-time favourite foods. We should probably issue a warning though: try this once, and you'll be so addicted that you'll probably make a batch ten times bigger than you need the second time around.

Day 1. Place the olives in a large food-grade bucket or stockpot and cover with unchlorinated water. Leave to soak for 24 hours.

Day 2. Drain the olives and cover with fresh water again.

Day 3. Change the water again.

Day 4. Place 5 litres of unchlorinated water and the salt in a stockpot. Bring to the boil then remove from the heat.

Meanwhile, distribute the garlic, herbs, chillies and lemon slices evenly between five 2 litre jars. Drain the olives and add them to the jars. Fill the jars to the brim with the hot brine, top with a fennel flower to keep the olives submerged and seal.

Leave the olives to ferment for 6 months before eating. They will keep for at least 2 years, but ours will be gone by the time the next season's batch is ready!

Notes.

If a fine, white mould forms on the surface of your olives, this is totally fine – just scrape it off. But if you see any colourful or black mould, discard the batch and start again. Your olives should smell and taste delicious. They should be firm, not soft and mushy.

See pages 186–87 for more information on preservation, and pages 188–89 for more information on fermentation.

The jars may overflow during fermentation, so it may be best to place them on small plates.

FIELD NOTES

On fennel flowers. Fennel flowers grow wild on roadsides everywhere! Look out for the bright yellow flowers towards the end of summer and all through autumn into winter. We always have fennel flowering in the garden. Just leave a Florence fennel bulb to go to seed in your garden and you too will have your very own fennel flowers.

Preserved lemons.

MAKES 1 X 1 LITRE JAR
TIME: 10 MINUTES
+ 30 DAYS FERMENTING

1 cinnamon stick

2 bay leaves

½ teaspoon black peppercorns

3 tablespoons unrefined salt

10 lemons

This recipe ferments lemons in their own juice with salt to create a strong, salty but bright lemon flavour. There generally isn't much reason to preserve lemons, as they will sit on the tree year round, so this is more about the flavour and adding a little more lactobacilli to your food, rather than actual preservation. They're awesome in rice dishes, warm salads and are great for developing Middle Eastern flavours (see pages 291 and 297 for recipes). You will only need a small amount of preserved lemon in a dish, so one jar will last you for a very long time!

Place the cinnamon, bay leaves, black peppercorns and 1–2 teaspoons of salt in the bottom of a 1 litre jar.

Quarter a lemon from the top down, stopping 1 cm from the bottom so that it still holds together. Sprinkle salt on the inside and press the quarters back together. Stuff the lemon into the jar and sprinkle some salt on top. Repeat for the other lemons. Once all of the lemons are in the jar, squash them down to release their juices, and sprinkle over any remaining salt.

Seal the jar and leave it in a warm, dark place that you will walk past often and give it a shake each day or so over about 30 days. They will last on the shelf for around a year, or refrigerate to stabilise for even longer.

Preservation guide 2: bottling

Bottling (canning, jarring and jam making) is more about *maintaining* the taste and nutrition of a food than it is about *transforming* and *enhancing* it, as fermentation does. These techniques have only been around for as long as jars, cans, sugar and vinegar have been readily available, but they are wonderful techniques with lots of positives. Many vitamins and minerals remain intact through the process, and bottled foods allow us to enjoy a much-enhanced repertoire of out-of-season flavours throughout the year.

Bottling pasteurises (heats to 72°C) the food we are preserving to reduce bad bacteria populations to harmless levels, and then holds the food in a vacuum so that no new airborne bacteria can enter, thus maintaining it in a stable state. Because some bacteria survive pasteurisation (the point isn't to kill them but to reduce them to harmless levels), we always use one of two key ingredients to prevent the survivors from multiplying and destroying all our hard work: sugar or vinegar (or another acid).

KEY INGREDIENTS

Sugar. Sugars act, like salt, to preserve food through osmosis (see page 187). For more information on how much sugar to use, see our spiced cherries recipe on page 224 and spiced apricot jam recipe on page 226.

Vinegar. Vinegar and other acids preserve by creating an environment with such a low pH (high acidity) that bacteria cannot grow (see page 187). Most vinegars are much more acidic than this, so as long as your pickles contain at least a 5:1 ratio of fruit/veg to vinegar, your final preserve will be safely acidic.

BOTTLING TECHNIQUES

The final step when bottling, of course, is the actual bottling process itself. There are two techniques.

1. The 'hot jar, hot liquid, hot lid' method.

Sterilise. Place the jars or bottles in a 100°C oven or a saucepan of boiling water (they don't have to be submerged, steam sterilises too!) and leave them there until you're ready to bottle. Sterilise the lids in boiling water only – never in the oven, as the seals will melt. Sterilise other utensils, like funnels and spoons, in boiling water.

Fill. Your preserve must be HOT (72–80°C) before bottling. Remove the jars or bottles from the oven or water and fill to within 1 cm of the top. Do this in small batches so that everything is still super hot when sealed.

Clean. Wipe the lips of the jars with a clean, dry cloth.

Seal. Be careful not to over-tighten the lids, as this may break the seal (it's not how tight you screw the lids on that seals, but the vacuum created when the jars cool). Allow the jars to cool to room temperature on the bench.

Check. Once cooled, the lids should have sucked down. If they haven't, the bottling wasn't done quickly enough (so everything wasn't hot enough) or there is a fault in the lid. It's best to re-bottle with a new lid with the 'classic water bath' method.

Store. Store in a cool, dark place. Once opened, store in the fridge.

2. The 'classic water bath' method.

Fill. Fill clean jars or bottles to within 1 cm of the lips.

Seal. Screw on the lids so that they're firmly in position, but be careful not to over-tighten them, as this may actually break the seal (it's not actually how tight you screw the lids on that seals, but the vacuum created when the jars cool).

Place in the water bath. Place as many jars as fit in a single layer in the biggest, deepest pot you have. Jars must be the same or a very similar height.

Add water. Fill the pot with water to within about 5 cm from the top of the shortest jar.

Heat. Cover and gently heat the water to 72–80°C. Maintain in this heat range for 15–20 minutes. What we are doing here is pasteurising everything – jars or bottles, contents and lids – all at the same time, so you need to give the contents time to heat to 72°C.

Cool. Check that the lids are still firmly in place and lightly tighten if necessary (but again, don't over-tighten them!). Cool to room temperature either on the bench or in the water bath.

Check. Once cooled, the lids should have sucked down. If they haven't, there is a fault in the lid. Repeat the steps with a new lid or a whole new jar or bottle and lid.

Store. Store in a cool, dark place. Once opened, store in the fridge.

Key points.
- To prevent bad bacteria from growing, bottling requires the addition of an acid (such as vinegar) to create a low pH environment OR the addition of sugar to dehydrate the food.
- We use high temperatures to 1. Pasteurise and kill any bad bacteria, and 2. Create a vacuum seal, so nothing 'bad' can get in afterwards.
- The aim of bottling is to create a delicious range of foods to enjoy out of season all year round.

Pear & eggplant kasundi.

This spicy and rich eggplant and pear chutney has an awesome balance of acidity, sweetness, spice and fruitiness, making it an amazing condiment for any meal. Honestly, if you are feeling super lazy, just make some rice, add this and some yoghurt (and maybe some chickpeas) and you have a great meal.

Place all part 1 ingredients in a stockpot and fry for about 5 minutes over a medium heat until fragrant.

Place all part 2 ingredients in a blender or food processer and blend into a paste.

Add the paste to the pot and fry until fragrant. Add all part 3 ingredients, cover and bring to the boil, stirring constantly to make sure nothing sticks to the bottom (it will take about 10 minutes to bring to the boil). Continue to simmer with the lid on for about 1 hour, stirring often, until the pear, eggplant and tomatoes are beginning to fall apart.

Reduce the heat to a low simmer and cook, uncovered, for a further 4–5 hours until it becomes a really thick sauce. Stir occasionally while it cooks, but be careful, as the mixture may become 'volcanic'. The kasundi should have reduced by at least half by this stage.

When your kasundi is ready, bottle as per the 'hot jar, hot liquid, hot lid' method (see page 215).

Store in a cool, dark place. The kasundi will keep for at least 1–2 years unopened. Once opened, store in the fridge for up to 3 months.

Notes.

While reducing, make sure you check the mixture often to ensure it's not sticking. If you're not watching, it can easily stick to the bottom of the pan and ruin the whole batch.

The strength of chilli powders and whole chillies can vary enormously, so please adjust to taste.

See pages 214–15 for more information on bottling.

To make a vegan version of this recipe, replace the honey with unrefined sugar.

MAKES ABOUT 2 LITRES
TIME: 6 HOURS

Part 1

110 ml extra-virgin olive oil

2 tablespoons yellow mustard seeds

2 tablespoons black mustard seeds

2 tablespoons ground turmeric

2 tablespoons chilli powder

3 teaspoons cumin seeds

3 teaspoons fennel seeds

1 heaped teaspoon garam masala

Part 2

1 large or 2–3 small garlic bulbs, peeled

5 dried red chillies

3 tablespoons ground ginger

3½ tablespoons white wine vinegar

Part 3

1.6 kg ripe tomatoes, cut into chunks

3 eggplants (about 800 g in total), cut into small chunks

4 pears (about 800 g in total), cut into small chunks

300 ml white wine vinegar

140 g unrefined sugar (e.g. rapadura)

50 g unprocessed honey

1 tablespoon unrefined salt

Vinegar pickles.

Master recipe.

Follow this recipe with the combinations listed opposite to fill your pantry with pickles!

MAKES 1 X 1 LITRE JAR
TIME: 15 MINUTES
+ 8 HOURS CURING

vegetables, as indicated

unrefined salt

juice of 1 lemon

250 ml (1 cup) white wine vinegar

3 tablespoons unrefined sugar (e.g. rapadura)

garlic, spices and herbs, as indicated

Cure the vegetables. In a non-reactive bowl, toss the vegetables in 5% of their weight of salt, cover and leave to cure at room temperature for 8 hours or overnight. Once cured, drain, wash and set aside.

Sterilise the jar and lid. Place a 1 litre jar and its lid in a saucepan of water, bring to the boil and leave to simmer while you make your pickles.

Blanch the vegetables. Bring another saucepan of water to the boil, add the lemon juice and vegetables, return to the boil and simmer for 2 minutes. Drain and set aside.

Make the pickling liquid. Add the vinegar, sugar, spices, 250 ml (1 cup) of water and ¼ teaspoon of salt to the pan and bring to the boil.

Jar the vegetables. Remove the jar from the water and drain. Add the herbs, fill with the hot vegetables and cover with the hot pickling liquid to 1 cm below the lip (make sure you get all of the spices in there too). Immediately take the lid out of the water and seal tightly without over tightening. Leave to cool on the kitchen bench. The lid should suck down. If it doesn't, reseal with a new lid as per the 'classic water bath' method (see page 215).

Store in a cool, dark place. Best eaten after 3 months and will keep for at least a year. Once opened, store in the fridge.

Wild mushrooms.

Wild mushrooms are one of the most delicious things in the world and they are only around for a brief season, so they are an essential treat to preserve! See the mushroom gathering guide on page 83.

Vegetables (fungi in this case!)

1 kg wild mushrooms, cleaned, left whole if small or cut as desired

Spices

6 black peppercorns

2 garlic cloves

Herbs

1 tarragon or rosemary sprig

Notes.

Mushrooms pack very tightly, so halve the pickling liquid for this recipe.

To clean wild mushrooms, tidy up the bases of the stems first, then grab a barely damp, soft cloth and lightly rub away any dirt on top of the cap. A light shake will usually dislodge any grime in the gills.

Garlic three ways.

As garlic grows it has awesome little tendrils called 'scapes' that are super sweet and juicy, which then develop heads with seeds that are like mini garlic cloves. The scapes don't store like garlic, so it's great to pickle them!

Vegetables

8 garlic bulbs (about 400 g in total), cloves separated and peeled

30–40 garlic scapes (about 260 g in total), cut into 2–3 cm pieces

20–30 garlic seed heads

Spices

1 teaspoon anise seeds

1 teaspoon juniper berries

1 teaspoon black peppercorns

Note. Skip the curing step for this pickle.

Leftover veg.

This is what you do when you need to clear out the veggie drawer at the end of the week. It's also awesome for things like cabbage cores that you often may have left over after making preserves like sauerkraut (see page 204).

Vegetables

600 g any vegetable you think will pickle nicely, trimmed and cut into appropriately sized pieces (we love using carrots, cabbage cores – so good! – capsicums, eggplant, cauliflower, chillies, green beans – everything tastes great pickled!)

Spices

¼ teaspoon yellow mustard seeds

¼ teaspoon black peppercorns

¼ teaspoon coriander seeds

a few fine slices of French shallot or onion

1 garlic clove

Passata.

Now, everyone has a way of making passata. We think ours is largely 'grassroots', how we imagine it was done back in the day – there are no fancy food mills or peeling of tomatoes (we don't peel them before eating them fresh in summer, so why peel them for winter!), and it's not limited to one specific variety. It's just good-quality, beautiful, red, heirloom tomatoes in a jar. We like to reduce it down until quite thick, so that when it comes to using it, it's ready to go – additionally, it's a lot less bottling! This is one of the most used preserves on our shelf. The aim is always to bottle enough to last throughout the winter and spring to follow, until tomatoes are back in season the next summer.

Place the tomatoes in a stockpot, cover and slowly bring to the boil, stirring occasionally to make sure nothing sticks to the bottom and burns. Simmer with the lid on, stirring occasionally, until the tomatoes have fallen apart and the liquid rises to the top (about 1 hour).

At this point, remove the lid, give the mixture a really good stir and simmer for another 2 hours, or until the sauce is the consistency of a thick soup. Stir occasionally to make sure nothing sticks to the bottom.

We like our passata as a chunky sauce, but if you prefer it smoother, simply blend with a hand-held blender.

To bottle, follow the 'classic water bath' method (see page 215). Store in a cool, dark place, where it will keep for 1–2 years unopened. Once opened, store in the fridge for up to 2 weeks.

Notes.

This recipe can vary a lot, depending on what type of tomatoes you use, so use it as a guide.

Please adjust this recipe to suit the amount of tomatoes you have – we generally do about 15–20 kg at a time! More tomatoes will mean the cooking times will be longer for each stage, so adjust the cooking times to suit. It takes us around 8 hours for a 15–20 kg pot of passata to cook down.

See pages 214–15 for more information on bottling.

MAKES ABOUT 1 LITRE
TIME: 3 HOURS

2 kg very ripe tomatoes (whatever type you've got), cored and cut into big chunks or just halved

FIELD NOTES

On picking the right tomato. You may be wondering why we can preserve tomatoes without vinegar, sugar or salt. It's because they inherently contain a high enough level of acidity (low pH) to preserve naturally. But make sure you choose heirloom tomatoes, not those that have been hybridised, genetically modified or picked green and chemically ripened. It's not only for flavour, but also because those tomatoes often won't preserve, as they have been bred specifically to have *less* acidity!

Green & red tomato ketchup.

MAKES ABOUT 1.2 LITRES
TIME: 3 HOURS

1 large onion, finely diced

extra-virgin olive oil

2 garlic cloves, crushed

3 teaspoons ground allspice

1 teaspoon ground cinnamon

1 teaspoon ground black pepper

1 teaspoon ground ginger

1 teaspoon celery seeds

½ teaspoon ground mustard seeds

2 cloves

80 g (½ cup) unrefined sugar
(e.g. rapadura)

1 kg ripe tomatoes, chopped into
small chunks

800 g green (unripe) tomatoes,
chopped into small chunks

3 tablespoons apple cider vinegar

1 tablespoon molasses

1 tablespoon unrefined salt

A super-flavoursome ketchup, full of warming spices and an earthy, sweet flavour that is great on pretty much anything. You can make this throughout the tomato season, although admittedly we make it at the end (in autumn before the frost kills all of the tomato plants!), throwing all of the last tomatoes in a pot, green, red, split, small and all! It is generally the last thing that we make and preserve. We have good memories of drinking wine with friends while making this in the biggest pot you can imagine, and blitzing it with a massive commercial hand blender – you can never have too much ketchup.

In a stockpot, sweat the onion with a big glug of oil over a low heat. Once the onion begins to break down, add the garlic and spices and fry until fragrant. Add the sugar and a handful of the tomatoes and fry for about 5 minutes until they start to break down and caramelise.

Add the remaining ingredients, cover and bring to the boil. Reduce the heat and simmer for about 30 minutes, covered, stirring often to ensure nothing sticks to the bottom.

Take the pot off the heat and blitz the mixture with a hand-held blender until combined. Return the pot to the stove and simmer, uncovered, for about 1–1½ hours until it becomes a thick sauce (be careful, as the mixture may become 'volcanic'). The ketchup should have reduced by at least half at this stage.

When your ketchup is ready, bottle as per the 'hot jar, hot liquid, hot lid' method (see page 215). It will keep in a cool, dark place for 1½ years or more. Once opened, store in the fridge for up to 3 months.

Notes.

If you can't source green tomatoes, replace with red tomatoes – the ketchup just won't have such an earthy flavour. It might also be a little sweeter, so you may need to add less sugar – experiment. The flavour and sweetness will also vary massively depending on the tomato varieties you use (our tomatoes are naturally sweet!), as well as the ripeness of the red tomatoes and how long you reduce the sauce for – adjust the sugar and salt to taste.

See pages 214–15 for more information on bottling.

Fruit bottling with minimum sugar – spiced cherries.

MAKES 4 X 1 LITRE JARS
TIME: 35 MINUTES

5 kg cherries, pitted

4 cinnamon sticks

1 tablespoon anise seeds

1 vanilla bean, split and halved
(or 1 teaspoon vanilla extract)

300 g unrefined sugar
(e.g. rapadura), plus extra

All summer and autumn we get busy preserving fruit. Usually, we keep it simple and preserve plain fruit in its own juice, so that we can use it for a variety of different dishes. But, over the years, we have discovered some truly memorable fruit and spice combinations, and these spiced cherries are one of them. You can use this same technique to bottle other fruit also. Just follow the steps outlined below.

Juice 3 kg of the cherries (use a cold-press juicer if possible) to yield about 2 litres of cherry juice. Strain through a single layer of muslin and discard the pulp.

Divide the cinnamon, anise, vanilla and sugar between four 1 litre jars, then distribute the remaining cherries evenly among the jars. Fill to 1 cm from the top with cherry juice (if you fall short, you can top up with a mix of water and sugar at a 4:1 ratio).

Follow the 'classic water bath' method (see page 215) to seal the jars.

Store in a cool, dark place. The cherries are best eaten after 3 months and will keep for at least a year. Once opened, store in the fridge.

FIELD NOTES

Preservation with minimal sugar.
For bottled whole fruit to preserve for any length of time the syrup needs to have a certain sugar content. The sweeter the syrup, the longer the fruit will keep for. We only aim to preserve fruit for about 1 year because after that there will be a new harvest and a new bounty to preserve! But if you'd like to preserve for longer than this, here are the ratios of sugar to water:

1:4 sugar or honey to water = at least 12 months
1:3 sugar or honey to water = at least 18 months
1:2 sugar or honey to water = at least 2 years
1:1 sugar or honey to water = pretty much forever!

Your syrup may be just sugar/honey and water, or sugar/honey and the juice of the fruit you are using, or a combination of both. Regardless, the end result needs to have a sugar level of at least 25%. On average, fruit juice is around 10% sugar, although some fruit juices are sweeter. Here's a quick guide showing the sugar percentage of various fruits:

grape juice 16% sugar content
apple juice 11% sugar content
cherry juice 10% sugar content
orange juice 9% sugar content

To achieve the 25% sugar level needed to preserve fruit in its own juice for at least 1 year, we need to sweeten the juice. For these spiced cherries, our juice is already 10%, so we'll need to add just 15 per cent sugar to the amount of juice required. If you are unsure of the sweetness of your fruit, assume 10% as a general rule.

Jam making with minimum sugar – spiced apricot jam.

MAKES ABOUT 5 LITRES
TIME: 3 HOURS

6.5 kg apricots, stones removed, quartered

17 cardamom pods

5 cinnamon sticks

10 star anise

3 cloves

1 kg lemons, halved and juiced, reserve the skins and pips

1 kg unprocessed honey

Apricots are one of the earliest fruits to come back in season after a cold winter. They are so delicious, but they don't store well in cold storage (unlike apples), so you will need to preserve them if you want to enjoy them between seasons. Some people get very particular about their jam, having to have it perfectly set, but we prefer it a bit more relaxed and a little less set. This recipe doesn't use added pectin (unlike many jam recipes), but instead uses lemon pips to naturally add pectin.

It also only uses the natural sugars in honey to preserve the apricots and is designed to be used within a year. We freestyle this recipe every year, so it's always a little different. This is the one and only time we recorded a written version of the recipe – so here you have it, our summer of 2014/15 spiced apricot jam. Enjoy!

Place a small plate in the freezer.

Place the apricots, cardamom, cinnamon, star anise, cloves, lemon juice, lemon skins and 2 teaspoons of the lemon pips in a stockpot, cover and bring to the boil. Reduce the heat to a simmer and cook, covered, for 2 hours or so until the mixture begins to thicken.

Add the honey to the pot and continue to simmer, uncovered, for about 30 minutes – don't let it boil, as it will become toffee-like if it becomes too hot.

Once you are happy with the thickness, pull out the lemon skins. Place a very small drop of the jam onto the cold plate. It should stiffen and set like jam. If it doesn't, add more lemon pips and continue to simmer with the lid on for another 30 minutes or so before checking again.

When your jam is ready, bottle as per the 'hot jar, hot liquid, hot lid' method (see page 215).

The jam will keep for at least a year stored in a cool, dark place. Once opened, store in the fridge.

Notes.

When we say whole lemon skins, we literally mean the whole thing, not peeled or grated – just whatever is left after juicing them.

You need at least 2 heaped teaspoons of pips, more is even better, for the jam to set – it's a great idea to collect these over time whenever you use lemons.

Mix up the spices or do away with them completely for a simpler jam. Additionally, if you want to use sugar in place of honey in this recipe, simply replace the honey with the same amount of sugar.

See pages 214–15 for more information on preservation and bottling.

FIELD NOTES

On making jam with minimal sugar. The more modern way (post industrialisation) to make jams is to use so much sugar that it would never go bad on the shelf. We see it a little differently. We see jams as a great way to preserve fruit for one year or so, until the next season. The total sugar content for one-year preservation needs to be 25%. We assume an average of 10% natural sugar for all fruits (see field notes on page 224 for more info), so we need to add another 15% sugar to make our jam preserve for that one year, which is about a sixth of the total weight of the fruit. That is how this recipe is designed, and you can use it for any sweet fruit. If you want your jam to last for longer, increase the ratio of sugar to fruit using the following guide:

1:6 sugar or honey to uncooked fruit = 1 year shelf life
1:4 sugar or honey to uncooked fruit = 1½ years shelf life
1:2.5 sugar or honey to uncooked fruit = 2 years+ shelf life

Please note that this is based on our experience with preserving and is a conservative guide. For us, jams prepared using these ratios have lasted much longer on the shelf, however it does depend on storage conditions and climatic factors.

Preservation guide 3: drying and curing

Drying and curing are the most ancient forms of food preservation. Even in the days before the village, people were drying and curing foods to survive. Bad bacteria need water to do their work – a dry environment won't necessarily kill them (as with pasteurisation), but it will definitely force them into a state of dormancy that effectively does the same job. So when we dry and cure foods we are trying to remove as much water as we can. The terms drying and curing are used fairly interchangeably, but drying *usually* refers to drying foods *without* the addition of other ingredients, whereas curing *usually* refers to drying foods *with* the addition of other ingredients, like salt or sugar. Usually, plants are better suited to drying, whereas animal foods are better suited to curing because they contain fats that are prone to oxidisation unless protected by salt.

DRYING

Drying involves removing moisture purely through evaporation. Traditionally, this was done in the sun. But these days, dehydrators exist just for the purpose. You don't have to get *every* water molecule out. In fact, you usually just take it to around 10% moisture, give or take. At moisture levels this low, bad bacteria grind to a halt. It is an incredibly effective preservation method – dried herbs, grains and beans have all been found in Egyptian tombs in pretty much perfect condition, despite them being more than 4,000 years old.

Grains, beans, peas, lentils, nuts and seeds. As discussed in the traditional preparation notes (see pages 138–49), seeds contain their own natural enzyme inhibitors, so they are inherently very stable when dried. The process is very simple: leave the seeds in the sun or a dehydrator until they are brittle and dry. Air circulation is key, and dehydrators are built precisely to maximise airflow. If drying in the sun, just make sure to move everything around regularly so that one side doesn't dry while the other side stays moist.

Herbs. The leaves of herbs are so fine that they can simply be hung up inside to dry in small bunches. Dried herbs make great teas. For example, we dry peppermint, chamomile, nettle, rosemary, anise hyssop and lemongrass for tea.

Fungi. Mushrooms have such a short season that they have long been dried to enjoy their dense, savoury flavour throughout the year. So long as there is good air circulation, drying mushrooms is super easy. Just dry them in the sun or a dehydrator until they are completely brittle. If drying in the sun, just like seeds, remember to move them regularly to ensure even drying.

Fruits. Fruits don't need to be quite so dry because their naturally high sugar content helps to preserve them via osmosis (see page 187). Dry your fruits until they are firm and rubbery, and then store in airtight containers to prevent rehydration from moisture in the atmosphere.

CURING

Curing is based on the same principle of drying, except that it employs salt and sugar to speed up the process and to prevent bacterial growth before the food is fully dry. Salt is also particularly effective at preventing the oxidation (rancidification) of fats.

Because of the presence of salt and sugar as preservatives, cured foods don't need to be *as* dry as foods dried only through means of evaporation, which makes them very pleasant to eat just as they are – think salami, bacon (see page 230) and cured tuna in oil (see page 233).

But because cured foods aren't *completely* dry, they aren't infinitely stable either. It is more about extending shelf life than preserving the food for years and years. Some cured foods are stable at room temperature, others do best cellared below 12°C, or refrigerated.

Meat. It is safer to cure meat with salt rather than simply drying purely through means of evaporation. So we cure it.

Traditional homemade bacon.

MAKES 1 KG
TIME: 2 HOURS AND 15 MINUTES
+ 21 DAYS TO CURE

½ teaspoon black peppercorns

1 teaspoon coriander seeds

1 tablespoon unrefined salt

1 heaped tablespoon unrefined sugar (e.g. rapadura)

1 garlic clove, finely chopped

1 kg pork belly

1 cup wood chips
(oak, black wattle, chestnut, grape vine or from any fruit tree)

Special equipment

2 woks

strong metal hook

small round metal rack

meat thermometer

This is the traditional way to make bacon. These days, most bacon is made using nitrates to speed up the curing process – taking one to two days – and to make the bacon look pink, but recent studies have suggested that nitrates are carcinogenic. When you make it the traditional way, the whole process takes 21 days, and it's actually a grey–brown colour on the outside once cured – this is how it *should* look.

We got this recipe and learnt the process through trading with an amazing man called Mike Patrick, who is the absolute pro at smoking everything. These days, smoking your own meat can seem complicated, with people building whole smokehouses just for curing meat, but actually you can do it on your stove and this recipe makes it achievable for everyone.

Day 1. Grind the peppercorns and coriander seeds using a mortar and pestle or blitz them in a blender. Add the salt, sugar and garlic and continue to grind or blitz until evenly combined.

Place the pork belly on a baking tray and rub all sides with the salt and spice mixture. Make sure you rub thoroughly and cover all of the pork. Place the pork in the fridge in a deep-sided tray, uncovered. Flip the pork belly every day for the next 10 days.

Day 11. Wash the pork thoroughly with cold water and pat dry with a tea towel. Hang in the fridge using the metal hook for 10 days (you may need to take a shelf out).

Day 21. It's bacon day. Get a wok and place the wood chips in the bottom, place the rack over the wood chips and place the pork belly on the rack. Insert a thermometer into the centre of the bacon at the thickest point. Place the second wok upside down on top so that it forms a lid and seals – it should look like a big clam. Place on the stove and turn the heat to high. Once it begins to smoke, reduce the heat to medium–high and smoke for about 2 hours (it doesn't get too smoky, but turn the exhaust fan on and open the windows anyway) until the internal temperature of the bacon reaches 65°C.

Remove the bacon from the smoker and leave on the bench to cool. Slice into 4–5 cm-wide strips before refrigerating or freezing. It will keep in the fridge for at least 1 month, or in the freezer for 6–12 months.

Note. Slow and consistent heat while cooking will achieve the best results, so try not to open the woks while cooking. 'If you're lookin', you ain't cookin'.' – MIKE

Homemade 'canned' tuna.

The first time we tried home-preserved tuna it was gifted to us by one of our country neighbours, Cal. He said to us 'once you try this, guys, you'll never eat tinned tuna again', and he was right. It tastes nothing like store-bought, tinned tuna, and it is a whole world of deliciousness. This is a recipe that calls for a party. Get one or two fish to preserve enough for the year, process them over two days – with the first day for cooking and the second day for bottling – drink some good wine and have a celebration!

Day 1. Combine the salt and water to make a 10% brine solution. You'll need enough to cover all of the fish.

Clean and gut the tuna. Remove the head and tail and, so there is no waste, set aside to make a tuna-head stock (see our waste bone stock recipe on page 180). Using a cleaver or large knife, cut the tuna crossways into 5 cm slabs.

Place all of the tuna pieces in a very large stockpot and pour in the brine, making sure the tuna is completely covered. Bring to the boil, then reduce the heat and simmer for 3 hours to cure and cook the tuna.

Lift the cooked tuna out of the pot, place in a very large colander (or several smaller ones) and drain over the sink. Put the metal racks over some tea towels and place the tuna on the racks. Cover with tea towels and leave overnight to drain.

Day 2. Place a little oil, 1–2 bay leaves, some chilli to taste and a teaspoon of peppercorns in each jar. Add the chunks of tuna, packing them in gently as you go (keep them as chunky as possible and remove any big bones). Fill the jars with oil, making sure to fill all the way to the top to cover the tuna. Screw on the lids so they are firmly in position, taking care not to over-tighten. Follow the 'classic water bath' method (see page 215) to seal.

You can eat the tuna after 1 month, but the flavour is best at 3 months. Place the jars in the fridge around the 3–4 month mark to ensure that they remain stable (better safe than sorry).

Notes.

Don't debone the tuna before cooking or it will fall apart into tiny pieces.

Make sure you open all of your windows and doors, or preferably do this outside, so your house doesn't smell like tuna for a week afterwards!

FIELD NOTES

On purchasing or catching tuna. Albacore tuna isn't as prized as yellowfin or bluefin tuna, so it's best to use here, as it's often the 'throwaway' catch for many fishermen (see page 83 for more information).

MAKES A 1 YEAR SUPPLY
OF TUNA FOR 2–4 PEOPLE
TIME: 6 HOURS
+ OVERNIGHT DRAINING

1–1.5 kg unrefined salt

10–15 litres unchlorinated water

1 whole tuna (about 17–25 kg)

To jar

extra-virgin olive oil

bay leaves

chilli flakes or whole dried chillies

black peppercorns

Special equipment

very large stockpot (15 litres plus, depending on the size of the tuna)

lots of jars with lids

metal racks

Dried persimmons.

TIME: ABOUT 4 WEEKS DRYING

freshly picked astringent
persimmons (see field notes)

Persimmons are an amazing and very underutilised temperate-climate fruit. In Japan, dried persimmons are known as *hoshigaki* and are a popular traditional delicacy. There is a lot of misinformation out there on how to make these, and if you get it wrong you will have all sorts of colourful moulds growing on them. But if they are covered in a delicious sugary coating, it means you've nailed it – the moisture has evaporated and all that is left is sugar. They are a *perfect* temperate-climate substitute for dates (you will see that we use them throughout this book) and are amazing on cheeseboards and in cakes. Plus, they store well on the shelf.

Pick your persimmons when they are totally orange/yellow in colour (no green) and still *very* firm, leaving a 't-piece' of stem attached (this makes them easier to hang later). If yours – like ours always do – begin to get eaten by possums or other wild animals before they fully ripen to orange/yellow, just pick them at whatever stage they're at (as far along as possible). Early-picked persimmons will still make amazing *hoshigaki*; they just won't be as sweet.

Peel the persimmons, leaving only the t-piece of stem, making sure there is no peel left on the fruit. String the persimmons up from their t-pieces (there are so many different techniques for this!), and then hang the strings so that the persimmons don't touch anything or each other in a well-ventilated and sunny spot inside. If you need some extra air circulation, you can put a fan on low to help out.

After 10–14 days, massage each piece of fruit *very* gently and briefly. Every few days, massage them again. If you forget to massage them, don't worry too much – they will still dry but just won't be as soft in texture. They should be dry within about 4 weeks, depending on the weather, the size of the fruit etc. You will know when they are ready; they will be a dark brown colour and have started to develop a white coating, which is the sugar (not mould!).

Store them in an airtight container on the pantry shelf. Enjoy in cakes, on cheese boards, or as a snack on their own.

FIELD NOTES

On persimmon varieties. There are two types of persimmon: astringent and non-astringent. Astringent varieties have so much tannin when picked that they are completely unpalatable, whereas non-astringent varieties can be eaten freshly picked, and are crisp like an apple. At first glance then, non-astringent varieties may seem like the way to go. But it's actually the astringent varieties that are prized. Astringent persimmons reach their full potential off the tree, with their tannins transforming as the starches break down into an intensely sweet jelly. Fully ripened, astringent varieties are a completely underrated delicacy. Because of their fierce sweetness, only use astringent persimmons for this technique – their flavour is unmatched.

Peeled and ready to hang.

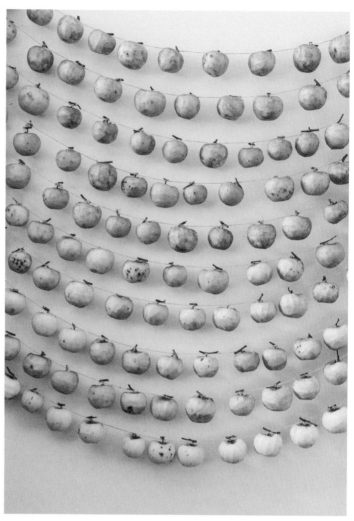

Freshly hung.

Drying.

Preservation guide 4: storing your harvest

Keeping summer and autumn harvests fresh throughout the winter is so easy! It's all about keeping your vegetables and fruit from drying out. It used to be that everyone had a little storage cellar just for this purpose, which would sit at about 12°C all year round. With fridges becoming so common, cellars have fallen out of favour, but they are a home feature we'd love to see return. If you're lucky enough to have one, use it! Or build one – go on. The key is a cool, dark, dry room with great air circulation.

Cellar or not, here's our simple guide to keeping your produce fresh for as long as possible.

Apples, pears and quinces. Harvest these after the autumn equinox and before the first frost. Wrap only perfectly unblemished fruit individually in newspaper and store in open crates or cardboard boxes in a dark, dry place with good air circulation at 3–12°C.

Potatoes. Harvest potatoes after the autumn equinox and before the first frost. Immediately wash them clean of any dirt and allow to dry completely. Store in a dark, dry place with good air circulation at 3–12°C.

Pumpkins. Harvest pumpkins after the autumn equinox and before the first frost. Brush them clean of any dirt and leave in the sun to dry and cure for at least 3–4 clear, sunny days, turning occasionally. Store in a dark, dry place with good air circulation, no warmer than 20°C.

Sweet potatoes. Harvest sweet potatoes after the autumn equinox and before the first frost. Immediately wash them clean of dirt and cure in a hot (25–30°C) and very humid room for 5–10 days – we cure ours in a warm shed up on shelves with wet towels or buckets of water on the floor for humidity. Air-dry the cured sweet potatoes in a single layer, turning occasionally for several days – we dry them in airy crates in a shady spot. Finally, store in open crates or cardboard boxes in a dark, dry place with good air circulation at 10–15°C.

Garlic. There are two kinds of garlic, 'hard neck' and 'soft neck', and both are harvested in early to mid-summer. We harvest hard-neck types when the lower 3–4 leaves have yellowed and dried, but the upper 5–6 are still green. We harvest soft-neck types when the tops have completely fallen over. Harvest on a dry day and brush clean of dirt or wash very gently before placing in a dry, shady spot with excellent air circulation for 10–14 days to cure. Hanging bunches of 10–12 plants from the roof of a breezy carport works perfectly – we cure ours on airy, shaded racks. After curing, we remove the tops (although they can be left in woven bundles) and store in a dry, dark place at 3–20°C.

Onions and French shallots. Harvest onions and shallots in summer when their tops have fallen over. Harvest on a dry day and brush clean of dirt or wash gently before placing in a dry, shady spot with excellent air circulation for 2–4 weeks to cure. Like garlic, hanging these in bunches of 10–12 plants from the roof of a breezy carport works perfectly. After curing, we remove the tops (although they can be left in woven bundles also) and store in a dry, dark place at 3–20°C.

Root vegetables. We store carrots, turnips, beets, Jerusalem artichokes and parsnips in the ground in the garden all winter long. But if you want to harvest them before winter sets in, there is a trick to keeping them fresh for many months. Grab a sturdy wooden or cardboard box with a lid and enough clean, barely moist sand to fill it. Place 2–3 cm of sand in the bottom of the box, then a single layer of freshly harvested clean roots with the tops removed. Cover with another 2–3 cm of sand and repeat until the box is full. Cover and store in a cool, dry place at 3–12°C.

Hanging tomatoes. Hanging tomatoes you say? Yes, tomatoes can be stored outside the passata bottle too! This is the best winter treat. When we experimented with this the first time, there was a lot of doubt that it would work. But it did. At the very end of autumn, when the tomatoes have stopped ripening, pull up a few plants, roots and all, that have semi-ripe and/or green tomatoes on them. Wash the roots and hang the plants upside down in your pantry or cellar. A month later, they will start to ripen and will continue to do so slowly for another month or so. It feels so special to have a few ripe tomatoes as a treat in the depths of winter. This is particularly amazing for very cold parts of the world that have very little fresh food in the winter months!

Key points.
- Foods stored in this way utilise their natural skin (or we create a skin with sand) to protect against bad bacteria entering.
- Stable, cool temperatures keep enzymes dormant and bad bacteria from growing.

Morning rituals.

Food to make the day feel special.

Simple man's cold brew.

MAKES 300 ML
SERVES 4
TIME: 5 MINUTES
+ 12 HOURS BREWING

Cold brew coffee

100 g (1 cup) responsibly
sourced coffee beans, ground
to a fine–medium grind
(a bit coarser than espresso)

To serve

75 ml cold-brew coffee

190 ml milk of your choice
or cold water

1 teaspoon vanilla extract

1 tablespoon unrefined sugar
(e.g. rapadura)

unrefined salt

Special equipment

muslin cloth or a nut bag

The perfect grind

This recipe is all about stripping coffee back to the essentials and using equipment you already have at home. You don't need heaps of equipment to make great coffee. Additionally, cold brewing reduces the acidity of the coffee by over two-thirds, keeping the acidity of your diet low and therefore you healthier!

Place the ground coffee in a large jar and add 500 ml (2 cups) cold water, pouring it in a circular motion to make sure you cover all of the coffee grinds. Put the lid on and place it in the fridge overnight (or up to 12 hours), or leave it on the bench at room temperature for 5 hours.

Place several layers of muslin over another jar (or use a nut bag) and strain the coffee. Store the black coffee in a jar in the fridge for up to 4 days.

To serve, divide the coffee into jars or cups, add milk or water, vanilla, sugar and a tiny pinch of salt and combine well. Pre-make small jars for an easy coffee during the week, or serve immediately over ice.

FIELD NOTES

On sourcing coffee. We don't have the climate or altitude to grow coffee where we are, yet it is something that we've chosen to have in our lives. This is because we know and trust the people who source it for us – we trade coffee for flowers and discuss the ins and outs of the coffee we are about to drink. See the *Trade* and *Seek* chapters for more information.

On growing coffee. When grown in an ideal climate, coffee, like any crop, grows happily without the need for chemicals. However, the reality of coffee farming means that it is often grown in less than ideal environments and therefore chemical use is high. In many places where coffee is grown, it is still common to use very harsh chemicals that have long been banned in developed countries.

We need to think beyond ourselves when drinking that cup of morning coffee – about the effects of those chemicals on the soil and the people working with them. Fortunately, there are amazing people producing amazing chemical-free and responsibly sourced coffee beans. So please support them and the farmers behind their coffee, so that we can encourage more farmers to grow their coffee beans well. Let's make change.

On freshness. Coffee is always more delicious when it is freshly ground using beans that were roasted less than two weeks ago. Pick good beans that aren't super darkly roasted. It's like burning a cake – it's never as good.

The perfect grind. The grind of the coffee can affect the flavour a lot. For this recipe, if the coffee tastes bitter, try a coarser grind. If it's too weak, try a finer grind.

Authentic chai.

Chai made from scratch with all its essential ingredients – this is something that makes our home feel like our home. As it starts to get cold, and throughout winter, we often have a pot of this on the stove to keep us warm and to share with friends. It is full of warming spices and decongestant herbs. Matt is the master of this recipe. He has good memories of spending time with India's charismatic *chai wallahs*, sweating beside cauldrons of the thick bubbling liquid over open fires. The key to real chai flavour is making sure that you get the mixture to a rollicking boil just before straining – that heat changes everything. Do this and you too will be a chai master. – LENTIL

Place the spices and salt in a saucepan with 600 ml of water and bring to the boil. Reduce the heat, cover and simmer for 15 minutes.

Add the remaining ingredients to the pan and slowly bring to the boil over a medium heat, stirring constantly to avoid sticking. Bring to a rolling boil, and then reduce the heat and boil gently for 1 minute. Remove the pan from the heat and strain.

Serve and enjoy, or place in the fridge to cool and serve as iced chai.

Note. If this isn't sweet enough for you, feel free to sweeten to taste.

MAKES 1 LITRE (SERVES 4–6)
TIME: 30 MINUTES

a knob of ginger, finely sliced

8 cardamom pods

5 star anise

2 cinnamon sticks

3 cloves

1 teaspoon ground cinnamon

a pinch of ground nutmeg

a pinch of unrefined salt

600 ml milk of your choice

1 tablespoon unrefined sugar (e.g. rapadura) or unprocessed honey

3 teaspoons black tea leaves

No-bake muesli bars.

This is a super-easy recipe for a quick and healthy breakfast or snack. These are kind of like a healthy baklava and are incredibly addictive! We store ours in the freezer to keep them fresh and more nutritious, ensuring the oats, nuts and seeds don't go rancid.

MAKES 18–20 BARS
TIME: 10 MINUTES + ABOUT 2 HOURS FREEZING TIME

150 g (½ cup) unprocessed honey

150 g tahini

70 g butter

200 g (1½ cups) gluten-free rolled oats (see note on page 140)

80 g (½ cup) sunflower seeds

80 g (½ cup) flaxseeds

60 g (⅓ cup) almonds

80 g (½ cup) pumpkin seeds

80 g (½ cup) sesame seeds

60 g (⅓ cup) chia seeds

Line a 30 cm x 15 cm baking tray with baking paper.

Melt the honey, tahini and butter in a small saucepan over a low heat, stirring until combined.

Place the oats, sunflower seeds, flaxseeds, almonds and pumpkin seeds in a blender and pulse until combined but still slightly chunky.

Pour into a bowl and add the sesame seeds and chia. Pour in the hot tahini mixture and massage everything together with your hands until combined.

Press the mixture firmly and evenly into the lined tray – it should be about 1 cm thick. Use the back of a wet spoon to smooth the top. Place in the freezer until set (around 2 hours).

Once set, cut into about 6 cm x 3 cm slices and store in an airtight container in the freezer. They will keep for at least 6 months.

Ginger snaps

In our modern world, cookies are often considered 'bad' for you, but this isn't always the case. Like the charismatic Greeks on the island of Symi, one of the longest living populations in the world, we are big fans of a cookie and coffee or tea for breakfast. This recipe is an awesome start to the day, with lots of nuts, fruit, endorphin-releasing spices and good oils.

MAKES ABOUT 50 COOKIES
TIME: 30 MINUTES + COOLING TIME

2 egg whites

a pinch of unrefined salt

70 g sultanas

25 g (⅓ cup) walnuts

200 g (2 cups) almond meal, plus extra for rolling

115 g white rice flour

80 g (½ cup) unrefined sugar (e.g. rapadura)

1 teaspoon ground cinnamon

1 tablespoon ground ginger

1 teaspoon bicarbonate of soda

150 ml extra-virgin olive oil

Place the egg whites and salt in a high-powered blender and blend until just fluffy. Add the sultanas and walnuts and blend again until just combined. Add the remaining ingredients and pulse until the mixture forms a thick paste.

Tip the mixture onto baking paper or a silicone oven mat and roll into a log. Cover and refrigerate for a few hours until really cold and firm.

Preheat the oven to 150°C fan-forced. Line baking trays with silicone baking mats or baking paper.

Dust the bench with extra almond meal. Divide the chilled dough into a few pieces and roll into 5 mm thick sheets. Cut into 4 cm x 4 cm squares, or use cookie cutters for fun! Bake for 15–20 minutes until just brown. Cool on a cooling rack and store in an airtight container.

Tonic.

MAKES 200 ML (ENOUGH FOR 1–2 PEOPLE)
TIME: 5 MINUTES

1 orange, peeled

½ grapefruit, peeled

1 small lemon, peeled

a knob of fresh turmeric

a knob of ginger

10 oregano sprigs (leaves picked if the stalks are older)

5 mint sprigs

1 fresh or dried chilli (if you are game!)

1 teaspoon apple cider vinegar

Juice all of the ingredients except the vinegar, and then stir in the vinegar well. Drink anytime, or as a 'cure all' when feeling a little unwell.

Note. If possible, use a cold-press juicer.

Summer fruit 'smoothie'.

MAKES 375 ML (ENOUGH FOR 1–2 PEOPLE)
TIME: 5 MINUTES

1 small to medium cucumber

4 nectarines, stones removed

4 peaches, stones removed

15 mint sprigs

¼ lemon, peeled

Juice all of the ingredients and stir to combine.

Note. If possible, use a cold-press juicer.

Apricot & cacao nib smoothie.

MAKES 375 ML (ENOUGH FOR 1–2 PEOPLE)
TIME: 5 MINUTES

190 g (¾ cup) natural yoghurt (see page 170)

3 frozen apricots, stones removed

a handful of kale

1½ tablespoons responsibly sourced cacao nibs

1½ teaspoons bee pollen

3 teaspoons unprocessed honey

10 ice cubes

Blend all of the ingredients in a high-powered blender until smooth.

Gooseberry lassi.

MAKES 400 ML (ENOUGH FOR 1–2 PEOPLE)
TIME: 5 MINUTES

250 g (1 cup) runny natural yoghurt (see page 170), very cold

80 g cape gooseberries

1 tablespoon unrefined sugar (e.g rapadura)

a pinch of unrefined salt

1 cardamom pod

1 tablespoon semi-dried rose petals (if you don't grow roses, ask a neighbour)

Blend all of the ingredients in a high-powered blender until smooth. Serve super cold!

Note. When replacing gooseberries with other fruit, you'll need to increase the amount of fruit to around 150 g, as gooseberries are strong in flavour compared to other fruit.

Toasted muesli.

Muesli is always a good way to start the day –
fruity, nutty, a tiny bit sweet and a little crunchy.
This recipe is all about the cinnamon, which is said to
release endorphins, so it will make you happy too!

MAKES 650 G
TIME: 50 MINUTES

400 g (3 cups) gluten-free rolled oats (see note on
page 140)

90 g (heaped ½ cup) pumpkin seeds

90 g (½ cup) almonds, roughly chopped

3 tablespoons flaxseeds

3 tablespoons sesame seeds

3 teaspoons ground cinnamon

½ teaspoon ground ginger

1 teaspoon vanilla extract

a pinch of unrefined salt

2 tablespoons unprocessed honey

4 tablespoons bee pollen

40 g (¼ cup) dried wild plums or dried sour cherries

Preheat the oven to 140°C fan-forced.

Place all of the ingredients except the honey, pollen
and plums in a deep baking tray and toss well to
combine. Drizzle the honey over the top and stir
to coat. Bake for 30–40 minutes, stirring every
10 minutes or so to evenly toast the muesli.

Stir through the bee pollen and wild plums. Cool
before storing in an airtight jar in the freezer to
prevent the muesli from becoming rancid.

FIELD NOTES

On muesli. When you buy muesli in a packet it will
often taste a little bitter – this is the rancidity of the oats
(see notes on the importance of rolling them fresh on
page 140). Make it at home to ensure that you are
getting oats in their freshest form, allowing your body to
absorb good oils and vitamins. Additionally, pre-soak it
(as in the bircher recipe opposite) to further aid digestion.

Traditional bircher.

The original bircher recipe was called 'the dish',
and is from a book titled *Fruit Dishes and Raw
Vegetables* by M. Bircher-Benner and Max E.
Bircher (1936). The original recipe was more like
a sweet and watery breakfast soup with a few
oats and nuts. Our recipe is a variation of the
original, using similar ingredients but in different
quantities to make it less sweet and soupy – much
more suited to our taste! And it's a really easy
way to prepare your morning grains well.

SERVES 1
TIME: 10 MINUTES + SOAKING OVERNIGHT

75 g (½ cup) gluten-free toasted muesli (see opposite)

juice of 1 large lemon

1 tablespoon 'top milk' (where cream settles at the top of
fresh milk) or a mix of cream and milk

1 tablespoon natural yoghurt (see page 170)

1 teaspoon unprocessed honey

1 large apple

1 tablespoon chopped almonds

1 tablespoon chopped walnuts

fresh fruit, to serve

Day 1. Combine the muesli, lemon juice and
170 ml of water in a bowl or container, cover
and leave on the bench overnight to soak.

Day 2. Mix the top milk, yoghurt and honey into
the muesli. Grate the apple, skin and all, into the
mixture, frequently stirring it through to stop
the apple from browning. Sprinkle the almonds,
walnuts and fruit on top and serve immediately.

Toast #1: Spring peas, broad beans & flowers.

This dish is full of the things that shine in spring: peas, broad beans, herbs and edible flowers.

SERVES 4
TIME: 25 MINUTES

100 ml extra-virgin olive oil

350 g (2 cups) podded broad beans and peas

unrefined salt

ground black pepper

a big handful of parsley, stalks and all, finely chopped

a big handful of mint, leaves picked and finely chopped

2 garlic cloves, crushed

2 dried chillies

½ lemon

4–8 slices of gluten-free sourdough bread (see page 152)

4–8 eggs

To serve

lemon

ricotta (see page 176)

unrefined salt

ground black pepper

edible flowers (we used nasturtiums, violas, cornflowers, brassica flowers and calendula) (optional)

Heat 80 ml of the olive oil in a heavy-based frying pan over a low heat. Add the broad beans, peas and a pinch of salt and pepper. Fry for about 10 minutes.

Grind the parsley, mint, garlic, chilli and remaining oil to a paste using a mortar and pestle or a blender. Add to the the broad beans and fry for 2–3 minutes. Take off the heat and add a squeeze of lemon juice.

Boil the eggs for 6 minutes and toast the bread.

To serve, peel and halve the eggs. Spoon the broad bean mix on the toast, then top with the eggs, a squeeze of lemon, some ricotta, a pinch of salt and pepper and the flowers (if using). Good morning!

Toast #2: Tomatoes, green tahini & toasted sesame.

So simple, but so good. Back when I was a speech therapist, there was one cafe near my work that served green tahini and tomatoes on toast – it made my mornings. I hope this recipe does the same for you. – LENTIL

SERVES 4
TIME: 5 MINUTES

4–8 slices of gluten-free sourdough bread (see page 152)

120–140 g green tahini (see page 268)

To serve

finely chopped garlic chives

toasted sesame oil

4 very ripe heirloom salad tomatoes, cut into thick slices

toasted sesame seeds

unrefined salt

ground black pepper

Toast the bread and spread on a thick layer of green tahini. Sprinkle with the garlic chives and splash on some sesame oil. Lay the sliced tomato on top, sprinkle with sesame seeds and season with a pinch of salt and pepper.

FIELD NOTES

On broad bean tips. You could also add a handful of broad bean tips to the recipe opposite. It is unlikely you will be able to find them in markets, but when you grow your own broad beans you will have an abundance of them! Don't cut the tips of your plants until they have reached their full height and set all of their pods, or you may be reducing your harvest. They taste just like broad beans, but, funnily enough, leafier. If you do have some, steam lightly and add to the herb mixture.

Greens & kimchi pancakes.

SERVES 4–6 (6–8 MEDIUM PANCAKES)
TIME: 20 MINUTES

Pancakes

½ batch of soured buckwheat pancake batter (see page 158)

150 g (1 packed cup) kimchi (see page 206)

2 tablespoons kimchi liquid

80 g mixed Asian greens (e.g. bok choy, tatsoi, mustard greens, yao choy, amaranth and upland cress), finely sliced

30 g pickled garlic (see page 219), finely chopped (optional)

1 large spring onion or onion shoot, finely chopped

70 g white rice flour

2 tablespoons unrefined sugar (e.g. rapadura)

extra-virgin olive oil, for frying

Sauce

100 ml rice wine vinegar

80 ml (⅓ cup) tamari

2 teaspoons toasted sesame oil

2 teaspoons unprocessed honey

2 teaspoons kimchi liquid

2 tablespoons finely chopped spring onion or onion shoot

2 green or red chillies, finely chopped

a pinch of unrefined sea salt

To serve

eggs (as many as you like!)

mayonnaise (see page 182)

toasted sesame seeds

kimchi (see page 206)

Fermented pickles, fresh greens, a little bit of chilli spice and an egg make for a delicious and nutrient-rich savoury breakfast! These pancakes are sweet and savoury, eggy and tangy, and are a super-filling way to start the day. This recipe is not only great for breakfast, but also works as a meal anytime of the day, from breakfast through to dinner, year round. If you want something simpler, make a batch of pancakes to keep in the fridge and just spread with butter for an easy breakfast.

Place the pancake batter and all of the pancake ingredients in a large bowl and mix well.

Heat a heavy-based frying pan until medium–hot (if you put a little splash of water in it, it will sizzle). Add a splash of oil to the pan and spoon in 2 big tablespoons of the pancake mix. Pat down the mix with the back of a spoon to make it as thin as you can – this is key, it should be about 20 cm in diameter. Fry for 2–3 minutes until the pancake starts to brown and become crispy underneath.

Flip and push down firmly with a spatula to flatten. Cook for a further 1–2 minutes and flip once more. Fry for 1 more minute to get it extra crispy.

Repeat for the remaining mixture. Place the pancakes in a tea towel or cover with a plate to keep them warm while the rest are cooking.

Meanwhile, place the sauce ingredients in a jar and shake to combine.

Fry the eggs to your preference.

To serve, place the pancakes on plates, top with fried eggs, a spoonful of mayonnaise, a sprinkling of sesame seeds and a spoonful of kimchi. Pour the sauce over the top and serve.

Sweet five-grain porridge.

SERVES 6
TIME: 1 HOUR
+ 12–24 HOURS SOURING

100 g (½ cup) brown rice
100 g (½ cup) millet
100 g (½ cup) buckwheat
100 g (½ cup) quinoa, washed
100 g (½ cup) gluten-free groats (whole oat kernels) (see note on page 140)
3 tablespoons apple cider vinegar
3 tablespoons chia seeds
2 dried persimmons (see page 234) or pitted dates, finely sliced
2 teaspoons ground cinnamon
1 teaspoon ground ginger
1 teaspoon vanilla extract
1 tablespoon unprocessed honey
1 litre (4 cups) milk of your choice

We are big on warming foods in winter, and porridge is one of the most fundamental. This porridge is slightly sweet, with a velvety texture and kick of ginger. We roll the grains fresh by hand with our oat roller, then we sour them overnight before cooking. I don't think we'll ever get sick of rolling the grains by hand – there is such a simple joy in it. Porridge is something we have tried so many different combinations for, but this recipe is up there with the best. Freshly rolled oats, brown rice, quinoa, millet and buckwheat cooked down with chia and milk and topped with preserved wild plums, quinces and cherries from freshly opened jars from the past growing season. Then come the edible flowers – there aren't many cut flowers around in winter, but there are actually a large range of edible flowers. This is food as it used to be. This porridge will keep for at least a week in the fridge, so we just make a big batch and heat it on the stove each morning with a bit of extra milk or water.

Day 1. Run the grains through an oat-roller. (If you don't have an oat-roller, simply keep the grains whole and replace the groats with rolled oats.) Place the grains in a large bowl with the vinegar and 1 litre (4 cups) of water. Cover and stand at room temperature for 12–24 hours.

Day 2. Transfer the soured grains and soaking liquid to a large heavy-based saucepan along with 500 ml (2 cups) of water. Add the remaining ingredients except for 250 ml (1 cup) of milk and bring to the boil over a high heat, stirring constantly to prevent it from sticking. Reduce the heat to low and cook for about 30 minutes with the lid on, stirring every 10 minutes or so, while gradually adding the remaining milk. If after 30 minutes it's still a bit thick, stir in a little more water or milk.

Serve in bowls with whatever toppings your heart desires – we used preserved cherries, quinces, wild plums, violas and unprocessed honey.

Notes.

If you are using whole grains (not rolled) expect a longer cooking time. If some of these grains aren't grown locally to you, just replace them with any other whole grains that are.

For a vegan version of this recipe, replace the honey with unrefined sugar.

Chia, flax & basil seed pudding.

SERVES 2
TIME: 10 MINUTES
+ OVERNIGHT SOAKING

60 g (⅓ cup) chia seeds

2 tablespoons flaxseeds, freshly ground

1 tablespoon basil seeds (or replace with chia)

3 plums (about 80 g), stones removed

1 heaped tablespoon unprocessed honey dissolved in a splash of hot water

1 teaspoon vanilla extract

To serve

plums, diced

basil leaves, torn

mint leaves, torn

natural yoghurt (see page 170) and/or cream

This is a super-refreshing summer breakfast. The plums make it light and tangy and it's a great source of slow-release energy throughout the morning. Super easy to make in jars the night before for a takeaway breakfast the next morning.

Combine the chia, flaxseeds and basil seeds in a bowl, or divide equally between two jars.

Place the plums, honey, vanilla and 250 ml (1 cup) of water in a blender and process until smooth. Pour over the seed mixture and combine thoroughly. Refrigerate for 6 hours or so until set.

To serve, toss the diced plums with the herbs and place on top of the pudding. Add a spoonful of yoghurt and/or cream, if desired, and serve.

Note. For a vegan version of this recipe, simply omit the yoghurt or cream and replace the honey with unrefined sugar, a date or a dried persimmon.

FIELD NOTES

On chia seeds. Like their South American cousins, quinoa and amaranth, chia seeds have become popular in recent years as a so-called superfood, and they are indeed a wonderful thing. What most people don't realise, though, is the massive impact this has had on huge numbers of people in countries like Bolivia and Peru. These seeds were staple foods for many communities, but their growing demand as a global commodity has led to huge price increases locally, which are far higher than most people can afford. To replace these staples, the people have turned to cheap, highly refined white flours and packaged food shipped in from the Western world, leading to mass malnourishment.

Both quinoa and chia are grown extensively in Australia now, and that is all that we will buy. At the time of writing, no Australian farms grow amaranth, so we either grow our own or go without. For further discussion on sourcing foods from far away responsibly, please refer to the *Seek* chapter.

On basil seeds. Basil seeds act in a similar way to chia seeds. So if it's the end of the season and your basil plants are beginning to go to flower and then set seed, don't stress – collect the seeds and use them for cooking!

Life-changing gluten-free sourdough crumpets.

So good, so easy, and *fun* – need we say more? These are free of all the 'things' and super good for you, using a long-ferment sourdough method. These should turn out full of bubbles and 'crumpetness', be a little crispy on the outside and soft and fluffy on the inside. They are neither too sweet nor too savoury, so are perfect for both uses – if you want them a bit sweeter, just add a little more sugar. Our favourite topping is fresh honeycomb from the bees, ricotta (see page 176) and some leftover coffee grounds sprinkled on top. Pre-make these and store them in the fridge or freezer, and put them in the toaster for an easy breakfast.

Day 1. In a large jug, dissolve the sourdough culture in the water. In a separate large bowl, combine the flours, sugar and a pinch of salt. Add the liquid to the dry ingredients and stir well to combine. Add the oil to the mixture and whisk until smooth. Place the bowl in a warm place for 24 hours.

Day 2. When ready, the batter should smell good and have small bubbles on top. Dissolve the bicarbonate of soda in a little water and add it to the batter. Whisk lightly and set aside for about 5 minutes until lots of bubbles appear on the top. The batter should be super airy, bubbly and fluffy!

Heat a knob of butter in a cast-iron skillet over a medium heat. Grease the crumpet rings with butter and place in the skillet. Ladle the batter into the rings to a height of about 1.5 cm (about ⅓ cup), cover the pan and cook for 4–5 minutes. When ready, bubbles will appear on top and a skin will form. At this point, remove the rings and flip the crumpets, browning the other side for just 30 seconds or so. Place on a cooling rack to cool.

Serve warm, eat cold, toast later or freeze.

Notes.

If your pan isn't hot enough, crumpets can become doughy and bubbles won't form. If it's too hot the same will happen – you want a medium–hot pan, this is key.

For a vegan and dairy-free version of this recipe, use cold-pressed sunflower oil or extra-virgin olive oil instead of butter to cook the crumpets.

MAKES ABOUT 15 CRUMPETS
TIME: 30 MINUTES
+ 24 HOURS FERMENTATION

50 g (2 tablespoons) gluten-free sourdough culture (see page 142)

800 ml unchlorinated water (unchlorinated water is essential for the fermentation to work)

250 g buckwheat flour

250 g white rice flour

2 tablespoons unrefined sugar (e.g. rapadura)

unrefined salt

180 ml (¾ cup) cold-pressed sunflower oil or extra-virgin olive oil, plus extra

1 heaped teaspoon bicarbonate of soda

unsalted butter, for frying

Special equipment

crumpet rings (at least 3 cm deep)

Beans & eggs.

SERVES 4
TIME: 3 HOURS 15 MINUTES

½ cup dried cannellini beans, soaked overnight (as per preparation guide on page 147)

extra-virgin olive oil

1 large onion, diced

1 large red capsicum, coarsely chopped

1 dried chilli

3 garlic cloves, crushed

1 tablespoon ground cumin

1 tablespoon sweet paprika

1½ teaspoons ground black pepper

1 teaspoon ground cinnamon or 1 cinnamon stick

1 teaspoon ground turmeric

½ teaspoon ground coriander

2 bay leaves

500 ml (2 cups) passata (see page 221)

300 g fat hen (see page 84), leaves picked and coarsely chopped or any other dark, leafy green (see note)

2 teaspoons unrefined sugar (e.g. rapadura)

½ teaspoon unrefined salt

4 eggs

1 lemon

3 parsley sprigs, stalks and all, finely chopped

This is our combination of what we consider two of the best breakfast dishes there are: baked beans and shakshuka. I first ate shakshuka when a friend made it for me in northern Israel as a hangover cure. The sharpness and spice of the shakshuka sauce paired with the deep savoury yolkiness of the egg was just magic. Adding white beans into the mix goes so well that I'm surprised it's not the way this classic breakfast has always been made! Use the reddest red passata you've got for this one – the colours in the finished dish are magnificent! We make the beans the day or night before and then just bake them in the morning – so easy if you're moving a little slower than usual. — MATT

Drain and rinse the beans.

Heat a splash of oil in a cast-iron pot over a medium heat. Sauté the onion, capsicum and chilli until the onions are soft but not yet brown. Add the garlic, spices and bay leaves and stir well. Cover and cook for 2–3 minutes until fragrant, stirring occasionally (it's okay if everything sticks a bit at this stage – just add a little more oil if it's too dry).

Add the beans, stir well, cover and leave for another 2–3 minutes. Add enough water to *just* cover the beans, stir well and bring to the boil. Reduce to a simmer, cover and cook until the beans are butter-soft (about 2½–3 hours).

When the beans are ready, remove the pot from the heat and stir in the passata, fat hen, sugar, salt and 2 tablespoons of oil. At this point we usually leave the beans to cool, and then pop them in the fridge to bake the following morning – but feel free to head straight into baking.

Preheat the oven to 180°C fan-forced.

You can either distribute the beans and gravy into four mini cast-iron pots or ramekins, or place in one deep, ovenproof frying pan. Bake uncovered for 45 minutes.

Remove the pots from the oven and gently crack an egg into each one (or crack all eggs into the one pan) and bake uncovered until the eggs are just set, about 6–7 minutes. Serve steaming hot with a little squeeze of lemon and parsley sprinkled on top.

Notes.

Fat hen can be replaced with any other deep and strongly flavoured cooking green, like silverbeet/chard, spinach, warrigal greens, collard greens or kale.

For a vegan version of this recipe, simply omit the eggs.

Sweet potato & almond breakfast bread.

MAKES 1 X 900 G LOAF (SERVES 8)
TIME: 1 HOUR

3 eggs

110 g (⅓ cup) unprocessed honey

125 ml (½ cup) extra-virgin olive oil

200 g (2 cups) almond meal

60 g buckwheat flour

1 teaspoon ground cinnamon

1 teaspoon vanilla extract

1 teaspoon bicarbonate of soda

a pinch of unrefined salt

juice of ½ small lemon

2 tablespoons chia seeds

45 g (½ cup) walnuts, cut into small chunks

300 g sweet potato, cooked and mashed to a puree

Bananas don't grow where we are, as it's too cold. So this is our version of banana bread, using sweet potatoes instead. An easy breakfast full of lots of good stuff – sweet potatoes, almonds, chia, honey, eggs, olive oil – and it's refined sugar free, dairy free and gluten free – it's free of all the things! It's an awesome combination of flavours that just work together, and it will get your day off to a good start – slice it, toast it and cover with butter.

Preheat the oven to 160°C fan-forced.

Place the eggs, honey, olive oil, almond meal, buckwheat flour, cinnamon, vanilla, bicarbonate of soda, salt and lemon juice in a high-powered blender. Stir with a spoon first, and then process on high until everything is combined and the mixture becomes a thick paste. Pour into a bowl and fold in the chia seeds, walnuts and sweet potato until just combined (don't over mix). Set aside for 10 minutes.

Liberally oil a 20 cm x 10 cm bread tin. Spoon the batter into the tin, tapping the bottom on the bench to even out the mixture. Bake for 45–50 minutes, or until a skewer inserted into the centre comes out clean. Place on a cooling rack to cool completely, before storing in the fridge in an airtight container, or freezing. Toast slices for an easy breakfast.

Note. It is key that the sweet potato is *really* well mashed!

FIELD NOTES

On growing sweet potatoes. Sweet potatoes are an incredibly ancient crop and are super easy to grow. We used to get told that we couldn't grow them in our temperate climate, but we decided to ignore the naysayers one year, and have been growing abundant, healthy crops of sweet potatoes ever since.

As with potatoes, sweet potatoes are most easily grown by sprouting a tuber from last year's harvest. It's a very simple process; all it takes is a little patience. Towards the end of winter we fill seedling trays with a single layer of sweet potatoes and just barely cover them with soil. We keep them moist, but not wet, and over the following weeks little green sprouts called 'slips' begin to grow. When the slips are about 10 cm tall, we gently separate them from their seed tuber right at the base and pop them in a glass of water. They sprout delicate white roots over the next few days and are then ready to plant in the garden! The process can also be done without soil, by suspending sweet potatoes in glasses of water. We have successfully used this technique, but we find the soil technique easier, because you don't have to keep changing the water.

The sweet potato greens will also creep on a trellis. Growing them in this way concentrates all of the tubers in the one place, making it a great technique for the home garden. See the *Grow* chapter for more information.

To share.

Little bits and pieces.

Green tahini.

Something special happens when you combine coriander, parsley, tahini and a little acidity. This is so good with tomatoes, oil, salt, pepper and fresh sourdough bread – an autumn favourite. See an awesome breakfast suggestion using green tahini on page 252.

MAKES ABOUT 900 G
TIME: 10 MINUTES

300 g tahini

125 ml (½ cup) extra-virgin olive oil

3½ tablespoons lemon juice

1½ tablespoons apple cider vinegar

100 g coriander, stalks and all, roughly chopped

100 g parsley, stalks and all, roughly chopped

2 garlic cloves

½ teaspoon unrefined salt

¼ teaspoon ground black pepper

Place all of the ingredients in a blender with 190 ml of water and blend until they form a thick paste.

It will keep in an airtight container in the fridge for a week or more.

Hummus with green chilli oil.

There seem to be a million hummus recipes, and we feel like we've tried them all! This one is our hands-down favourite. It's silky, deeply savoury and perfectly spiced, and it's completely addictive with the green chilli oil – a brilliant combination.

MAKES 500 ML
TIME: 10 MINUTES

Hummus

260 g (1½ cups) cooked chickpeas
(as per preparation guide on page 147)

100 ml extra-virgin olive oil

3 tablespoons lemon juice

2½ tablespoons ground cumin

½ teaspoon unrefined salt

¼ teaspoon ground black pepper

1 garlic clove, roughly chopped

100 g hulled tahini

ground sumac, to serve

Green chilli oil

1 hot green chilli (fresh or dried), finely chopped

3 tablespoons extra-virgin olive oil

Place the chickpeas, olive oil, lemon juice, cumin, salt, pepper, garlic and 125 ml (½ cup) of water in a blender and blend until well combined. Add the tahini and blend again until combined.

For the chilli oil, grind the chilli and oil using a mortar and pestle until combined.

Place the hummus in a bowl and drizzle over the chilli oil. Sprinkle some sumac over the top and serve.

Olive tapenade.

Throughout rural Australia you will find olives growing wild – they grow on the riverbanks where we live – as they are a super hardy plant and their seeds are spread rapidly by birds. The fruit of wild trees is generally smaller than fruit from the Kalamata groves, but it's super tasty. Every year we harvest and preserve them (see page 210), and we always seem to preserve more than we can eat! So this is a classic tapenade we have on hand for quick sandwiches, or a simple summer pasta with fresh cherry tomatoes, basil and feta. Pitting olives might seem like a chore, but if there was ever a reason to do it, this is it – and you only use a little at a time, so a little bit goes a long way!

MAKES 375 ML
TIME: 20 MINUTES

400 g (4 cups) brined olives (see page 210), pitted (you should end up with about 2 cups pitted olives)

8 anchovy fillets

4 garlic cloves, sliced

juice of 2 lemons

100 g parsley, stalks and all, finely chopped

10 thyme sprigs, leaves picked

1 teaspoon ground black pepper

1 dried red chilli

2 tablespoons extra-virgin olive oil

Place all of the ingredients in a blender and blend to your desired consistency, adding a little more lemon juice to balance the salt, if needed. Serve immediately, or store in a jar with a little olive oil poured on top to seal for up to 6 months in the fridge (although it never lasts that long in our hungry house!).

Note. If your olives are particularly salty, try soaking them overnight in cold water before pitting.

Roast beetroot & lemon dip.

There is just something special that happens when you take a super-earthy vegetable like beetroot and combine it with tangy yoghurt and lemon – a perfect balance. Dips like this are the best thing to have in the fridge for when you want to eat vegetables but just don't have the time to prepare them.

MAKES 800 ML
TIME: 1 HOUR

1 kg beetroot

1 lemon, quartered and pips removed, plus extra lemon juice

4 garlic cloves, peeled

extra-virgin olive oil

1½ teaspoons coriander seeds

½ teaspoon ground cinnamon

1½ teaspoons sweet paprika

100 g walnuts

250 g (1 cup) natural yoghurt (see page 170)

¼ teaspoon unrefined salt, plus extra

Preheat the oven to 180°C fan-forced.

Remove the beet tops and cut into quarters. Place the beets, lemon quarters and garlic on a baking tray, drizzle with a little olive oil, sprinkle over the spices and mix thoroughly with your hands. Roast for about 40 minutes until the beets are soft on the inside and crisp on the outside. Set aside to cool.

Once cool enough to touch, tip the contents of the tray into a blender (make sure you get all of the lemon and toasted seeds in there!). Add the walnuts, yoghurt, salt and 1 tablespoon of olive oil and blend until smooth. Adjust with lemon juice and salt if necessary.

Rillettes (ree-yet).

Slow-cooked meat, fresh herbs, sweet spices and port – in a jar. Amazing! Perfect for share plates and easy ploughman-style meals. We make this after we make waste bone stock (see page 180), using the remaining meat from the bones. While this is a great recipe for using that leftover meat, you can of course just use slow-cooked pulled meat pieces that you have precooked.

MAKES 620 G
TIME: 15 MINUTES

600 g pulled pork

10 thyme sprigs, leaves picked

1 teaspoon unrefined salt

2 teaspoons ground nutmeg

1 teaspoon ground black pepper

zest and juice of 1 lemon

2 tablespoons tawny port or sherry

1 tablespoon stock (see page 180) or water

50 g lard, melted (see page 179) or extra-virgin olive oil or butter

Place all of the ingredients in a blender except the lard and pulse on low until just combined – don't blend on high or it will become a paste, and you want it to stay a little chunky.

Divide the rillettes into jars, leaving about 1 cm of space at the top, cover with a thin layer of lard and seal. The rillettes will keep for up to 3 weeks in the fridge if the lard seal remains unbroken, but only a week once it has. Or freeze for up to 3 months.

Pâté.

This pâté is brimming with B vitamins from the liver. It's also earthy, sweet and completely moreish!

MAKES 400 G
TIME: 20 MINUTES + 8–12 HOURS SOAKING

600 g liver (we used kangaroo, but lamb and poultry livers are also amazing), trimmed

1 teaspoon unrefined salt, plus extra

300 g butter, cubed

1 French shallot, finely chopped

10 thyme sprigs, leaves picked

4 allspice berries, ground

1 teaspoon ground black pepper

150 ml tawny port or sherry

Soak the liver in water with a pinch of salt for 8 hours or overnight to draw out the blood and impurities.

Strain the purged liver and pat dry. If using chicken livers, leave whole. If using a larger liver, cut into chunks roughly similar to the size of a chicken liver.

Melt a few cubes of the butter in a large skillet or frying pan over a medium heat. Add the shallots, thyme and spices and sauté until the shallots have softened. Transfer to a blender and return the skillet to the heat without wiping clean.

Sauté the liver with a little more butter until browned on the outside but still just pink on the inside. Add to the blender and again return the skillet to the heat without wiping clean.

Add the port or sherry to the skillet and bring to the boil. Reduce the heat and simmer for a few minutes until thick. Add to the blender with all but 50 g of the remaining butter and blend until smooth. Divide the pâté between jars, leaving 1 cm space at the top.

Melt the remaining butter and pour a thin layer on top of each jar. Set in the fridge for at least 2 hours before eating. The pâté will keep for up to 3 weeks in the fridge if the butter seal remains unbroken, but only 1 week once it has. Freeze for up to 3 months.

Baked polenta crisps.

Have leftover polenta? This is what you want to do with it. These are super delicious – crispy corn with just a little bit of spice. They pair perfectly with labne (see page 171) or any of our dips (see pages 268–69).

Preheat the oven to 130°C. Grease two large baking trays liberally with butter.

Using wet hands, spread the polenta onto the trays, pressing down to form a very thin layer (about 1–2 mm thick). Basically, you want to get the polenta as thin as you can without it breaking apart.

Brush on 3 tablespoons of oil with a pastry brush then sprinkle with salt, pepper, garlic, chilli and za'atar. Brush again to even out the ingredients and bake for 50–60 minutes until crispy and thin. They should be super thin, almost transparent in parts, crisp and easy to break apart. They should not be burnt, just browned.

When your polenta sheets are ready, break up into corn-chip-sized crisps and serve immediately. These are incredible with any of our dips (see pages 268–69) or, our favourite, fresh labne sprinkled with paprika and drizzled with olive oil.

SERVES 4
TIME: 1 HOUR 5 MINUTES

4 cups cooked polenta (as per preparation guide on page 145)

3 tablespoons extra-virgin olive oil, plus extra

½ teaspoon unrefined salt

½ teaspoon ground black pepper

2 garlic cloves, crushed

3 dried chillies, finely chopped

1 tablespoon ground za'atar (see field notes)

FIELD NOTES

On growing za'atar. These days, the term za'atar has come to represent a herb and spice blend that includes sesame seeds, oregano, basil thyme, thyme proper, savoury (a woody herb) and sometimes other spices like caraway and sumac. But this was not always the case. Za'atar is actually a rare wild herb – otherwise known as biblical hyssop or wild hyssop – which, when you taste it, kind of makes you feel like the spice blend za'atar was created as a really great 'I know this isn't the real deal but it's pretty close at least, right?' kinda substitute. The reality is that za'atar *is* a lot like oregano. But it is also incredibly similar to basil thyme. And thyme proper. *And* savoury. All at the same time! Although za'atar the spice mix is a close substitute (and delicious), there is nothing quite like the original.

Fortunately, we don't have to mimic anymore. The seeds of this desert mountain herb are now readily available, and we highly recommend growing your own. If you know someone with a plant, you can even just break off a branch near the base, pop it in a glass of water until little roots begin to sprout, and then plant it straight in the soil. It is incredibly hardy and a super-rewarding herb to grow.

Pan-fried cardoon chips.

SERVES 4–6
TIME: 40 MINUTES

8–10 cardoon stalks (about 450 g in total), prepared (see field notes and diagram below) and cut into 10 cm batons

ghee (see page 166), for frying

340 g (2 cups) finely ground white rice flour

unrefined salt

ground black pepper

6 eggs

To serve

⅓ cup mayonnaise (see page 182)

1 tablespoon mustard (see page 182)

ketchup (see page 222)

Cardoons are a mystery vegetable. Before we grew them we had no idea what to do with them, nor had we ever eaten them before. They look like an artichoke plant, but they don't have such big edible heads. Instead you eat their stalks, which look like giant celery stalks. The bad news is that you probably won't be able to find cardoons in stores. The good news is they are one of the easiest plants to grow, and you can often find them growing in the wild. While they taste a little like an artichoke, they have a unique flavour that is light and a little bit smoky. This is by far the greatest thing you can do with a cardoon.

Cook the cardoons in boiling salted water (salty like the sea!) for 15–20 minutes until soft. Drain and pat dry with a tea towel.

Combine the mayonnaise and mustard in one small serving bowl or ramekin, and place the ketchup in another.

Heat 0.5–1 cm of ghee in a large frying pan over a medium–high heat.

Meanwhile, divide the rice flour between two small bowls and season with a pinch of salt and pepper. Whisk the eggs in a third bowl. Working in batches, coat the cardoons in the egg, then the first bowl of rice flour, then back into the egg and finally into the second bowl of rice flour.

Fry the cardoons for about 5 minutes on each side until brown.

Serve immediately with the mustard-mayonnaise and ketchup on the side.

Note. As this recipe requires frying at a high heat, we use ghee for its very high smoke point – plus it's delicious! See page 166 for instructions on making your own ghee.

FIELD NOTES

On growing cardoons. You can either grow a cardoon from seed, or by digging up its root system and replanting it. To plant it from rootstock, cut off the top of the plant, dig a big hole and put it in the ground. Its root system is one of the hardiest we have ever seen; it can be transported and even cut up a little and it will still grow. It requires little water and loves full sun! It will also produce big, beautiful, purple flowers for you, and its leaves act as great mulch in the garden.

On preparing cardoons. Cut the plant at the base, one section at a time. You want the big thick stalks that are flatter and paler (often the young stalks), and discard anything hollow, along with the top leaves and any debris. Trim the edges of the cardoon with a sharp knife. Using a vegetable peeler, peel the ridged side of the stalk, removing any stringy sections. Scrape the smooth inside section with a spoon to remove the fine skin and place in water with a squeeze of lemon juice to prevent browning. Your cardoon is now prepared.

Pickled cabbage rolls.

Everything about these makes me happy: the flavour of the fermented cabbage, the rice, olives, tomatoes, herbs, spices, olive oil and the overall crunch and richness. They are literally one of my favourite things on the whole planet. If I could just eat these with pickles and our bread for the rest of my life, I would probably be the happiest little lady in the world. It's like there is something genetically wired in me to love these. – LENTIL

For the filling, place the onion, garlic, capsicum, passata, olives, herbs and olive oil in a blender and blend on low for 20 seconds until just combined.

Heat a large frying pan over a medium heat and quickly fry the pepper and paprika with a little extra olive oil until fragrant. Add the contents of the blender to the pan and simmer, covered, for about 20 minutes. By this time it should have become a thick and fragrant sauce. Add the rice, salt and lemon juice to the pan, turn off the heat and stir gently.

Meanwhile, make the sauce by sweating the onion and pepper with a splash of oil in a saucepan over a medium heat. Add the remaining ingredients and whisk to combine. Simmer, covered, for 20–30 minutes.

While the sauce cooks, take a whole cabbage leaf and cut off most of the hard outer vein with a small knife, being careful not to break the leaf. Place a spoonful of stuffing mixture into the lower middle of the leaf and wrap up like a parcel (see diagram below). Repeat until all of the filling is used.

Once rolled, place the cabbage rolls in a shallow baking dish and pour the hot sauce over the top. Cover, leave to cool to room temperature (your cabbage rolls will gently poach as they cool) and then refrigerate.

Eat these cold. We love to serve them with hummus and sourdough bread.

Note. If you don't have fermented cabbage, simply blanch the large outer leaves of the largest cabbage you can find in boiling water with a big splash of vinegar and a big pinch of salt until *just* soft.

MAKES 15–25 CABBAGE ROLLS
TIME: 50 MINUTES

Cabbage rolls

2 large onions, roughly chopped

2 garlic cloves

1 red capsicum, cut into chunks

125 ml (½ cup) thick passata (see page 221)

100 g black olives, pitted

a small handful of dill, stalks and all, finely chopped

a small handful of parsley, stalks and all, finely chopped

5 oregano sprigs, leaves picked and finely chopped

125 ml (½ cup) extra-virgin olive oil, plus extra

½ teaspoon ground black pepper

1 teaspoon sweet paprika

3 cups cooked brown rice (as per preparation guide on page 141)

½ teaspoon unrefined salt

80 ml (⅓ cup) lemon juice

15–25 fermented cabbage leaves (see page 201) or blanched cabbage leaves (see note)

Sauce

1 large onion, diced

½ teaspoon ground black pepper

3 tablespoons extra-virgin olive oil

500 ml (2 cups) passata (see page 221)

⅓ bunch of parsley (about 50 g), stalks and all, finely chopped

2 teaspoons unrefined sugar (e.g. rapadura)

1 teaspoon apple cider vinegar

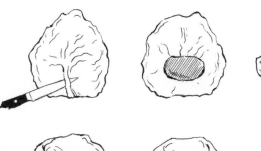

Salt & pepper peppers.

extra-virgin olive oil

400 g padron or other sweet green peppers

unrefined salt

ground black pepper

It really doesn't get any simpler than this. I was first introduced to these incredible gems by Andy (mentor #2). We'd just harvested the first haul of padron peppers for the season, and Andy had a little game he wanted to play. He fried a big batch up as below and sat us all down. Padron peppers are a type of green-picked pepper that are like Russian roulette to eat. Most of them are deliciously fruity and sweet, with only the faintest chilli heat. But every now and then (about one in six) they're crazy HOT!! And so we sat around the table and played the game, taking it in turns to blindly grab a pepper and start munching before the heat (or not) kicked in. Every year since, we've grown a new variety of peppers in our patch just to make this dish. This is a super-fast, incredibly delicious and achingly addictive snack for all occasions. – MATT

Place a cast-iron skillet over a medium heat and add a glug of oil. Add as many peppers as will fit in a single layer in the pan and scatter over a generous pinch of salt and pepper.

Cover and steam-fry for about 10 minutes, shaking and checking occasionally, until the peppers are blistered, a bit blackened and melt-in-your-mouth soft.

Serve in batches as soon as they're ready and repeat until all peppers are cooked. They're still great after they've cooled too.

Vegetables.

To include in every meal.

Caponata.

SERVES 4 AS A SIDE OR 2 AS A MAIN
TIME: 45 MINUTES

1 onion, diced

1 dried chilli, torn into pieces

½ teaspoon ground black pepper

extra-virgin olive oil

3 garlic cloves, crushed

1 large red capsicum,
roughly chopped

1 large eggplant, roughly chopped

1 tablespoon balsamic vinegar

1 teaspoon unrefined sugar
(e.g. rapadura)

½ teaspoon unrefined salt

350 g very ripe cooking tomatoes
(see field notes), roughly chopped

100 g black olives (see page 210),
pitted

5 parsley sprigs, stalks and all,
finely chopped

5 Greek oregano sprigs, leaves
picked and finely chopped

½ cup well-packed basil leaves,
torn

½ lemon

Maybe it's my Italian heritage coming out, but I think there is no other dish so perfect for warm autumn days, and none so wonderful a celebration of autumn's bright vegetables than the humble caponata! Our version of caponata isn't just about eggplant like most are. Here, the fruity, sweet red capsicum and super ripe and jammy tomatoes demand equal attention. And so they should. Combined, the trio is more magical than any one of them on their own. Add to that last season's preserved olives and you have a dish that will hopefully become as much a staple in your home as it has in ours. – MATT

Place a large, shallow frying pan over a medium–high heat. Sauté the onion, chilli and pepper in a generous splash of oil until the onion has softened but not yet started to brown. Add the garlic and continue to sauté until the garlic begins to brown.

Add the capsicum, eggplant, balsamic, sugar and salt and continue to cook for 10 minutes, stirring occasionally – add a little water to the pan if it starts to stick. Add the tomatoes, olives, parsley and oregano, stir well and cover. Cook, stirring occasionally, until the eggplant has completely broken down (about 15–20 minutes).

Remove from the heat, stir through the basil, squeeze over the lemon and drizzle with a generous splash of oil. Serve hot or cold with buttered sourdough and plenty of red wine!

FIELD NOTES

On tomatoes. There are two types of tomatoes: salad and cooking. Salad tomatoes – or slicing tomatoes – are juicier and sweeter raw. Common varieties are cherry-type and beefsteak-type tomatoes. Cooking tomatoes – often called saucing, sauce, paste or bottling tomatoes – are much denser, and their sweetness really sings after cooking. Common types are Roma and Amish paste. In both cases, home-grown tomatoes, picked fully ripe straight off the vine, leave all other tomatoes for dead. If you can, plant yourself a tomato plant. If you can't, steer clear of the supermarket and head to the farmers' market, because if there's one thing supermarkets do not do well, it's tomatoes.

Sweet & spicy turnips.

SERVES 4
TIME: 45 MINUTES

600 g small to medium turnips and their tops (see note)

extra-virgin olive oil

unrefined salt

Reduction

45 g (⅓ cup) sultanas

45 g prunes, pitted

1 teaspoon unrefined sugar (e.g. rapadura)

1 dried chilli

juice of ½ a lemon

juice of ½ an orange

1 clove

1 star anise

To serve

3 tablespoons toasted almonds, roughly chopped

3 tablespoons toasted pumpkin seeds

a handful of sultanas

There is a common misconception that all turnips are good for is soup. But turnips are, in fact, delicious when partnered with the right flavours, and the tops are a fantastic cooking green, tasting a bit like spicy broccoli.

Preheat the oven to 180°C fan-forced.

Cut any medium-sized turnips in half and leave any smaller ones whole. Add them to a saucepan of boiling salted water (salty like the sea!) and boil for 8–10 minutes until just tender.

Drain, pat dry, place on a baking tray and bake for 5 minutes. Coat the turnips in oil, season with a pinch of salt and roast for 20–30 minutes until soft and golden.

While the turnips are cooking, make the reduction. Place the sultanas, prunes, sugar, chilli, lemon juice, orange juice and 125 ml (½ cup) of water in a blender and process until smooth. Tip the mixture into a heavy-based saucepan and add the clove and star anise. Bring to the boil then reduce the heat to low. Cook, uncovered, until the mixture thickens (about 20 minutes).

About 5 or so minutes before the reduction is ready, strip the leaves from the stalks of the turnip tops. Cut the leaves coarsely, and slice the stalks finely.

Heat a big splash of oil in a frying pan over a medium heat. Add the turnip tops and sauté until wilted. Add a splash of water and season, then cover and cook until the tops have softened.

To serve, add the cooked turnips and tops to a large bowl and spoon over the reduction. Sprinkle the almonds, pumpkin seeds and sultanas on top and finish with a splash of oil.

Note. If you can't get turnips with tops for this recipe, use kale as a substitute for the tops. And if you can't get turnips themselves (or swede, turnip's cousin), try the dish with kale and an entirely different root vegetable like carrots.

FIELD NOTES

On growing turnips. Turnips are always more delicious after a frost, because once they get frozen in the ground they become sweeter in flavour. When you grow them well, you should also get big, luscious green tops to use as cooking greens.

On boiling vegetables. When boiling or blanching vegetables, always liberally salt the water. It is a wonderful way to bring out the natural flavour of the vegetables and enhance their digestibility, while also ensuring all of the nutrients remain in your food, rather than leaching out into the water. Don't worry, it won't make things taste salty, just seasoned. The salt blocks the water-soluble vitamins from crossing the cell walls of the vegetable, keeping them right where you want them. And their stunning colour is testament to the nutrient density that is retained.

Melted miso eggplant with green beans.

SERVES 4 AS A SIDE OR 2 AS A MAIN
TIME: 30 MINUTES

toasted sesame oil

1 large eggplant, sliced into
1.5 cm-thick rounds

350 g green beans

1 tablespoon light and/or black
sesame seeds, lightly toasted

Marinade

1 tablespoon mirin

1 tablespoon miso
(your choice of dark or light)

Dressing

1 tablespoon tahini

1 tablespoon mirin

1 tablespoon lemon juice

When the first eggplants of the season ripen, this is the dish we make. It really is the best method for cooking eggplants! They just dissolve into a creamy, sweet and savoury miso mess of deliciousness that can't be beaten. We've found green beans to be the ultimate companion. They stay crisp and fresh by comparison – the perfect contrast. We trade for all of our traditional Japanese ferments with our awesome friends Yumi and Taka. Thanks legends! One day we will nail making them ourselves. This is great as a side dish or main. Pair it with basic steamed brown *koshihikari* rice and a glass of saké – now this is food!

For the marinade, place the mirin and miso in a shallow bowl with 2 tablespoons of water and mix to form a thick sauce.

Heat a generous splash of sesame oil in a large cast-iron skillet over a medium heat. When hot, add a single layer of eggplant and fry for 1 minute on each side. Cover and steam-fry for an additional 2 minutes.

Remove the eggplant from the skillet. Place in a bowl, coat with the marinade and leave to soak. Repeat the process until all of the eggplant is cooked and marinating, adding more oil to the skillet as needed.

Place the beans in the skillet, cover and steam-fry for about 4 minutes, shaking occasionally, until soft and a little blackened. Remove from the skillet and set aside.

Return the marinated eggplant to the skillet in a single layer and fry on both sides until the flesh is totally 'melted' and the marinade has caramelised – you may need to do this in batches, depending on the size of your pan.

Meanwhile, combine the dressing ingredients and any remaining marinade in a jar and shake well.

Arrange the beans in a layer on a serving plate and top with the melted eggplant. Pour the dressing over the top and finish off with a sprinkle of sesame seeds. Serve steaming hot with rice and a cup of saké.

Honey leek cannelloni.

This is a simple dish, with a perfect balance of sweet and savoury flavours. It's a fun play on traditional Italian cannelloni and is all about using leeks when they're at their biggest. I think of it as a dish to celebrate the largest member of the allium family (onions, garlic, leeks, spring onions, garlic chives and chives are all alliums).

Preheat the oven to 190°C fan-forced.

Cut the leeks into 10 cm batons and blanch in a large saucepan of boiling salted water (salty like the sea!) for 2–4 minutes until just softened. Drain and refresh under cold water.

Gently push the centres out of the leeks with a chopstick or something similar (they should come out easily). You will now have several tubes of leek. Place the tubes on a tray and set aside. Finely chop the leek centres.

Sauté the chopped leek with a big knob of butter in a medium–hot frying pan until soft.

Transfer the sautéed leeks to a bowl. Add the ricotta, garlic, sumac, preserved lemon, honey, olive oil and a pinch of salt and mix well.

Using the back of a spoon, stuff the leek and ricotta mixture into the leek tubes and place on a baking tray. Drizzle the cannelloni with a little extra honey and oil, cover with another baking tray and bake for about 30 minutes until soft.

Once soft, remove the cover and turn the oven to the grill setting. Grill the cannelloni for a further 5 minutes until brown.

Note. Leftover stuffing mixture is great on toast, or with roast vegetables!

SERVES 4 (ABOUT 8 CANNELLONI)
TIME: 45 MINUTES

4 large leeks (about 1 kg in total), roots trimmed and dark green tops removed

a knob of butter

150 g ricotta (see page 176)

1 large garlic clove, crushed

½ teaspoon ground sumac

1 teaspoon finely chopped preserved lemon (see page 212)

1 tablespoon unprocessed honey, plus extra

1 tablespoon extra-virgin olive oil, plus extra

unrefined salt

FIELD NOTES

On growing leeks. You can basically grow leeks all year round, but they are at their biggest in autumn, winter and spring, which is when we recommend making this recipe. You can, of course, make these in summer, but they'll just be smaller.

End of summer fattoush.

SERVES 4 AS A SIDE OR 2 AS A MAIN
TIME: 25 MINUTES

Salad

2 soured wholegrain pizza bases
(see page 157)

4 very ripe heirloom salad
tomatoes, coarsely chopped

1 cos lettuce, outer leaves
discarded, heart coarsely chopped

2 Lebanese-style cucumbers, diced

4 radishes, finely sliced

a few very fine slices of red onion

8 parsley sprigs, stalks and all,
finely chopped

8 mint sprigs, leaves picked and
finely chopped

4 dill pickles (see page 198), diced

Dressing

80 ml (⅓ cup) extra-virgin olive oil

80 g (⅓ cup) natural yoghurt
(see page 170)

2 garlic cloves, crushed

juice of 1 lemon

⅓ cup dried za'atar leaves
(see note)

1 teaspoon ground sumac

1 teaspoon unrefined salt

½ teaspoon ground black pepper,

Fattoush is all about using up leftover flatbread. But we think it's so good that we cook whole batches of our soured wholegrain pizza bases just so we can make it! The toasted pizza bases bring a deep nuttiness that combines with the crisp lettuce, sweet tomatoes and piquant and salty yoghurt dressing to form an amazing flavour. The taste dances from sweet to tart to salty and back to sweet again so smoothly that you just have to go back for more. The key to this dish is using fresh vegetables. If you can, pick them straight out of your garden!

Preheat the oven to 180°C fan-forced.

Bake the pizza bases directly on the oven shelves for even heat circulation until crisply toasted. Set aside to cool.

Combine the dressing ingredients in a jar and shake well.

Combine the remaining salad ingredients in a large mixing bowl, pour over the dressing and mix thoroughly with your hands. Set aside for 15 minutes.

Just before serving, break the toasted pizza bases into bite-sized pieces and mix through the salad. This ensures the bread is still super crunchy when it hits the table. Enjoy.

Note. When we say za'atar, we mean the herb za'atar (wild hyssop – see field notes on page 275), not the spice mix that includes sesame seeds etc. If you can't find dried za'atar, we highly recommend you grow some. But in the meantime, substitute with dried Greek oregano or wild oregano.

Mixed grain & sprout pilaf.

SERVES 4 AS A SIDE OR 2 AS A MAIN
TIME: 20 MINUTES

extra-virgin olive oil

1 small onion or
French shallot, diced

1 carrot, grated

½ cup sultanas

1 teaspoon fennel seeds

1 teaspoon cumin seeds

1 teaspoon ground cinnamon
or 1 cinnamon stick

1 teaspoon ground black pepper

3 tablespoons coarsley
chopped almonds

3 tablespoons pumpkin seeds

1½ cups cooked mixed whole
gluten-free grains (e.g. brown
rice, buckwheat, quinoa) (as per
preparation guide on page 141)

1½ cups mixed sprouts
(e.g. mung bean, lentil)
(see sprouting guide on page 148)

½ teaspoon unrefined salt

juice of ½ lemon

10 mint sprigs, leaves picked
and finely chopped

While a pilaf wouldn't normally make it into a vegetables chapter, in this case we decided to make an exception. It's all about the sprouts. Sprouts, although grains and beans to begin with, are totally transformed by the sprouting process (see our guide on page 148). As such, they are much closer to a tiny young plant or vegetable than they are to the grain or bean they once were. And, given this salad contains as many sprouts as it does cooked grains – well, here we are. This is a wonderful, classic pilaf full of warm Middle Eastern flavours, bright mint freshness and just a little sweetness from the sultanas. The sprouts bring a textural crispness not common in a pilaf, and the nuts and seeds the expected crunch. A simple beautiful meal all on its own, or a versatile side dish.

Heat a generous splash of oil in a large, shallow frying pan over a medium heat. Sauté the onion, carrot, sultanas, spices and pepper until the onion is soft and beginning to brown.

Add the almonds and pumpkin seeds and continue cooking until lightly toasted and fragrant. Add the grains, sprouts and salt and mix thoroughly, adding a little oil if it's sticking too much.

When well combined, remove from the heat and add the lemon juice, a little more oil and the mint. Gently stir through and serve steaming hot.

Mustard, carrots, cauliflower & lentils.

Mustard, honey and carrots were just born to be together. Throw in cauliflower and lentils and you've got an incredible dish. This is a year-round dish in our house. Its flavour is grounded from the lentils and sharp from the lemon, and it packs a mustard punch. Combining vegetables with a pulse (peas, beans or lentils) always makes for a robust salad that carries enough depth to be eaten as a quick and super-healthy meal. We always have some cooked lentils or beans sitting in the fridge ready to go (see page 147) to add to salads like this.

Preheat the oven to 180°C fan-forced.

For the dressing, grind the mustard seeds using a mortar and pestle until about half are ground and half are just cracked. Add the remaining dressing ingredients and continue to grind gently until combined.

Cut the cauliflower into rough 4 cm florets and 1 cm-thick slices of stem and add to a bowl with the carrots. Add the mustard dressing and combine thoroughly with your hands. Spread the vegetables out on a baking tray in a single layer and roast for 1 hour, or until the vegetables are super tender on the inside and just beginning to blacken around the edges.

Meanwhile, for the vinaigrette, place the oil and lemon juice in a jar, season to taste, seal with the lid and shake well.

Place the mustard greens in a serving bowl, pour over the vinaigrette and roughly massage with your hands to bruise the leaves. Add the lentils and toss gently. Set aside for the flavours to come together while the vegetables continue to roast.

When the vegetables are ready, add them to the greens and lentils and gently combine. Serve immediately.

Notes.

Olive oil has a smoke point of around 200–210°C, so roasting at 180°C ensures the flavour of the vegetables, not burnt oil, is what you taste.

If you don't have a mortar and pestle, use a high-powered blender.

To make a vegan version of this recipe, replace the honey with unrefined sugar.

SERVES 4 AS A SIDE OR 2 AS A MAIN
TIME: 1 HOUR 15 MINUTES

½ head of cauliflower
(about 400 g)

400 g Dutch carrots
(or larger carrots cut to a similar size), trimmed to leave 1 cm of green stem

120 g mustard greens,
coarsely chopped

1½ cups cooked puy lentils (as per preparation guide on page 147)

Mustard dressing

1 tablespoon yellow mustard seeds

2 tablespoons extra-virgin olive oil

1 tablespoon unprocessed honey

¼ preserved lemon
(see page 212), finely chopped

Vinaigrette

2 tablespoons extra-virgin olive oil

juice of 1 large lemon

unrefined salt

ground black pepper

FIELD NOTES

On growing cauliflowers. You can grow cauliflowers all year round. Growing cauliflowers in peak summer can be a challenge, but with the right varieties and a whole lot of dill and garlic chives planted around them to ward off white cabbage moths, grubs and aphids, it's absolutely possible.

Fried paneer
& summer squash.

SERVES 4 AS A SIDE OR 2 AS A MAIN
TIME: 10 MINUTES

2 tablespoons butter

extra-virgin olive oil

1 kg summer squash (and/or
zucchini), cut into 6 mm slices

300–400 g paneer (see page 176),
cut into 6 mm slices

unrefined salt

ground black pepper

1 large lemon

Sometimes you just need something super quick, super simple and super tasty to put on the table. This is a celebration of the humble summer squash, one of our all-time favourite vegetables, and although simple, it should not be underestimated. Cooked in this way, summer squash is nutty and sweet, with overtones reminiscent of sweet corn. The paneer is a superb companion to the squash – a little chewy, just the right amount of oily and perfectly aromatic as the nigella seeds toast in the pan. Simple but not stupid.

Heat a small knob of butter and a splash of oil in a cast-iron skillet over a medium heat. Add equal amounts of squash and paneer slices in a single layer until the skillet is full. Sprinkle over a little pinch of salt and pepper and cook for 1–2 minutes until browned on the underside.

Flip the slices and sprinkle over another little pinch of salt and pepper. Cook for 1–2 minutes until browned – if the paneer starts to get too dark, just pop them on top of the squash slices until they are ready too.

Transfer the cooked slices to a serving plate and squeeze over some lemon juice. Repeat until all of the squash and paneer are cooked, adding more oil and butter as needed.

Serve steaming hot.

Note. Our paneer recipe (see page 176) includes nigella seeds. If you buy pre-made paneer, simply scatter some nigella seeds over each batch as it cooks – makes all the difference!

Mains.

Big meals to share, best paired with vegetables.

Chickpea & cauliflower bowls.

SERVES 4
TIME: 1 HOUR

120 g (½ cup) tahini

125 g (½ cup) natural yoghurt
(see page 170)

½ teaspoon unrefined salt

4 mint sprigs, leaves picked and
finely chopped

6 cups cooked chickpeas (as per
preparation guide on page 147),
cooking liquid reserved

2 soured wholegrain pizza bases
(see page 157), toasted until crisp,
broken into smallish pieces

Roasted cauliflower

1 head of cauliflower
(about 1 kg without leaves),
cut into small florets

1 large onion, diced

3 garlic cloves, crushed

2 teaspoons sweet paprika

2½ teaspoons ground cumin

1 teaspoon ground cinnamon

1 teaspoon ground black pepper

½ teaspoon unrefined salt

extra-virgin olive oil

To serve

3 tablespoons toasted pine nuts
or coarsely chopped almonds

ground sumac

ground cumin

dried chilli flakes (optional)

extra-virgin olive oil

This dish is based on chickpea 'fatteh' (meaning crushed or crumbs) – serious Syrian comfort food. The addition of spiced roast cauliflower to the classic chickpea, yoghurt and tahini combination offers a soft texture and earthy sweetness in perfect contrast to the crunch of the toasted bread and nuts. This is *super-tasty*, *super-nutrient-rich* food! When the colder months are upon you and you come in from outside feeling like you are freezing right to the bone, a warm bowl of these silky, yoghurty chickpeas will make you feel human again.

Preheat the oven to 180°C fan-forced.

Start with the roasted cauliflower. Combine all of the ingredients and a generous splash of oil in a large bowl and mix thoroughly with your hands. Spread in single layers on baking trays and bake for 45–50 minutes until the cauliflower is well cooked, crispy and almost black around the edges.

Meanwhile, place the tahini, yoghurt, salt and mint in a saucepan with half of the cooked chickpeas and 125 ml (½ cup) of the reserved chickpea cooking liquid. Crush the chickpeas with the back of a fork or potato masher and mix together until you form a thick, silky sauce. If it seems too runny, add more chickpeas, if too thick, add more of the reserved cooking liquid. And don't worry if it's not totally smooth.

Add 2 cups of the remaining chickpeas to the sauce and place the pan on the stove. Heat to just below a simmer but don't boil. Keep warm.

When the cauliflower is ready, divide half of the chickpea mixture between four bowls, followed by half of the cauliflower and half of the pizza base pieces. Cover with the remaining chickpea mixture, then top with the reserved plain chickpeas and the remaining cauliflower and pizza pieces. Sprinkle with the pine nuts, a pinch of sumac, cumin and chilli flakes (if using), and a generous drizzle of oil. Serve steaming hot.

Carp masgouf.

SERVES 8
TIME: 1 HOUR
+ 30 MINUTES MARINATING

1 x 1.5 kg carp
(prepared as per page 77)

2 dried persimmons
(see page 234) or pitted dates,
diced (see field notes)

80 ml (⅓ cup) extra-virgin olive oil

½ teaspoon unrefined salt

2 teaspoons ground black pepper

1 teaspoon ground turmeric

1¼ lemons (see field notes)

I was first served this dish in Syria by a proud Iraqi chef, and it remains one of the most delicious dishes of my life. Masgouf is the process of butterflying fish, marinating them in a blend of olive oil, salt, tamarind and turmeric and grilling them beside an open fire. Carp masgouf is so common and loved in Iraq that it has become the unofficial national dish there, and there are restaurants dedicated to it, complete with open ponds and massive flickering fire pits. If you can, do this on an open fire. AMAZING. It is a truly mouth-watering combination of sticky fish, lemon tang and sweetness from the persimmon (or tamarind if you're in the tropics). It also works excellently with other fatty fish like trout or salmon. – MATT

Reverse butterfly your carp by slicing along the top of the head (kitchen shears help here) then all along the back on one side of the spine, cutting through the ribs, all the way to the tail. Remove the entrails, clean thoroughly in cold water and pat dry.

Place the persimmon, olive oil, salt, pepper, turmeric and the juice of 1 lemon in a high-powered blender (or use a mortar and pestle) and blend to a smooth paste.

Place the carp on a tray skin-side down. Pour the marinade over the flesh and rub it in thoroughly with your hands. Set aside to marinate for 30 minutes (refrigerate if it's warm).

If cooking traditionally on a fire. Get your fire going. It only needs to be as wide at its base as your carp is long. The key here is hot coals, so let some hardwood burn strong for about half an hour before knocking it down to a flat bed of burning hot coals.

Place the carp flesh-side down on a metal rack and place the rack directly on or just above the hot coals. Cook for 3–5 minutes, or until the flesh has turned opaque and is beginning to char.

Remove the rack from the coals, carefully turn the carp skin-side down and place the rack back on the coals. Cook for another 3–5 minutes, or until the skin is crispy and charred. Remove the rack from the coals.

If cooking in the kitchen. Preheat the oven to 160°C on the top grill setting to replicate hot coals.

Place the marinated carp flesh-side up on a wire rack over a large roasting tray. Place the tray right at the bottom of the oven (as far away from your grill as the oven will allow) and grill until the flesh is opaque throughout and the exposed surface is getting nice and crispy (about 30 minutes).

Remove the carp from the oven. Turn the grill to its maximum setting.

Place the carp back in the oven, as close to the grill as possible without touching it, for 2 minutes until the flesh is beginning to char a little.

Carefully flip the whole fish over and place it skin-side up in the oven, as close to the grill as possible without touching it, for 2–4 minutes until the skin is crispy and beginning to char. Remove the cooked carp from the oven.

To serve. Serve flesh-side up with the remaining lemon juice squeezed over the top. Large floating bones can be easily removed with a fork before serving, and just pick out the smaller ones as you go. This dish goes beautifully with our mixed grain and sprout pilaf (see page 294) caponata (see page 284) and an end of summer fattoush (see page 292)!

FIELD NOTES

On carp. I know, I know. In Australia, carp would have to have the worst reputation of any fish. They are destroying our waterways, preying on our native fish and basically ruining everything good about the world. I know. To make matters worse, you can't even eat them! Right? Wrong. Carp are delicious. The carp family is one of the most eaten fish in the world. It is nutritious, fatty and succulent, with pure white flesh not unlike chicken. Traditional preparation is key (see page 77), or the carp will be tough and muddy tasting. – MATT

On tamarind. Traditionally, masgouf calls for tamarind. It's hard to get fresh tamarind where we are, but if you live in the tropics, substitute the lemon and persimmon in the marinade with 60 g of freshly prepared tamarind.

Wild mushroom & weed ravioli.

SERVES 4
TIME: 45 MINUTES

200 g pine mushrooms, very finely diced (see gathering notes on page 83)

a knob of butter

unrefined salt

ground black pepper

150 g ricotta (see page 176)

juice of ½ lemon

extra-virgin olive oil

500 g gluten-free or whole-wheat pasta dough (see pages 162–63)

almond meal, to serve

Pesto

70 g fat hen (see gathering notes on page 84)

70 g nettles (see gathering notes on page 84)

unrefined salt

ground black pepper

180 ml (¾ cup) extra-virgin olive oil

2 garlic cloves, crushed

juice of 1 small lemon

30 g (⅓ cup) almond meal

This dish is the very definition of autumn for us, with so many great memories of climbing hills in the silent forest to gather the ingredients. It is so simple, but the combination of flavours gathered from the wild are incredible – flavours you don't get anywhere else. Plus a lot of these ingredients – such as nettles, olive oil and garlic – are cleansing and so great for you in the lead-up to winter! If you can't forage your own weeds and mushrooms, see the notes for some replacement suggestions.

To make the ravioli filling, place the mushrooms in a medium–hot frying pan with the butter, a splash of water and a pinch of salt and pepper. Cover and sauté until the mushrooms fall apart.

Place the mushrooms, ricotta, lemon juice and a splash of oil in a small bowl and mash with a fork until well combined.

For the pesto, sauté the fat hen and nettles in a frying pan over a high heat with a splash of water and a big pinch of salt. Once wilted, remove from the heat and strip the leaves from the stalks as necessary – the young stalks will be fine, but discard the more mature stalks, as they will be tough.

Place the greens and remaining pesto ingredients in a blender (or use a mortar and pestle) and blend to a puree.

Roll the pasta dough out into rectangular sheets that are 10–12 cm wide (see page 162). Dot teaspoons of the ricotta filling evenly along one half of the pasta sheets. Fold the other half of the pasta over the ricotta filling and press around the edges to seal. Cut out the ravioli and trim the edges so that they're nice and neat.

Bring a saucepan of salted water to the boil over a medium–high heat. Carefully add the ravioli and cook for 2–3 minutes until just soft. Using a slotted spoon, lift the cooked ravioli out of the water into a colander to drain.

To serve, divide the ravioli between bowls, cover with pesto and finish with a splash of oil and a dusting of almond meal.

Notes.

Fat hen and nettles can be replaced with any other deep and strongly flavoured cooking green, like silverbeet/chard, spinach, warrigal greens, collard greens or kale.

If unavailable, pine mushrooms can be replaced with any other type of mushroom.

Honey, fig, bacon & zucchini pizzas.

This is a really simple dish, but the flavour combination is just out of this world. It is honestly one of the best pizzas we have ever eaten. It's got all the good stuff: some vegetables, some fruit, a little meat and some grains – an incredibly tasty and satisfying meal.

Preheat the oven to 250°C fan-forced.

Place the pizza bases onto greased baking trays. To each, add a good glug of oil, some garlic and a pinch of salt and pepper and spread out across the bases. Layer with the zucchini, bacon and figs and finish with a drizzle of honey. Bake for about 12 minutes until everything is just starting to brown and look caramelised.

To serve, transfer the cooked pizzas to wooden boards and sprinkle with freshly torn basil leaves. Cut into slices and enjoy!

SERVES 4
TIME: 15-20 MINUTES

4 soured wholegrain pizza bases (see page 157)

extra-virgin olive oil

4 garlic cloves, crushed

unrefined salt

ground black pepper

2 zucchini, finely sliced

200 g bacon (see page 230), finely sliced

10–15 small figs (600–800 g in total), sliced thickly or cut into quarters

1 tablespoon unprocessed honey

½ bunch of basil, leaves picked

Sprouted mung daal.

6 cups sprouted mung beans
(as per preparation guide
on page 148, but sprouted
for 2–3 days only)

⅓ cup ghee (see page 166)

40 g ginger, grated

4 dried chillies, finely chopped

12 fresh curry leaves

1 tablespoon ground turmeric

2 teaspoons cumin seeds

2 teaspoons yellow mustard seeds

1 teaspoon ground cinnamon

½ teaspoon asafoetida (hing)

1 teaspoon ground black pepper

4 garlic cloves, crushed

4 large tomatoes, diced
(or 200–250 ml passata,
see page 221)

2 teaspoons unprocessed honey

2 teaspoons apple cider vinegar

unrefined salt

180 g coconut paste,
dissolved in 500 ml water
(or 700 ml coconut cream)

To serve

cooked brown rice (as per
preparation guide on page 141)

a handful of fresh coriander, stalks
and all, finely chopped

natural yoghurt (see page 170)

pear and eggplant kasundi
(see page 217)

This nutrient-rich daal is full of invigorating spices and naturally sweet sprouts, with amazing toppings that make it that much better. It's a fantastic, warming dish for anytime of the year, and it has gotten us through many busy times. Make a big batch and eat it throughout the week – it always tastes better the next day anyway!

Wash the sprouts thoroughly and add to a heavy-based saucepan. Add just enough water to cover the sprouts, cover and bring to the boil. Reduce the heat to medium and simmer for 30 minutes. Once the water has been absorbed and the sprouts are soft, mash a little with a fork.

Meanwhile, add the ghee to a large saucepan over a low heat. Add the ginger, chilli, curry leaves, spices and pepper and fry until fragrant. Add the garlic and tomatoes and fry for a minute or so. Add the honey, vinegar, 1 teaspoon of salt and a splash of coconut cream, cover and simmer until it's all broken down (it should be ready by the time the sprouts are ready), stirring occasionally.

Add the sprouts and the remaining coconut cream to the spice mixture and cook for 10 minutes with the lid on, stirring occasionally. We like the consistency of the daal here, but if you prefer it thicker, take the lid off and simmer until you reach your desired consistency. Alternatively, if you prefer it runnier, add more water. Season to taste and serve over rice with coriander, a spoonful of yoghurt and some kasundi.

Notes.

It's important to only sprout the beans for a couple of days, otherwise they can become bitter when cooked.

This is a bit spicy, so alter the amount of chilli to your taste.

To make a vegan version of this recipe, replace the ghee with extra-virgin olive oil and the honey with unprocessed sugar, and omit the yoghurt.

FIELD NOTES

On growing tropical spices like curry leaves, ginger and turmeric.
This recipe and others in this book require some tropical spices. If, like us, you live somewhere that generally gets too cold to grow these, you can grow a plant or two of these in a big pot near a concrete wall that gets heaps of sun (or in a small greenhouse – see the *Grow* chapter for more information), and you will probably harvest enough for your own use!

Spring chicken soup.

SERVES 6
TIME: 45 MINUTES

extra-virgin olive oil (and butter, if desired)

1 large carrot, halved

4 celery stalks

10 thyme sprigs, leaves picked

1 bunch of parsley (about 150 g), stalks and leaves separated, each finely chopped

2 large spring onions (or ½ onion)

zest and juice of 3 lemons, zested skins reserved

1 teaspoon ground black pepper

6 shoots of spring garlic, finely chopped, green tops kept separate for garnish (or 4 garlic cloves, finely chopped)

2 litres chicken stock (see page 180)

unrefined salt

4 trimmed artichoke hearts (see page 314), soaked in lemon juice and water to prevent browning

280 g (2 cups) broad beans

325 g (1½ cups) pulled chicken (left over from making the stock, see page 180)

Where we live, spring can be very indecisive; it fluctuates between brutally hot, bitterly cold and everything in between – this is a soup for those bitterly cold days.

It's an easy, warming and humble dish to nourish your body, heal you if you're unwell and to share with your family – a combination of earthy artichokes, hearty broad beans, bright lemon and fortifying chicken stock. Chicken soup is always special to us because we make it from the chickens that we have hatched and hand raised (see the *Nurture* chapter for more information) – so there is so much respect in this dish. If you don't raise your own chickens, there are great producers who have carcasses from well-raised chickens that they will often give away or sell for minimal cost.

Heat a big glug of olive oil in a stockpot over a medium heat – if using butter, add a large knob of butter to the olive oil and wait for the foam to subside. Tie together the carrot and celery with kitchen twine and add to the pot. Add the thyme, parsley stalks, spring onions, lemon zest and pepper and fry until just browned. Add the garlic and fry for another 5 minutes or so. Add the lemon juice, lemon skins and chicken stock, season with salt and simmer for 20 minutes.

Throw in the artichoke hearts and simmer for 10 minutes.

Add the broad beans, parsley leaves and chicken and simmer for another 5 minutes. Take the pot off the heat and remove the carrot, celery, lemon skins and spring onions. Ladle the soup into bowls and sprinkle with the reserved garlic tops. Finish with a splash of oil and season with salt and pepper to taste.

Notes.

If you are after a more filling meal, this is also great served over brown rice (see page 141 for our preparation guide).

If you can't find fresh artichokes, use preserved artichoke hearts.

FIELD NOTES

On broad beans. Pick broad beans young, when the beans are around 1–2 cm, so that you can pop them out of their pods and simply cook them. As broad beans get older their husks get tougher, so you need to double-pod the beans before eating them – we don't recommend this, as it is lots of work! If the broad beans have reached this stage, simply dry them and use them as a dried bean (see page 147).

HOW TO PREPARE ARTICHOKE HEARTS

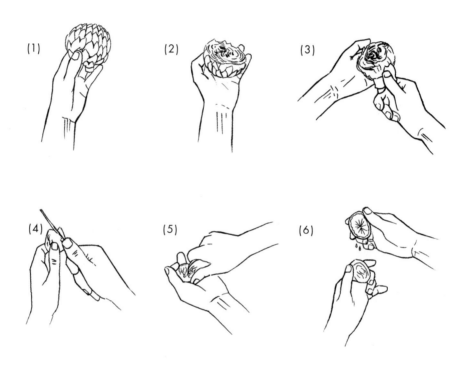

1) Begin with a whole globe artichoke.

2) Cut the top 3 cm off the artichoke to expose the centre.

3) Peel away the leaves.

4) Use a knife to trim off the green skin around the base.

5) Use a spoon to remove the hairy bits (the choke) from the heart.

6) Squeeze a little lemon juice over the heart to stop it from oxidising.

Vegetable & lentil shepherd's pie.

This is a deep winter dish for us, as it's super warming and hearty. It's perfect for using the end-of-the-week vegetables, and if you're feeling lazy, you can omit the pastry – just top with the mash, bake and enjoy.

Throw a big pinch of pepper and a splash of oil into a large, heavy-based saucepan over a medium heat. Add the onion, celery, chilli, savoury, thyme, oregano, rosemary, parsley stalks, bay leaves and celery seeds and sauté until fragrant and the onion is just browned. Add the lentils, garlic, tamari and bone and sauté for a few minutes. Add the carrot, sweet potato, potato, parsnip and turnip and sauté until just starting to brown. Add 1 litre (4 cups) of water, bring to the boil and then simmer, covered, for 2 hours or until everything is cooked down.

After 2 hours, remove the lid and cook for about 30 minutes until thick. Add the chopped parsley leaves and salt and pepper to taste.

To prepare the mash, place the sweet potato, potato, carrot and turnip in a small saucepan, sprinkle with a big pinch of salt and barely cover with water. Bring to the boil and simmer until soft. Drain and mash well with the oil and milk, adding salt and pepper to taste.

Preheat the oven to 180°C fan-forced. Grease your chosen pie tins – a couple of larger ones or a few smaller ones, whatever you prefer.

On a floured bench, roll the chilled pastry into balls, and then roll out into thin discs. Flip into the greased pie tins and pre-bake for 5–10 minutes until just brown – you can use pastry weights (we just use dried beans), though it's not crucial.

Fill the pie dishes with the lentil mixture and then cover with mash. Bake for about 20 minutes until the pastry and mash begin to brown a little.

Notes.

For a vegetarian version of this recipe, omit the bone and use 1 litre of vegetable stock (see page 180) instead of water.

Savoury is a woody herb that is great in meat and bean dishes with deep flavours.

SERVES 6–8
TIME: 3–3½ HOURS

ground black pepper

extra-virgin olive oil

1 onion, finely chopped

4 celery stalks and tops, finely chopped

2 dried chillies, finely chopped

2 fresh savoury sprigs (see note)

15–20 thyme sprigs, leaves picked and finely chopped

3–4 oregano sprigs, leaves picked and finely chopped

2 rosemary sprigs, leaves picked and finely chopped

½ bunch of parsley (about 60 g), stalks and leaves separated, each finely chopped

2 bay leaves

1 teaspoon celery seeds

320 g (1½ cups) puy lentils, soaked overnight (as per preparation guide on page 147) and drained

2 garlic cloves, crushed

3 tablespoons tamari

1 responsibly sourced lamb or beef bone

2 carrots, very finely diced

1 small sweet potato, very finely diced

4 small potatoes, very finely diced

2 parsnips, very finely diced

1 small turnip, very finely diced

unrefined salt

savoury gluten-free shortcrust pastry (see page 161), chilled

Mash

1 small sweet potato, cut into chunks

4 small potatoes, cut into chunks

2 carrots, cut into chunks

1 small turnip, cut into chunks

unrefined salt

a big splash of extra-virgin olive oil

a big splash of milk

ground black pepper

Wild rabbit stew on soft polenta.

SERVES 4–6
TIME: 5–7 HOURS

3–4 bacon rashers
(see page 230), diced

1 large onion, diced

extra-virgin olive oil

2 celery stalks including tops,
diced

2 carrots, diced

6 garlic cloves, finely chopped

1 teaspoon chilli flakes or
1 dried chilli

500 ml (2 cups) passata
(see page 221)

250 ml (1 cup) red wine

3 thyme sprigs, leaves picked

5 rosemary sprigs, leaves picked
and finely chopped

1 bunch of parsley (about 150 g),
stalks and all, finely chopped,
plus extra to serve

100 g brined olives
(see page 210), pitted

1 tablespoon butter

1 rabbit, halved or quartered
to fit in the pot

unrefined salt

ground black pepper

6 cups cooked polenta (as per
preparation guide on page 145)

This really has to be the best rabbit dish we have ever eaten. And it holds so many great memories for us. We were originally gifted it by a couple, Gay and Kathy, in New Zealand, in exchange for homemade hazelnut cookies. Not only did Gay and Kathy give us the handwritten recipe, but they also gave us all of the ingredients, including a rabbit they had hunted themselves. It was one of the most thoughtful things we have ever been given. We then traded the whole experience of this dish – from hunting and preparing the rabbit to cooking it – for a photographic print with one of our great friends (and photographer of this book), Shantanu.

Where we live, rabbits are plentiful and considered a pest (see page 78), so it's a very sustainable source of meat. Wild rabbit is quite often available at good butchers; farmed rabbit is even more common.

Preheat the oven to 180°C fan-forced.

In a large, deep frying pan, sauté the bacon and onion in a little oil until the onion is soft. Add the celery, carrot, garlic and chilli and sauté until just browned (around 10–15 minutes). Add the passata, wine, herbs, olives and 250 ml (1 cup) of water and simmer for 5–10 minutes.

Meanwhile, melt the butter in a cast-iron pot over a medium heat and brown the rabbit for 2–3 minutes on each side. Pour the sauce over the rabbit, season with salt and pepper and give the pot a little shake to settle everything in. Cover and place in the oven. Reduce the temperature to 150°C and cook for 2½ hours.

Turn the oven off but leave the pot in the oven so that the stew poaches for 2–4 hours (4 hours is best).

Prepare the polenta 30 minutes before you are ready to serve. Warm the stew on the stove.

To serve, place the polenta in bowls, top with the rabbit stew and sprinkle extra parsley on top.

Note. For a dairy-free version of this recipe, replace the butter with extra-virgin olive oil.

Wild duck ramen.

This is such a warming dish. Wild duck is the perfect meat in the lead-up to winter, which is also the perfect time to hunt them because all of their young have been raised to independence. Farmed and wild duck are full of B vitamins – just what our bodies need to buffer the onset of colder weather. This wintery ramen takes it one step further with a fortifying miso base and a Korean twist of kimchi to serve. This is a winter staple for us, but if you don't have access to wild duck, farmed duck is a perfect substitute, or experiment by replacing it with chicken or pork.

To make the broth, add a big splash of sesame oil to a stockpot over a medium heat and sauté the spring onion, garlic, ginger and chilli until the onion has softened. Add the sesame seeds and sauté for 1 minute. Add the miso, saké, mirin and a splash of the stock and stir until the miso has completely dissolved. Add the remaining stock, salt and pepper and bring to a simmer, skimming off any foam as it forms. Reduce to a bare simmer and cover while you prepare the remaining ingredients.

Place the eggs in a saucepan of boiling water and cook for 7 minutes. Remove from the pan and cool under running water. Peel immediately, halve lengthways and leave yolk-side up to allow the yolks to form skins.

Add the bicarbonate of soda to a large saucepan of boiling water – be warned, this will cause your water to froth! Add the pasta and cook until just soft. Drain, refresh under cold water and set aside.

Cook the corn, if using, in salted boiling water until just tender. Add the greens, blanch for a minute or so and drain. Cut the corn kernels from the cobs and set aside with the greens.

Portion out the pasta in four deep bowls, fill with broth and top with the greens, corn, duck, eggs, a sprinkle of sesame seeds, the reserved spring onion, a torn square of nori and some kimchi. Serve steaming hot.

FIELD NOTES

On cooking duck. Our favourite way to cook duck – except maybe for cassoulet(!) – is twice-cooked with crispy skin. Rub a whole duck inside and out with salt and pepper and leave on a wire rack in the fridge to cure for 4 hours. Preheat the oven to 80°C. Cut a lemon in half and place it in the duck's cavity, and then slow-cook it, uncovered, for 8 hours. Remove from the oven and brush all over with the fat that has rendered in the bottom of the pan. Turn the oven up to as high as it goes (usually about 250°C) and hard roast for about 20–25 minutes until the skin is crispy and golden. So good.

On making duck stock. We make ours from the leftover frame after making twice-cooked duck with crispy skin (above). See our recipe for waste bone stock on page 180.

SERVES 4
TIME: 30 MINUTES

2 eggs

2 teaspoons bicarbonate of soda

400 g fresh or 200 g dry gluten-free or whole-wheat pasta (see pages 162–63)

2 corn cobs (optional, but when corn is still in season during autumn, this is a must!)

340 g mustard greens (or pak choi, tatsoi or upland cress)

300 g leftover roast duck, sliced finely across the grain (see field notes)

sesame seeds, to serve

1 sheet of nori

kimchi (see page 206), to serve

Broth

toasted sesame oil

4 large spring onions, finely sliced (reserve some of the sliced green tops for garnish)

4 garlic cloves, finely chopped

60 g ginger, finely chopped

2 dried red chillies, finely chopped

2 tablespoons sesame seeds

2 tablespoons miso (we love dark miso)

2 tablespoons saké

2 tablespoons mirin

1.5 litres duck stock (see field notes)

1 teaspoon unrefined salt

2 teaspoons ground black pepper

Asparagus, broccoli, tuna & chilli crepes.

SERVES 4–6 (MAKES 15 CREPES)
TIME: 40 MINUTES

3 tablespoons extra-virgin olive oil

250 g preserved tuna
(see page 233)

6 spring garlic shoots (or 3 garlic
cloves), finely chopped

2 dried chillies, finely chopped

½ teaspoon ground black pepper

350 g asparagus, finely chopped

1 large head of broccoli or
broccoli shoots (about 350 g),
florets and stalk finely chopped

150 g mushrooms, finely sliced

juice of 1 lemon

1 batch of soured buckwheat
crepe batter (see page 158)

unrefined salt

freshly grated parmesan, to serve

This is always the first dish we make after the first asparagus harvest in spring and it is seriously so delicious. It is savoury, bright and naturally sweet from the asparagus and broccoli, with just a hint of chilli and a subtle sourness from the crepes. Growing asparagus requires patience, as the initial wait is a long one. So make the most of it – eat it until you can't eat it anymore.

Place a large heavy-based frying pan over a medium–high heat. Add a glug of olive oil to the pan and throw in the tuna, garlic, chilli and pepper. Cook for a few minutes until fragrant. Add the asparagus, broccoli and mushrooms, cover and allow the mixture to sweat, stirring occasionally.

Once the mushrooms have collapsed (about 10 minutes), add a big splash of water and the lemon juice. Cover and continue to sweat for a further 20–25 minutes, stirring occasionally, until all of the ingredients have fallen apart and the mixture it super fragrant. Add a little water as needed if the mixture is sticking to the pan.

Meanwhile, cook your crepes (see page 158).

Once the filling mixture is ready, add the remaining olive oil and season with salt. Reduce the heat to low while you finish cooking the crepes.

To serve, divide the mixture evenly between the crepes, top with parmesan, roll up and enjoy.

FIELD NOTES

On growing asparagus. Asparagus is a perennial plant. From seed, asparagus takes about 3–4 years until you get a crop. To begin, collect the red berries off the female plants in autumn/winter, and sow them thickly on top of a large, 30 cm-deep pot of soil, covering them with 2.5 cm more of soil. Keep well watered, and in the following spring/summer your baby asparagus crowns will form. The following winter, turn the pot upside down and separate all of the crowns, then plant them into the garden at 30 cm intervals. Don't pick the asparagus that spring – your crowns are developing their strength, so allow the plants to get tall, flower and seed. That winter, cut the ferns down at the base, sprinkle a little compost on top and mulch over thickly with straw. You can harvest a few of the biggest spears the following spring (just don't go too hard), then repeat the cutting, feeding and mulching in winter. And finally, in their third spring in the garden, and from now on, you can pick every spear that comes up through spring and into summer, repeating the winter mulching each year. Your asparagus crowns will bear heavily for at least 20 years. If you want to speed up the process, get some mature asparagus crowns from someone else's garden. Plant these in the ground, and you will only have to wait 2–3 years before you can pick them!

On picking asparagus. Once established, pick asparagus often during their season to encourage the spears to keep growing, otherwise they will shoot to the sky, think that their job is done and stop producing until next year.

Szechuan rice bowls with wild greens.

SERVES 4
TIME: 30 MINUTES
+ OVERNIGHT SOAKING

extra-virgin olive oil

1 large onion or 200 g French shallots, diced

1¼ teaspoons Szechuan peppercorns, lightly ground

6 whole dried chillies, torn into pieces

5 star anise

7–8 garlic cloves, crushed

5 cm piece of ginger, finely chopped

200 g traditional homemade bacon (see page 230) or fresh pork belly, diced

2½ teaspoons unrefined sugar (e.g. rapadura)

300 g wild mallow (see page 84), leaves picked (see notes for replacement suggestions)

300 g young wild radish leaves (see page 87), coarsely chopped (see notes for replacement suggestions)

1¼ teaspoons unrefined salt

1 lemon

4 cups cooked brown rice (as per preparation guide on page 141)

This dish is for chilli lovers and is just as good vegetarian with eggs (see notes below) as it is for omnivores with bacon! It's a silky, spicy bowl of rice and greens. The wild greens add unique flavours: the mallow (see page 84) is nutty and the wild radish (see page 87) pungent, an awesome combination. Hot chillies bring the fire, and the Szechuan pepper creates a tingling numbness in your mouth, while the garlic is pungent, the ginger tangy and the star anise sweetly subtle. This is a healthy and quick mid-week meal.

It's not at all traditional to use olive oil and lemon, but these ingredients are abundant to us and carry the Chinese flavours in this dish superbly.

Heat a large cast-iron skillet or wok over a medium heat and add a generous glug of oil. Fry the onion, Szechuan peppercorns, chilli and star anise until the onion is soft but not browned. Add the garlic, ginger, bacon and sugar and cook for a couple of minutes until the garlic begins to brown. Add the greens and salt, cover and cook for about 2 minutes. Add a splash of water to the pan and stir, cover and cook for another 2 minutes.

Uncover and stir-fry until all of the moisture has evaporated and the greens have completely collapsed.

Remove from the heat and add a splash more oil and a squeeze of lemon. Portion the rice out into bowls, top with the greens and serve steaming hot.

Notes.

Wild mallow and radish greens can be replaced with any other deep and strongly flavoured cooking green, like silverbeet/chard, spinach, warrigal greens, collard greens or kale.

To make a vegetarian version of this recipe, replace the diced bacon with 6 eggs. Simply whisk the eggs in a bowl and add them to the skillet after the greens have completely collapsed. Stir for a few minutes until the eggs are cooked through, then proceed with the recipe.

FIELD NOTES

On Szechuan pepper. When it comes to spicy food, the Chinese have the secret weapon. These incredible little seed husks come from a temperate-climate tree related to citrus, and they pack a citrusy numbness that allows you to eat otherwise completely unapproachable levels of chilli heat without blinking. If you love chilli, learn to love these little guys.

To celebrate.

Desserts for special occasions and celebrations.

Chocolate, espresso & mulberry cake.

To me, this is the ultimate celebration cake. It is super moist and almost pudding like, with some crunchiness from the hazelnuts, a slight fruitiness from the mulberries, and rich chocolate and espresso flavours. It's not super sweet, because that seems to be how I make everything – people say I am 'sugar blind' – so adjust the recipe if you like it sweeter. For me this cake is special, not only because it uses ingredients we see as 'sometimes foods' (chocolate and espresso), but also because it reminds me of my childhood. Hazelnuts were always used to make celebration sweets in the Maltese tradition, and I have so many memories of purple-stained hands and feet from picking mulberries. — LENTIL

Preheat the oven to 170°C fan-forced. Grease a round cake tin, about 20 cm in diameter.

Place the espresso and cacao in a bowl and mix until the cacao is dissolved.

In a separate bowl, beat the sugar and eggs until very thick, pale and fluffy. Beat in the honey and vanilla, followed by the remaining dry ingredients. Fold in the espresso mixture and oil until combined.

Spread the mulberries in the base of the cake tin. Pour the cake mixture on top and bake for 35–45 minutes in the upper part of the oven. Take a look after 30 minutes to make sure you don't overcook it. When the cake is ready, a skewer inserted in the centre will come out with some sticky crumbs on it, but it shouldn't be wet.

Rest the cake in the tin for 10 minutes or so before turning out onto a cooling rack. Eat hot or cold with fresh mulberries and cream or sour cream if you like. Store in an airtight container in the fridge.

Notes.

If you need to replace the mulberries, try blackberries. And if you can't source any berries at all, just omit them.

If using frozen berries, make sure you defrost them and pat them dry before using, otherwise it will affect the baking times and moisture content of the cake.

SERVES 8–10
TIME: 1 HOUR

125 ml (½ cup) espresso

50 g (½ cup) responsibly sourced cacao powder

70 g unrefined sugar (e.g. rapadura)

3 eggs

70 g unprocessed honey

1 teaspoon vanilla extract

80 g almond meal

80 g hazelnut meal

1 teaspoon bicarbonate of soda

2½ tablespoons extra-virgin olive oil

200 g mulberries, plus extra to serve

Dessert bowls.

SERVES 4
TIME: 40 MINUTES

1 kg seedless table grapes
(we prefer red or purple varieties
for looks but use whatever you
have), chilled

80 g (½ cup) shelled pistachios

2 teaspoons unrefined sugar
(e.g. rapadura)

3 mint sprigs, leaves picked

250 ml (1 cup) sour cream
(see page 167), mascarpone
or ice cream

1 lemon

When we need a simple, fast dessert that doesn't hold back on flavour, we turn to these little guys. Each bowl is perfectly balanced: there's the sweetness from the grapes, a little zing from the lemon, added complexity from the mint and crunch from the pistachios, all wrapped in silky sour cream, mascarpone or ice cream. We always make this in summer to celebrate the first grapes of the season, but you can substitute grapes with almost any other fruit – peaches and strawberries work especially well – just sweeten the syrup if you need to (grapes are so sweet they don't need any added sugar!). This simple dish makes any fruit you choose the real hero!

Place 600 g of the grapes in a high-powered blender and blend until completely smooth – be careful not to overblend and aerate the mix. (If your blender isn't quite powerful enough, push the blended pulp through a sieve to remove any large bits.)

Pour the blended grapes into a small saucepan and bring to a gentle simmer. Reduce by half, or until you can slide the end of a spoon across the bottom of the pan and see the base show through before the liquid comes back together. Place the syrup in the freezer to cool quickly, or refrigerate overnight.

Meanwhile, coarsely chop the pistachios and toast with the sugar in a small frying pan over a medium heat, moving constantly to avoid burning. Toast until the sugar has caramelised and the pistachios are *just* fragrant. Turn out into a bowl to cool.

Once the syrup has cooled completely, place it in the blender with two-thirds of the mint and blend until smooth, again being careful not to overblend.

When you are ready to serve, slice the remaining grapes in half and finely chop the remaining mint. Divide the grapes between four chilled bowls or jars and pour a little syrup over the grapes. Add the sour cream, mascarpone or ice cream and pour the remaining syrup over the top. Top with a little squeeze of lemon, a sprinkling of pistachios and some mint and serve immediately.

Beetroot and sour cream ice cream.

A creamy, earthy and slightly sweet ice cream with an amazing combination of flavours and beautiful colour!

MAKES ABOUT 850 ML
TIME: 35 MINUTES + COOLING TIME + CHURNING TIME

500 ml (2 cups) milk

250 ml (1 cup) beetroot juice
(about 2 large beetroots, juiced)

250 ml (1 cup) sour cream (see page 167)

1 teaspoon vanilla extract

80 g (½ cup) unrefined sugar (e.g. rapadura)

2 teaspoons psyllium husk

8 egg yolks, whisked

Special equipment

ice cream machine

thermometer

Place the milk, beetroot juice, sour cream and vanilla in a large, heavy-based saucepan over a medium heat and whisk until combined. Slowly whisk in the sugar and psyllium until dissolved. Whisk in the yolks, and continue to whisk until the mixture reaches 70°C – by this point it should have thickened. Leave on a low simmer with the lid off for 20 minutes, whisking often – be careful not to overheat, otherwise you will cook the egg.

Cool the mixture in the fridge before churning in an ice cream machine (as per the machine's instructions).

Once done, place the ice cream in the freezer and eat as desired.

Note. You may be tempted to cut out the step of simmering for 20 minutes in these ice cream recipes, however this is to ensure that all of the sugar has dissolved, the egg yolks and liquid have bound, and any excess water has evaporated (otherwise your ice cream will be icy!).

Spiced pumpkin, cookie & cacao ice cream.

An ice cream full of spice, crunch and the natural sweetness of pumpkin!

MAKES ABOUT 850 ML
TIME: 35 MINUTES + COOLING TIME + CHURNING TIME

500 ml (2 cups) milk

250 ml (1 cup) cream

200 g pumpkin, boiled and mashed

1 teaspoon vanilla extract

½ teaspoon ground ginger

1 teaspoon ground cinnamon

a pinch of unrefined salt

80 g (½ cup) unrefined sugar (e.g. rapadura)

2 teaspoons psyllium husk

6 egg yolks, whisked

1½ tablespoons responsibly sourced cacao nibs

5 ginger snaps (see page 246), cut into tiny pieces

Special equipment

ice cream machine

thermometer

Place the milk, cream, pumpkin, vanilla, spices and salt in a large, heavy-based saucepan over a medium heat and whisk until combined. Slowly whisk in the sugar and psyllium until dissolved. Blend with a hand-held blender until well combined. Whisk in the yolks, and continue to whisk until the mixture reaches 70°C – by this point it should have thickened. Leave on a low simmer with the lid off for 20 minutes, whisking often – be careful not to overheat, otherwise you will cook the egg.

Cool the mixture in the fridge before churning in an ice cream machine (as per the machine's instructions). Once the machine is running, add the cacao nibs.

Once done, mix in the ginger snaps and place the ice cream in the freezer. Eat as desired.

No-bake 'cherry ripe'.

A refreshing, healthy and easy summer dessert. This cake has three layers: a crunchy base, a textured fruit layer and a chocolate filling – a grown-up dessert, like an adult cherry ripe. Just omit the port for children and add a little extra orange juice, or omit the soaked fruit layer to make a super-simple frozen cake. Or if you want it more chocolatey, add a little more cacao powder to the filling ingredients. This recipe makes quite a lot because it stores for a long time in the freezer, making for a quick and healthy dessert or snack when we're craving something sweet.

For the soaked fruit, place the cherries, prunes and figs in a jug and cover with the port. Place a small weight (e.g. a stack of small plates) on top to keep the fruit submerged and extract the natural juices. Set aside for about 2 hours.

Meanwhile, thoroughly grease a bread tin, ceramic dish or cake tin that's about 30–40 cm long and about 10 cm wide (or a 30 cm diameter round tin, it doesn't matter too much – use whatever you've got) with the extra coconut oil.

For the base, place the cacao nibs and sunflower seeds in a blender and blend on low until they are like coarse flour. Transfer to a bowl and massage in all of the remaining ingredients with your hands until well combined. Firmly press this into the cake tin to create a base.

For the filling, place the coconut oil and cacao powder in a small saucepan over a low heat and stir until combined.

Place the persimmons or dates and orange juice in a blender and blitz. Transfer to a bowl along with the coconut oil and cacao mixture and stir in the almond or macadamia meal, orange zest and vanilla. Pour in the liquid from the soaking fruit and combine well.

To assemble, pour a very thin layer of filling mixture over the base and lay the soaked fruit on top. Pour over the remaining filling mixture and gently tap the base of the tin on the bench to settle the ingredients. Freeze until set (about 5 hours).

Once set, simply run a knife around the edge of the tin to loosen, and then turn upside down – it should pop out. Alternatively, turn upside down and run the base of the tin under hot water for a few seconds. To serve, cut into thick slices and stand for a few minutes to slightly soften. Store in an airtight container in the freezer for 6 months or more.

Note. If you can't find macadamia meal, simply blend 110 g of whole macadamia nuts in a high-powered blender to make a coarse flour.

SERVES 10–12
TIME: 25 MINUTES
+ SOAKING AND FREEZING TIME

125 ml (½ cup) coconut oil, plus extra for greasing

30 g (⅓ cup) responsibly sourced cacao powder

2 dried persimmons (see page 234) or pitted dates, finely chopped (or replace with 3 tablespoons unrefined sugar)

250 ml (1 cup) orange juice

110 g almond or macadamia meal

2 tablespoons orange zest

1 teaspoon vanilla extract

Soaked fruit

400 g fresh or preserved cherries (see page 224), pitted and halved

50 g prunes, pitted and finely sliced

50 g dried figs, finely sliced

80 ml (⅓ cup) port

Base

105 g responsibly sourced cacao nibs

90 g (¾ cup) sunflower seeds

100 ml melted coconut oil

75 g (¾ cup) almond meal

2 tablespoons unrefined sugar (e.g. rapadura)

Carrot crepes with burnt oranges.

SERVES 4
TIME: 20 MINUTES

4 oranges, peeled, pith cut off, sliced into 8 mm-thick rounds, pips removed

½ batch of soured buckwheat crepe batter (see page 158), substituting the milk with carrot juice

juice of 4 oranges

1 tablespoon unrefined sugar (e.g. rapadura)

1 teaspoon ground cinnamon

unrefined salt

125 ml (½ cup) unmarinated labne (see page 171)

¼ teaspoon ground cardamom

This dish is a celebration of all things orange and is an absolutely awesome combination of flavours. It is the perfect warm dessert in the depths of winter and early spring when you can't seem to find any fruits except citrus. But it's just as good, and super refreshing, served cold at the height of summer. The burnt oranges and their syrup are nutty and bittersweet. The crepes are subtle and earthy from the carrot juice and the labne ties everything together in sharp creaminess. A simple and incredibly rewarding dish.

Place a large, shallow frying pan over a medium heat. Add half of the orange slices and cook without moving for 2–4 minutes on each side until a little burnt.

Meanwhile, start cooking your crepes (see page 158).

Once the oranges have some good colour, pour half of the orange juice over them. Add the sugar, cinnamon and a pinch of salt and simmer, uncovered, until the juice turns to syrup (7–9 minutes). Once ready, set aside and repeat for the remaining orange slices.

When all of the crepes are ready, place them on plates and top with the burnt orange slices and labne. Drizzle over the syrup from the pan and sprinkle with cardamom. Alternatively, chill everything and serve cold.

Honey-soaked lemon, sour cream & olive oil cake.

SERVES 8–10
TIME: 1 HOUR

1 lemon

3 eggs

200 ml sour cream (see page 167)

80 g (½ cup) unrefined sugar
(e.g. rapadura)

160 g LSA (see page 149)

140 g millet flour (see note)

1 teaspoon bicarbonate of soda

100 ml extra-virgin olive oil

natural yoghurt (see page 170),
sour cream (see page 167)
or cream, to serve

Syrup

150 g (½ cup) unprocessed honey

100 ml water

3 tablespoons dried or semi-dried
rose petals (optional)

Gluten free and you would never know it! Full of the goodness of flaxseed, sunflower seeds, almonds and millet, this moist cake has an addictively sharp flavour from the lemon and sour cream, which works super well with the sweetness of honey. Trust us – it tastes like it's no good for you, but it is.

Add the whole lemon to a small saucepan and cover with water. Place the lid on and boil for about 20 minutes or until soft. Take the lemon out of the water and place in the fridge to cool.

Preheat the oven to 180°C. Grease a 20 cm round cake tin.

Beat the eggs and sour cream in a large mixing bowl until combined. Slowly add the sugar while beating until the mixture is light and smooth.

Combine the LSA, millet flour and bicarbonate of soda in a separate bowl.

Place the olive oil and whole lemon in a blender and blend until smooth.

Slowly fold half of the dry mixture into the egg mixture, followed by half of the lemon mixture. Fold in the remaining dry and lemon mixtures until well combined. Tip the batter into the prepared tin and bake for 30–40 minutes until a skewer inserted in the centre comes out clean. Leave in the tin for a few minutes, then turn out onto a cooling rack.

Meanwhile, heat the syrup ingredients in a small saucepan over a low heat until warm and combined. Pour the syrup into the empty cake tin and carefully return the cake to the tin to soak up the syrup.

Serve hot or cold with yoghurt, sour cream or cream.

Notes.

If you want a super-moist and sweet cake, double the syrup mixture.

If you can't find millet flour and don't have a grain mill, try grinding whole millet in your spice grinder.

If you don't grow roses, ask a neighbour!

Soured wholegrain doughnuts.

MAKES 16 SMALL DOUGHNUTS
TIME: 30 MINUTES
+ 6–12 HOURS SOURING

120 g whole-wheat flour

65 g (⅓ cup) unrefined sugar (e.g. rapadura), plus extra for dusting

½ teaspoon bicarbonate of soda

1 teaspoon ground cinnamon, plus extra for dusting

1 tablespoon unsalted butter

3 tablespoons milk

3 tablespoons natural yoghurt (see page 170)

1 teaspoon vanilla extract

1 egg, whisked

a pinch of unrefined salt

cold-pressed sunflower oil

Special equipment

cake pop moulds or a mini muffin tray

This recipe uses yoghurt and milk to sour the grains, which breaks down the hard-to-digest starches and creates a nice sharp flavour. They have the same cinnamon and textural goodness of a standard doughnut, but they're so much better for you, as they're baked, not fried, and are full of amazing, well-prepared whole grains. Enjoy guilt free.

Place all of the dry ingredients in a blender and blend until fine. Transfer to a mixing bowl, add the butter and massage with your hands until combined. Fold in the milk, yoghurt and vanilla until just combined – don't over mix (it will be a thick paste). Cover and leave the mixture to sit at room temperature for 6–12 hours to sour.

Preheat the oven to 200°C fan-forced. Grease your cake pop moulds or mini muffin tray with butter or sunflower oil.

Add the egg and salt to the soured mixture and combine gently with your hands or a cake spatula. Fill the moulds or muffin tray with the mixture and bake for 10 minutes. When cooked, the doughnuts should spring back when pressed.

Remove the doughnuts from the moulds or tray and brush with sunflower oil. Roll in a combined mix of extra cinnamon and sugar.

Place the doughnuts on a baking tray and back into the oven for 5 minutes to get hot and crispy. Serve on their own or with ice cream!

Note. If you don't have cake pop moulds or a mini muffin tray, use a standard muffin tray to make flat doughnuts – just bake them for an extra 3 minutes initially.

THE NEXT CHAPTER

This is the final page of our journey so far.

We are so thankful for every day we have had and for everything we have learnt on this farm. But it is time for us to leave what we have created here and move on to our next adventure.

Despite everything we have made and achieved here, every moment of hard work, the few tears and every seed we have sown, it feels right to leave. Because we know that we are leaving this land better than we found it. We know that others will enjoy the trees we have planted and seeds that were sown. We know that what we can do in the next paddock will be incredible, as we look back with confidence on what we achieved in this one. We will leave with our chickens, sheep, cows, dogs, bees, rhubarb, asparagus, globe artichokes… and wherever all of this is, we are home. And wherever we have each other, that is home.

We don't know where the next pages will take us. But we are excited about the days ahead.

To being brave and bold.

Until the next chapter.

THANK YOU

To every person who has picked up this book. From our hearts.

To my Maltese family (each and every one of you), for showing me what true love, food and community is. To my mum, Michelle, I hope you would be proud. To my dad, Russell, and brother, Lee, for your endless and forgiving support, and for always caring so deeply. – *Lentil*

To Quinto and Genoveffa (Nonno and Nonna), I wish you were here to share in this feast. To Brian and Jessica – for everything you have taught me, and for leading me down this path. To Andy and Jill – for opening doors and opening my mind, thank you so much for always giving with such generosity. To dad, Alister, and mum, Rosa, for your heartfelt generosity and support in helping us to turn the next page, to go on our next adventure. I love you. – *Matt*

To our extended family of friends. Especially: Matt Wilkinson – for your generous heart, endless support, unwavering enthusiasm and inability to sit down to read this book – we love you and wouldn't be here without you; Fran Haysey – for your passion and belief that we were good enough and for being the strongest support we could ask for; and Lachie McFarlane, for being you, as you no doubt will always be.

To the team behind this book. This has truly been a collaboration of people with passion, good hearts, amazing minds and great humour. Mary, thank you for giving us the opportunity to share our thoughts with the world. Jane and Marcus, thank you for editing those thoughts so that the world can understand them. Daniel, thank you for your incredible, sensitive design – we are so proud of what you have created. Flooze and Cammy, thank you for enthusiastically welcoming our recipes as the primary food source in your diet during the testing of this book – your constructive positivity and hilarious word use was phenomenally contagious and made us laugh daily. And of course, dear Shantanu, thank you for being as crazy as us, for changing our lives, literally, in the best way. Welcome to our family.

Thank you to all of you legends who have traded with us so enthusiastically. To mention a few: Sophie Harle, Fancy Mike, Ben Baldwin, Yumi and Taka, Sarah Withers and Andrew Kelly. It is so beautiful learning about and appreciating each other's skills, knowledge and abundances. We are often so removed from the appreciation of how much love and effort and skill goes into what other people do these days. When we have experienced it first hand, our entire world perspective has shifted.

And finally, to *everyone* who has touched our lives so far, you have changed us. From the deepest, most sparkly part of our hearts – thank you. You know who you are.

REFERENCES

We believe that learning should be a lifelong pursuit. We are so fortunate to have met mentors who've shared their wisdom and taught us hands on skills, and every day we experiment and learn from trial and error. While there are many things in life that have to be experienced to be truly understood, luckily, we don't have to figure everything out for ourselves. People from all around the world are exploring, experimenting and explaining, and a lot of this knowledge is freely available online. Throughout this book, we've referred to a few of the studies that have helped educate us along our journey, so if you want to learn more, you can use this as a starting point.

To find out more on the positive effect of human touch on plant growth (mentioned on page 13):

Cahill, J., Castelli, J. and Casper, B. (2002). Separate effects of human visitation and touch on plant growth and herbivory in an old-field community. *American Journal of Botany*, 89(9), pp.1401–1409.

For further information about the different nutrient profiles of heirloom vs hybridised plants, and how vitamin and mineral content has decreased over the past 40 years (we briefly touch on this on pages 52 and 128):

Davis, D., Epp, M. and Riordan, H. (2004). Changes in USDA Food Composition Data for 43 Garden Crops, 1950 to 1999. *Journal of the American College of Nutrition*, 23(6), pp.669–682.

Mayer, A. (1997). Historical changes in the mineral content of fruits and vegetables. *British Food Journal*, 99(6), pp.207–211.

Ekholm, P., Reinivuo, H., Mattila, P., Pakkala, H., Koponen, J., Happonen, A., Hellström, J. and Ovaskainen, M. (2007). Changes in the mineral and trace element contents of cereals, fruits and vegetables in Finland. *Journal of Food Composition and Analysis*, 20(6), pp.487–495.

Learn more about how your brain reacts to buying new things (we talk about the long lasting happiness of experiences over things on page 111):

Gilovich, T., Kumar, A. and Jampol, L. (2015). A wonderful life: experiential consumption and the pursuit of happiness. *Journal of Consumer Psychology*, 25(1), pp.152–165.

Cell Press, (2006). Pure Novelty Spurs The Brain. *ScienceDaily*. [online] Available at: http://www.sciencedaily.com/releases/2006/08/060826180547.htm.

If you'd like to learn more about how fermented foods can improve gut health and reduce allergies and disease (mentioned on page 127):

Adolfsson, O., Meydani, S. and Russell, R. (2004). Yogurt and gut function. *The American Journal of Clinical Nutrition*, 80(2), pp.245–256.

Selhub, E., Logan, A. and Bested, A. (2014). Fermented foods, microbiota, and mental health: ancient practice meets nutritional psychiatry. *J Physiol Anthropol*, 33(1), p.2.

Nelson, N. (2006). Migrant Studies Aid the Search for Factors Linked to Breast Cancer Risk. *JNCI Journal of the National Cancer Institute*, 98(7), pp.436–438.

These studies talk about the importance of using (and touching!) real soil (mentioned on page 127):

Matthews, D. and Jenks, S. (2013). Ingestion of Mycobacterium vaccae decreases anxiety-related behavior and improves learning in mice. *Behavioural Processes*, 96, pp.27–35.

Ege, M., Mayer, M., Normand, A., Genuneit, J., Cookson, W., Braun-Fahrländer, C., Heederik, D., Piarroux, R. and von Mutius, E. (2011). Exposure to Environmental Microorganisms and Childhood Asthma. *New England Journal of Medicine*, 364(8), pp.701–709.

For more information on why grains should be fermented before cooking (discussed on pages 127 and 138–40):

Rizzello, C., De Angelis, M., Di Cagno, R., Camarca, A., Silano, M., Losito, I., De Vincenzi, M., De Bari, M., Palmisano, F., Maurano, F., Gianfrani, C. and Gobbetti, M. (2007). Highly Efficient Gluten Degradation by Lactobacilli and Fungal Proteases during Food Processing: New Perspectives for Celiac Disease. *Applied and Environmental Microbiology*, 73(14), pp.4499–4507.

If you want to learn more about how milled grains go rancid and why this can be harmful (we mention this on page 140), this is a good place to start:

Ussing Larsen, J. (1995). *Aurions bagebog: fra korn til brød*. [Kbh.]: Olivia.

Learn more about avenin in connection with gluten intolerance here (mentioned on page 140):

Arentz-Hansen, H., Fleckenstein, B., Molberg, Ø., Scott, H., Koning, F., Jung, G., Roepstorff, P., Lundin, K. and Sollid, L. (2004). The Molecular Basis for Oat Intolerance in Patients with Celiac Disease. *PLoS Med*, 1(1), p.e1.

A PLUM BOOK

First published in 2016 by
Pan Macmillan Australia Pty Limited
Level 25, 1 Market Street,
Sydney, NSW 2000, Australia

Level 1, 15–19 Claremont Street,
South Yarra, Victoria 3141, Australia

Design and illustrations by Daniel New/OetomoNew
Photography by Shantanu Starick (with additional photography by Lentil Purbrick)
Styling by Matt and Lentil Purbrick
Editing by Marcus Ellis
Index by Frances Paterson
Typeset by Daniel New and Kirby Jones
Colour reproduction by Splitting Image Colour Studio
Printed and bound in China by 1010 Printing International Limited

A CIP catalogue record for this book is available from the National Library of Australia.

MIX
Paper from
responsible sources
FSC® C016973
www.fsc.org

ABOUT THE AUTHORS

Matt and Lentil began by selling the produce from their Central Victorian farm to some of Melbourne's top restaurants and cafes, encouraging chefs to adopt principles of local, real produce and sustainable farming and packaging. But they craved more. They wanted to extend the conversation. So they decided to open their van doors to the people of Melbourne, pulling up in forgotten side lanes to sell and trade their home-grown vegetables, flowers and produce 'like drug dealers for vegetarian hipsters'. They soon sold out week after week and their education became something sought after. They are now authors, educators, bloggers and advocates for sustainability and a bright future. *Grown & Gathered* is their first book.

'David Frenkiel, Green Kitchen Stories